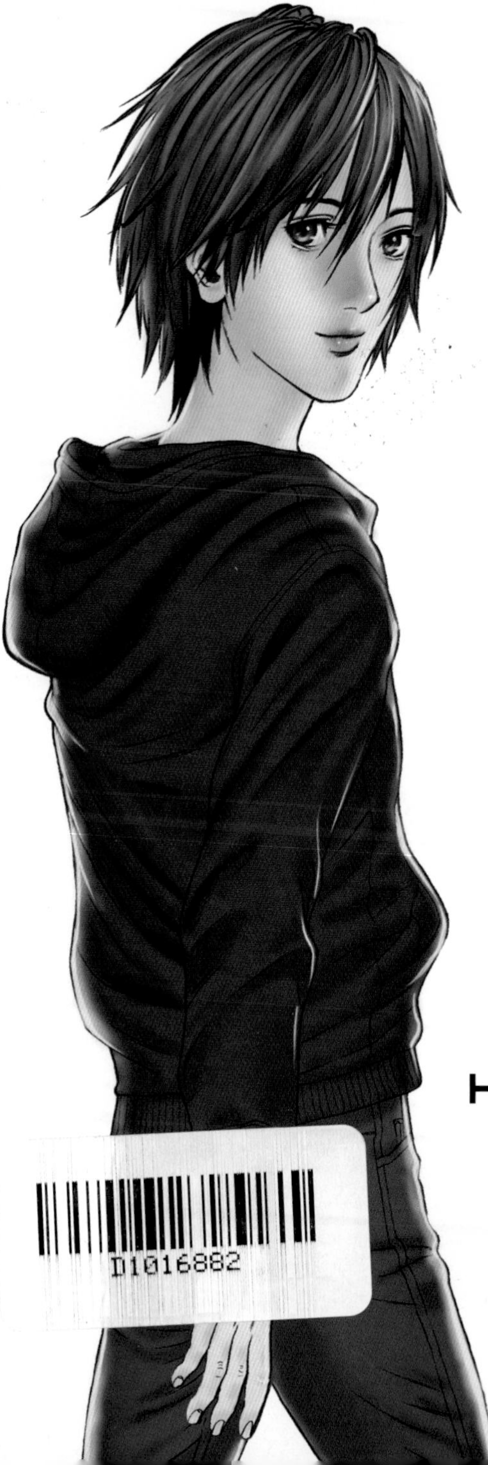

INUYASHIKI

10

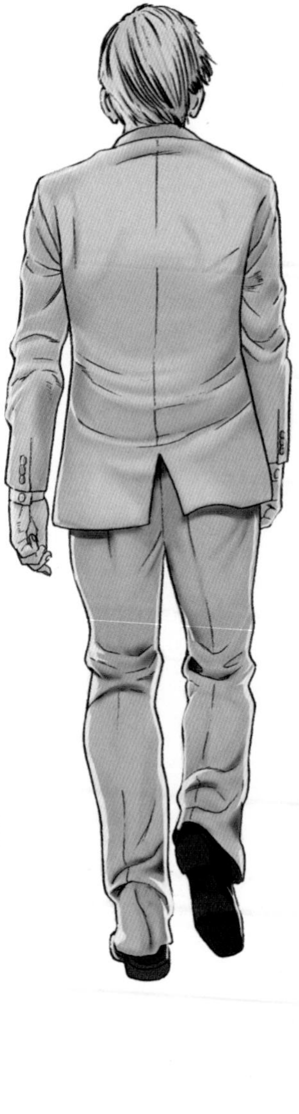

HIROYA OKU

CHAPTER 78: WHAT I CAN DO
3

CHAPTER 79: FATHER, THOU SHALT NOT DIE
25

CHAPTER 80: IF THIS WERE ARMAGEDDON
47

CHAPTER 81: STILL HE FOUGHT AGAINST DESPAIR
69

CHAPTER 82: WHY ARE YOU HERE...?
91

CHAPTER 83: FOR WHOSE SAKE?
115

CHAPTER 84: ICHIRO INUYASHIKI
137

FINAL CHAPTER: LAST HERO
161

INUYASHIKI 10 CONTENTS

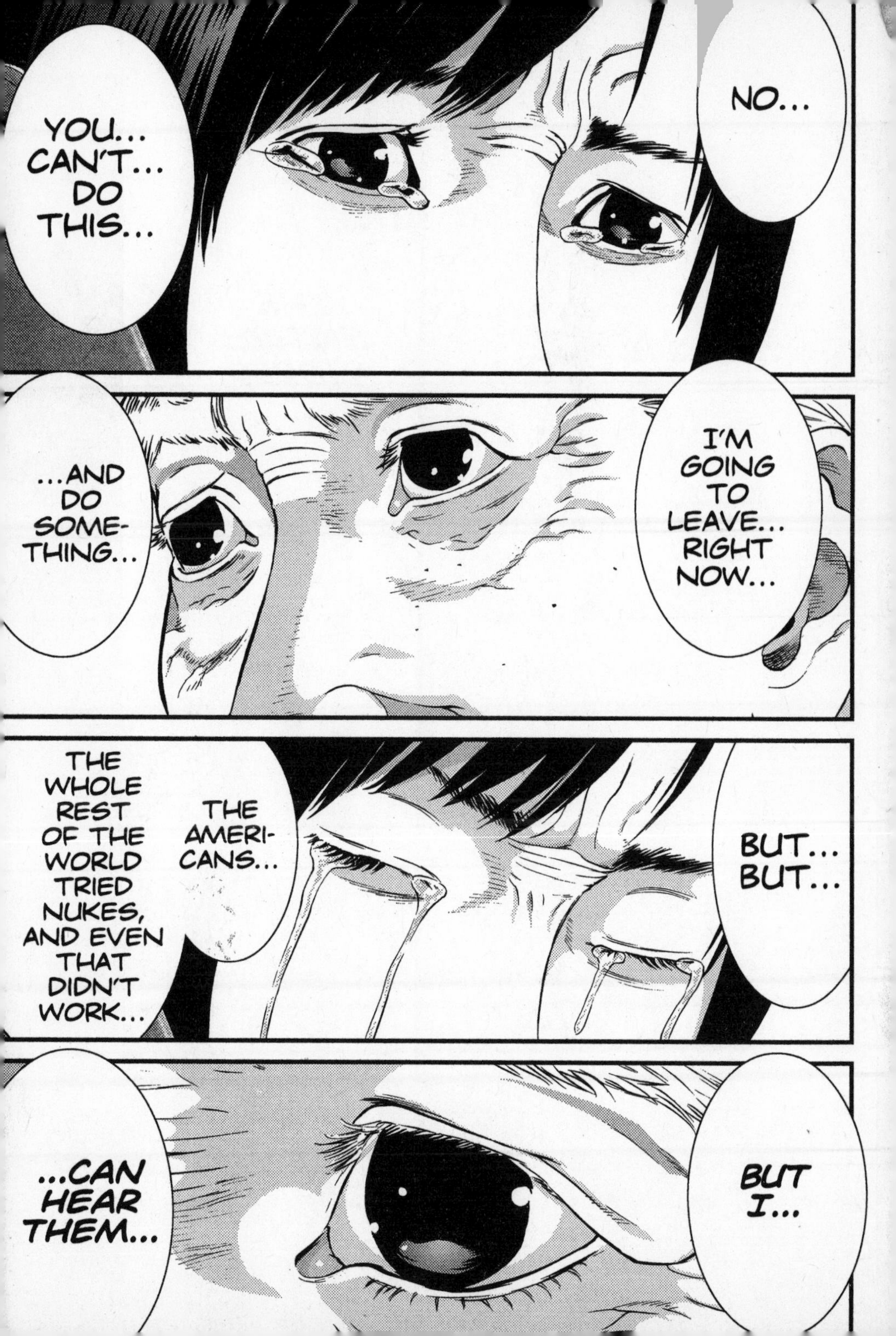
NO...
YOU... CAN'T... DO THIS...
I'M GOING TO LEAVE... RIGHT NOW...
...AND DO SOMETHING...
BUT... BUT...
THE AMERICANS...
THE WHOLE REST OF THE WORLD TRIED NUKES, AND EVEN THAT DIDN'T WORK...
BUT I...
...CAN HEAR THEM...

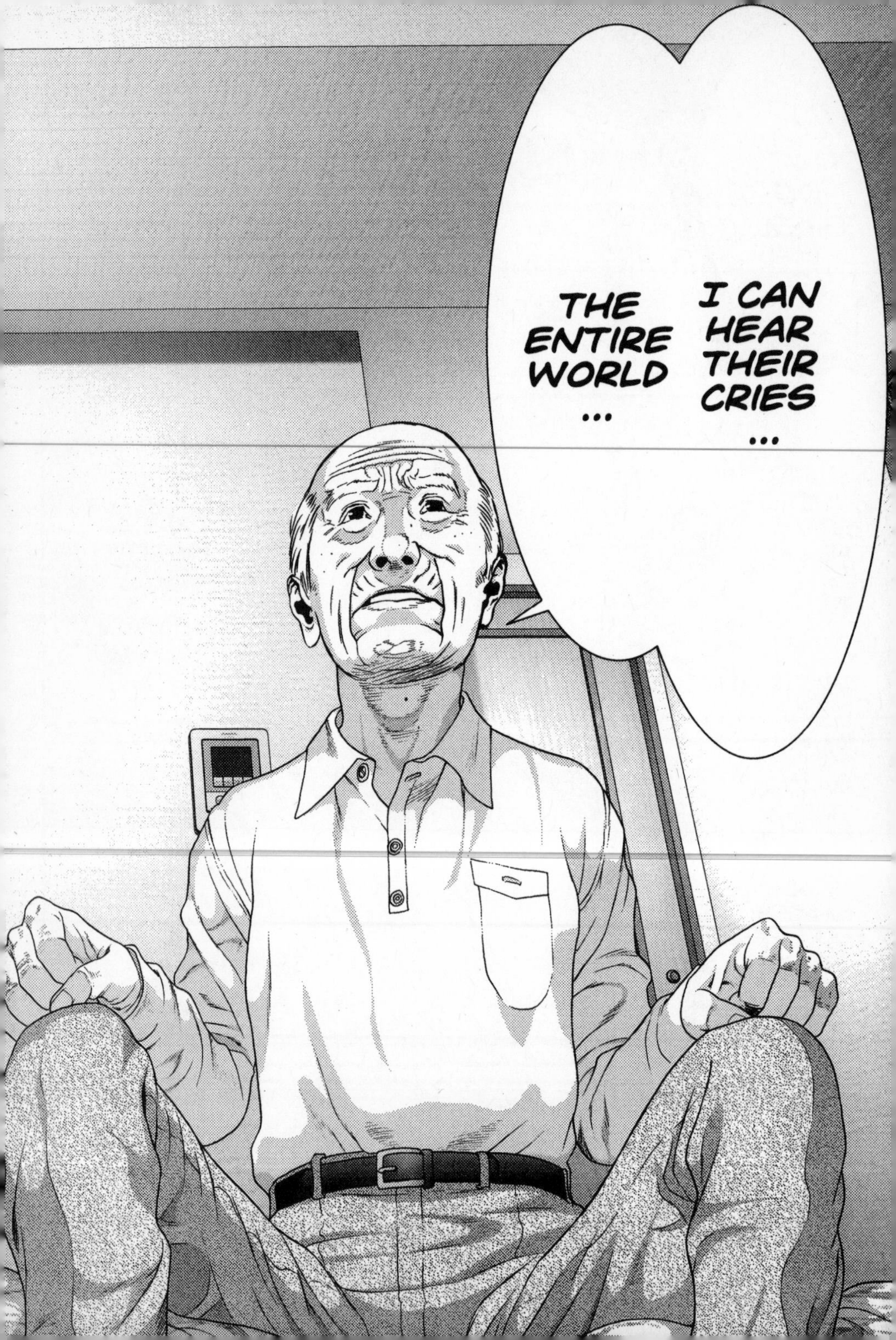
I CAN HEAR THEIR CRIES ...
THE ENTIRE WORLD ...

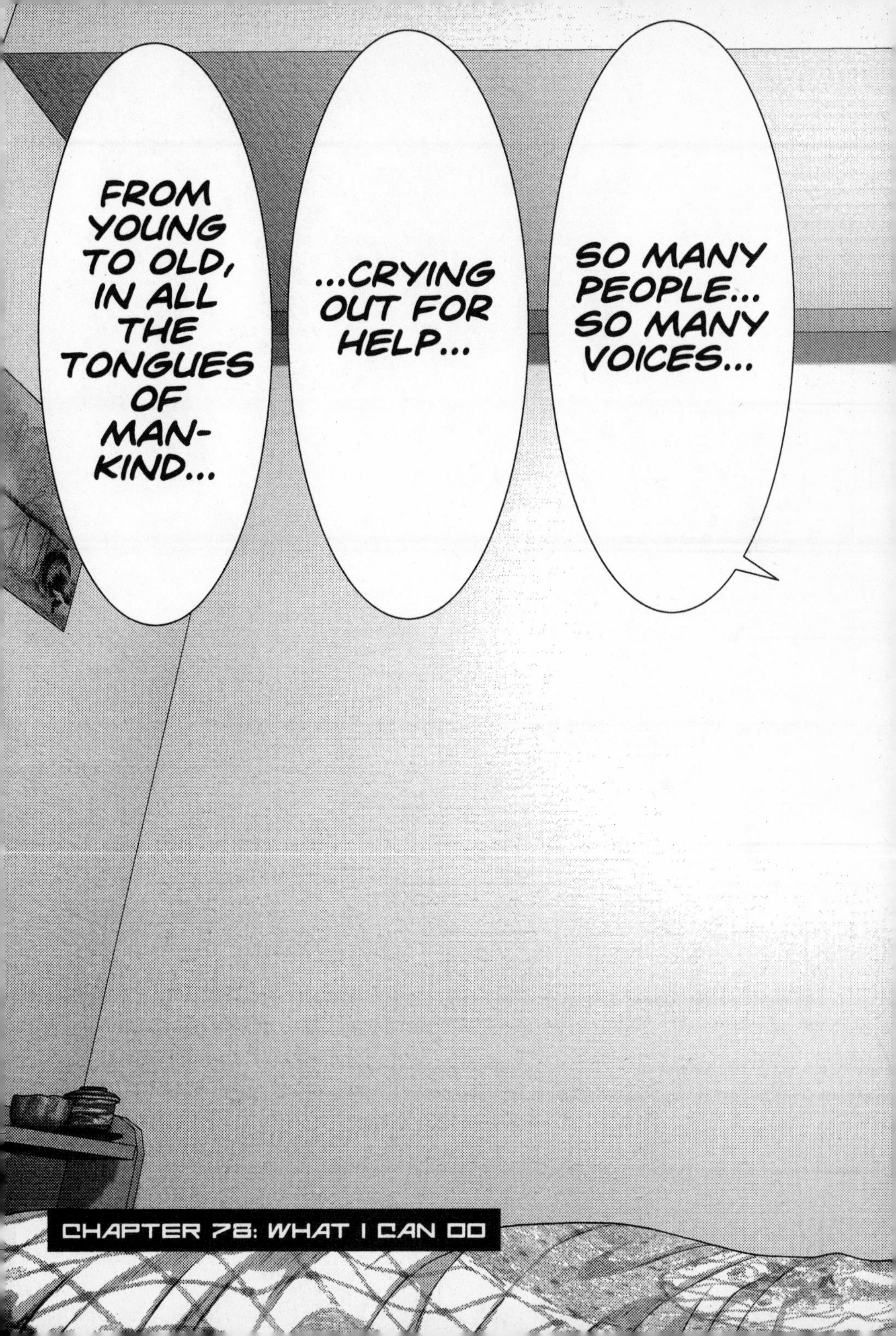
SO MANY PEOPLE... SO MANY VOICES...
...CRYING OUT FOR HELP...
FROM YOUNG TO OLD, IN ALL THE TONGUES OF MAN-KIND...
CHAPTER 78: WHAT I CAN DO

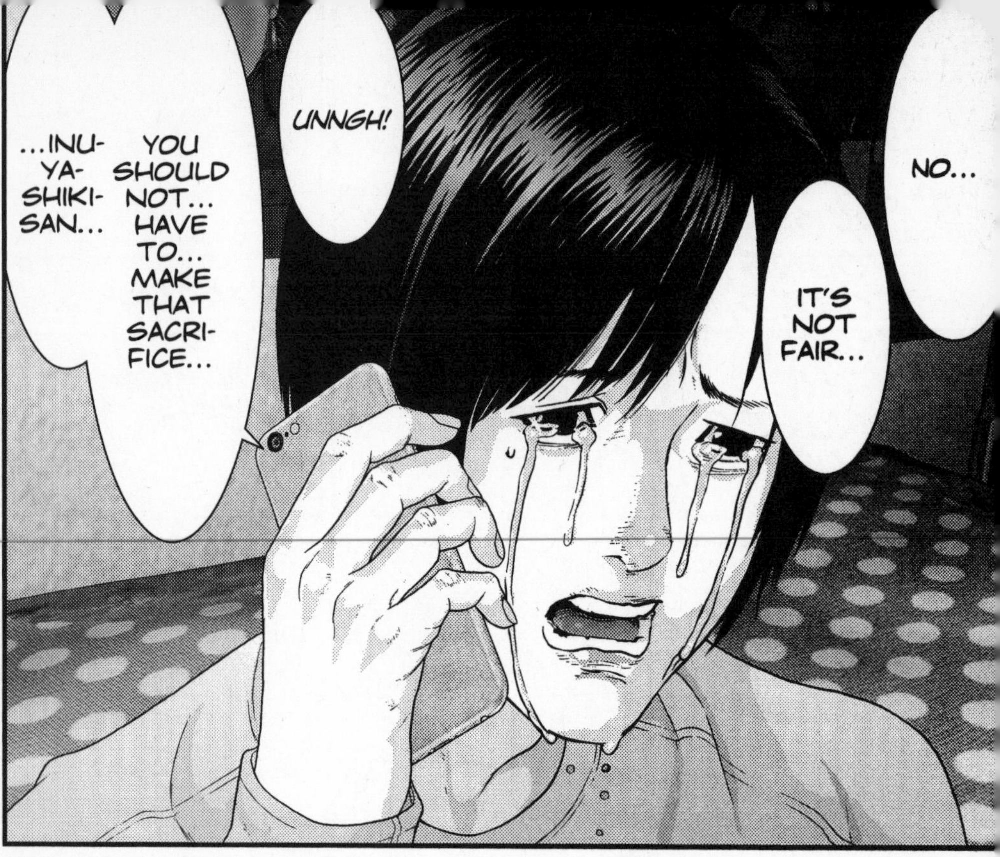
NO...
IT'S NOT FAIR...
UNNGH!
YOU SHOULD NOT... HAVE TO... MAKE THAT SACRIFICE... ...INUYASHIKI-SAN...
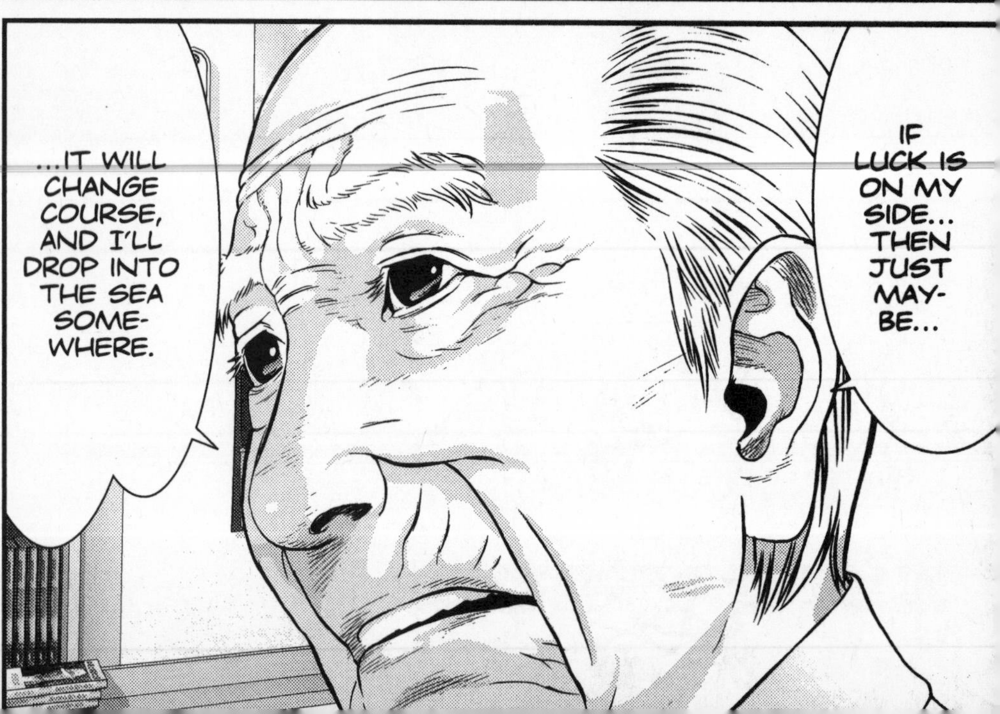
IF LUCK IS ON MY SIDE... THEN JUST MAYBE...
...IT WILL CHANGE COURSE, AND I'LL DROP INTO THE SEA SOMEWHERE.

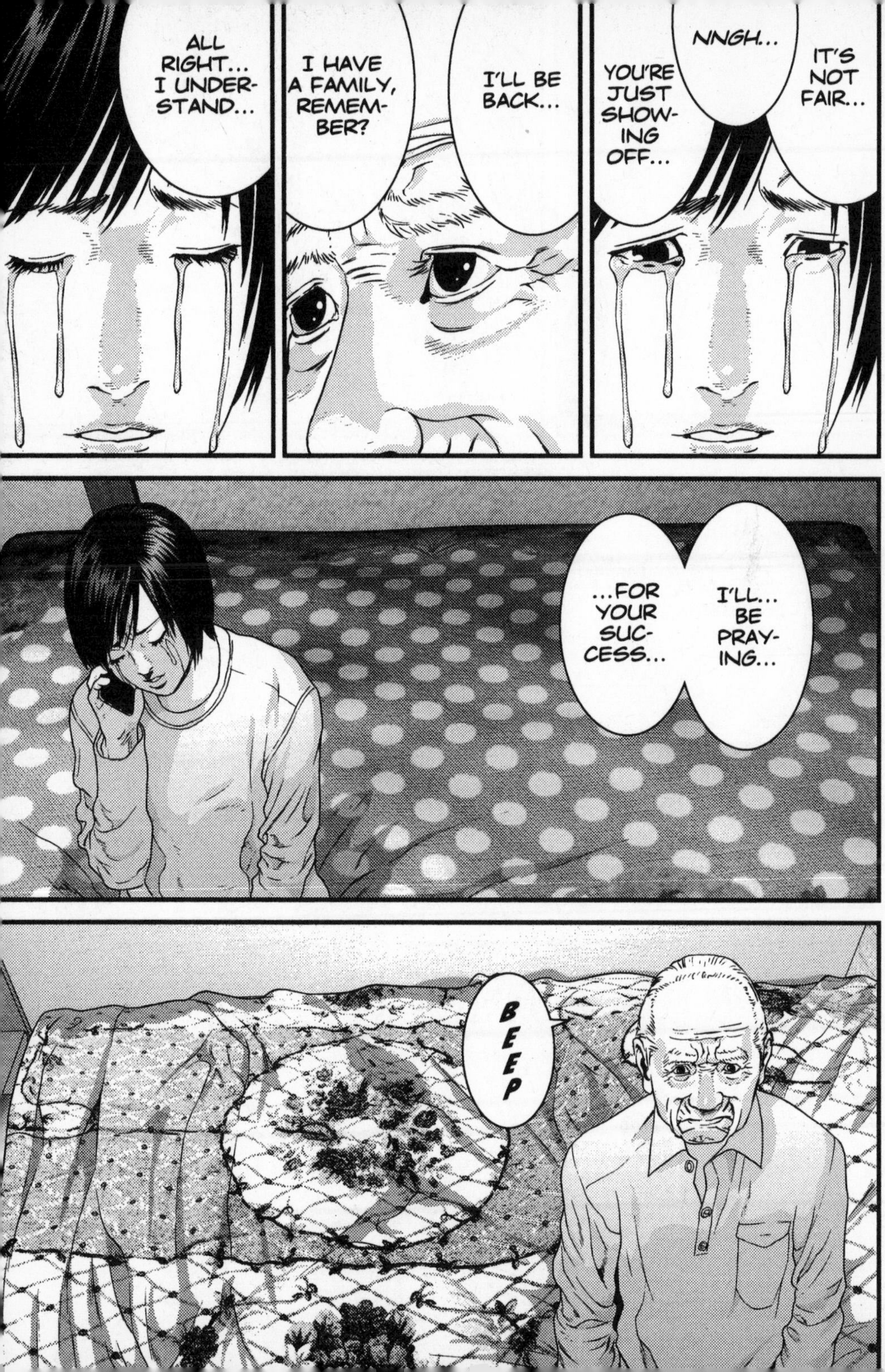
IT'S NOT FAIR...
NNGH...
YOU'RE JUST SHOWING-OFF...
I'LL BE BACK...
I HAVE A FAMILY, REMEMBER?
ALL RIGHT... I UNDERSTAND...
I'LL... BE PRAYING...
...FOR YOUR SUCCESS...
BEEP

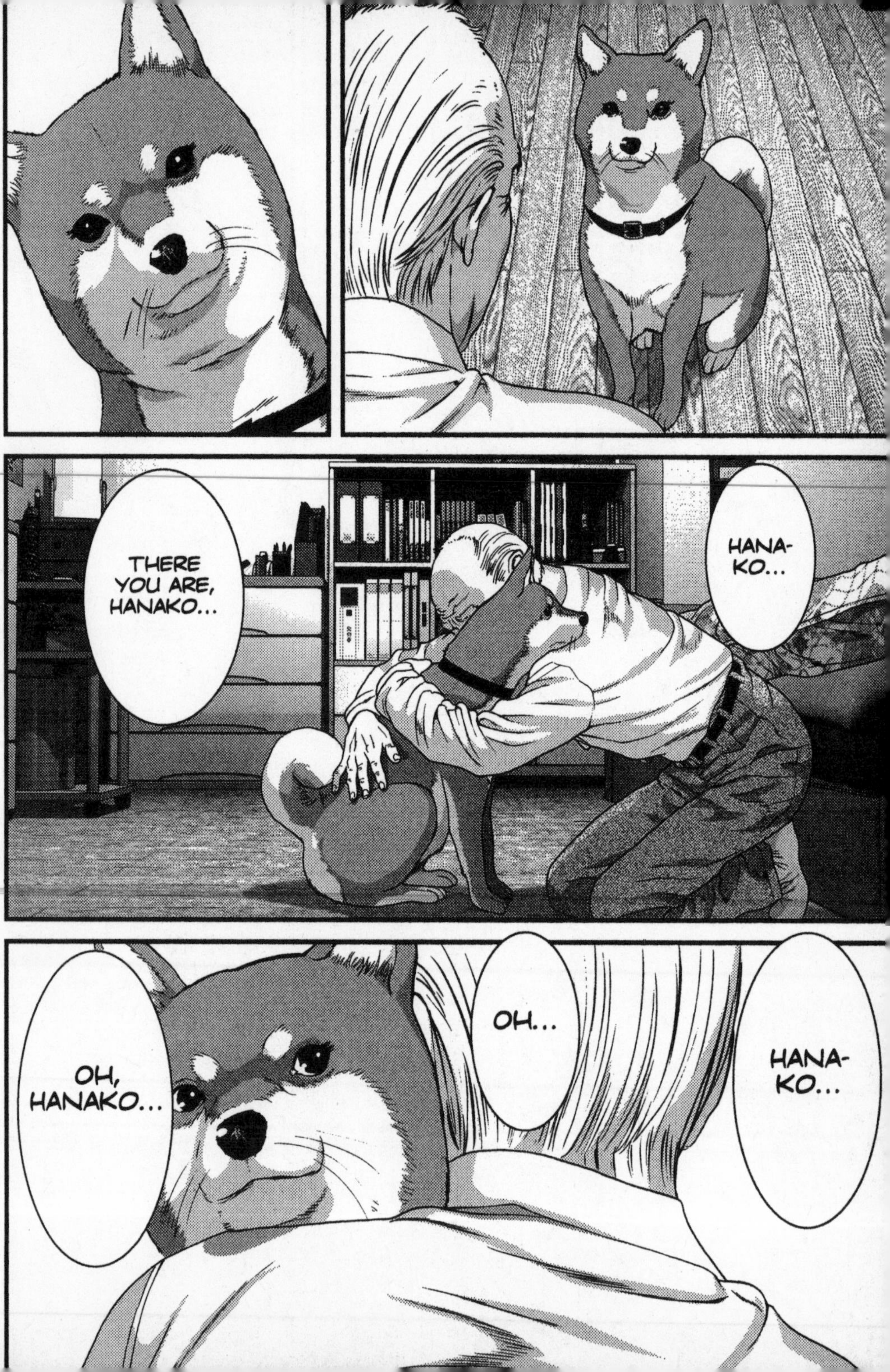
HANA-KO...
THERE YOU ARE, HANAKO...
HANA-KO...
OH...
OH, HANAKO...

ALL RIGHT... I'M HEAD-ING OUT NOW.

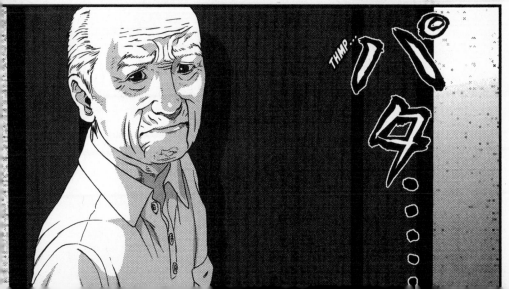

THMP...

FSHHHHHHHH

WELL, EVERY-ONE... I'M OFF...

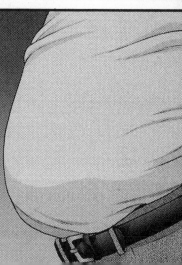

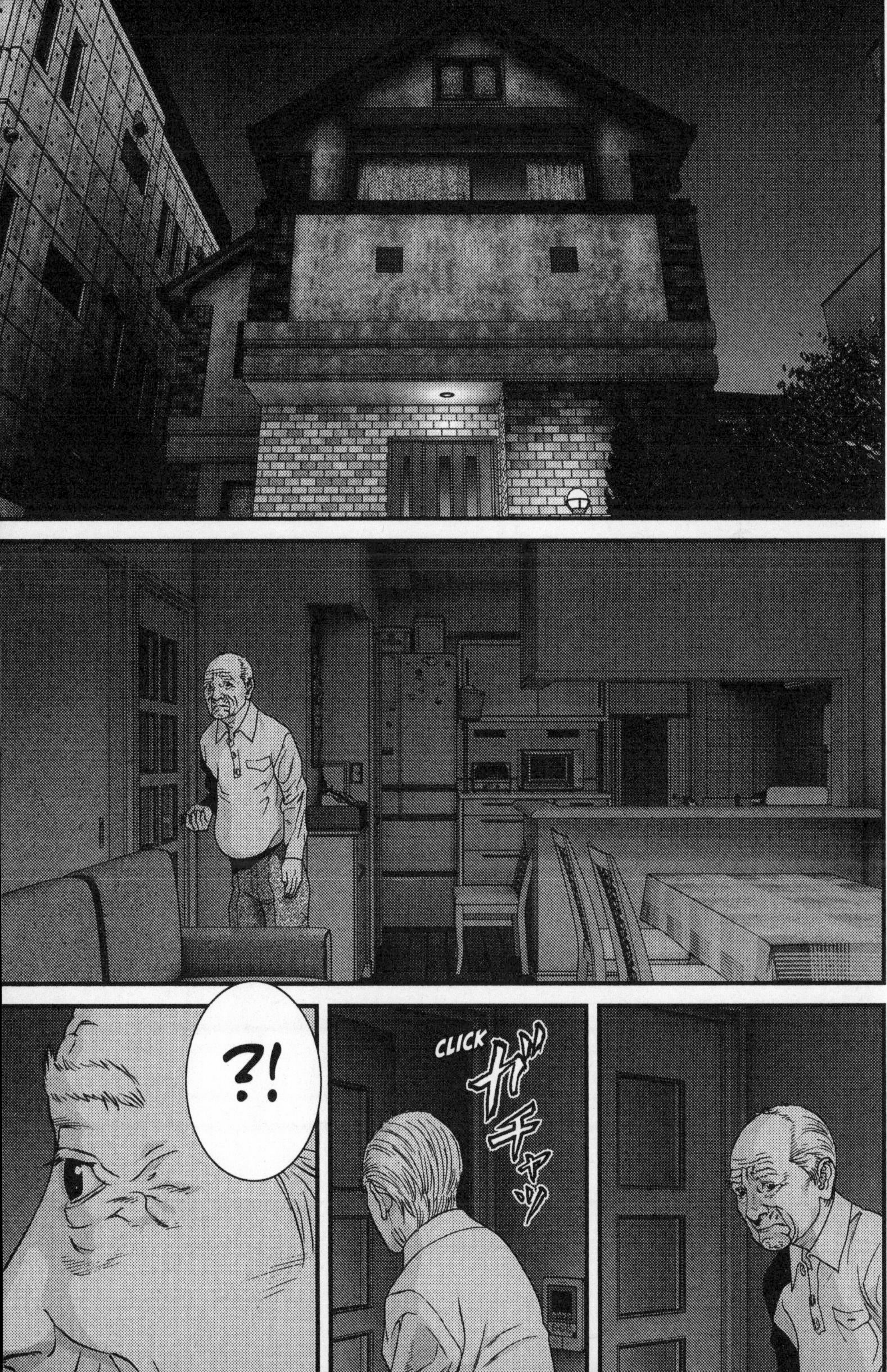
CLICK
ガチャッ
?!

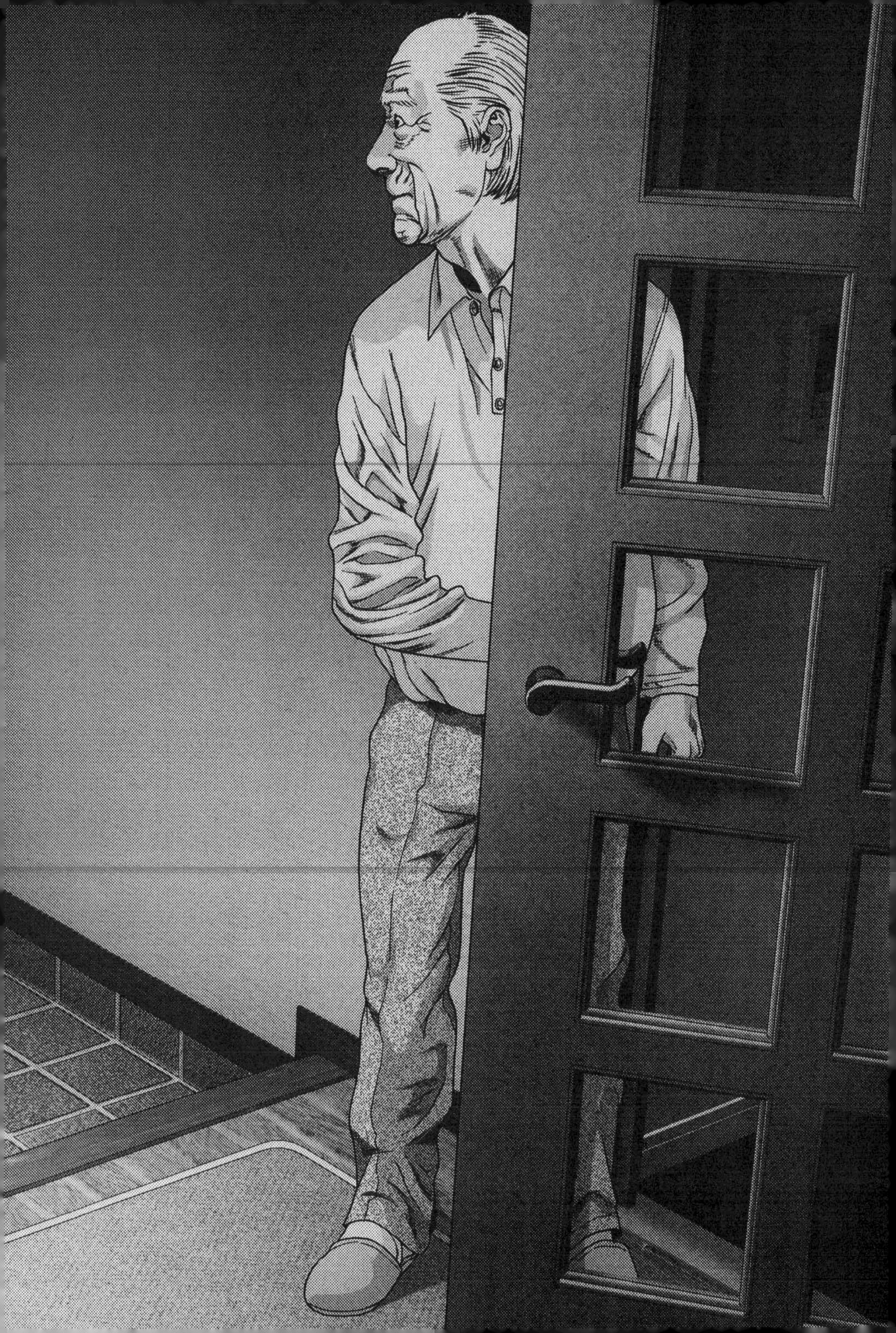

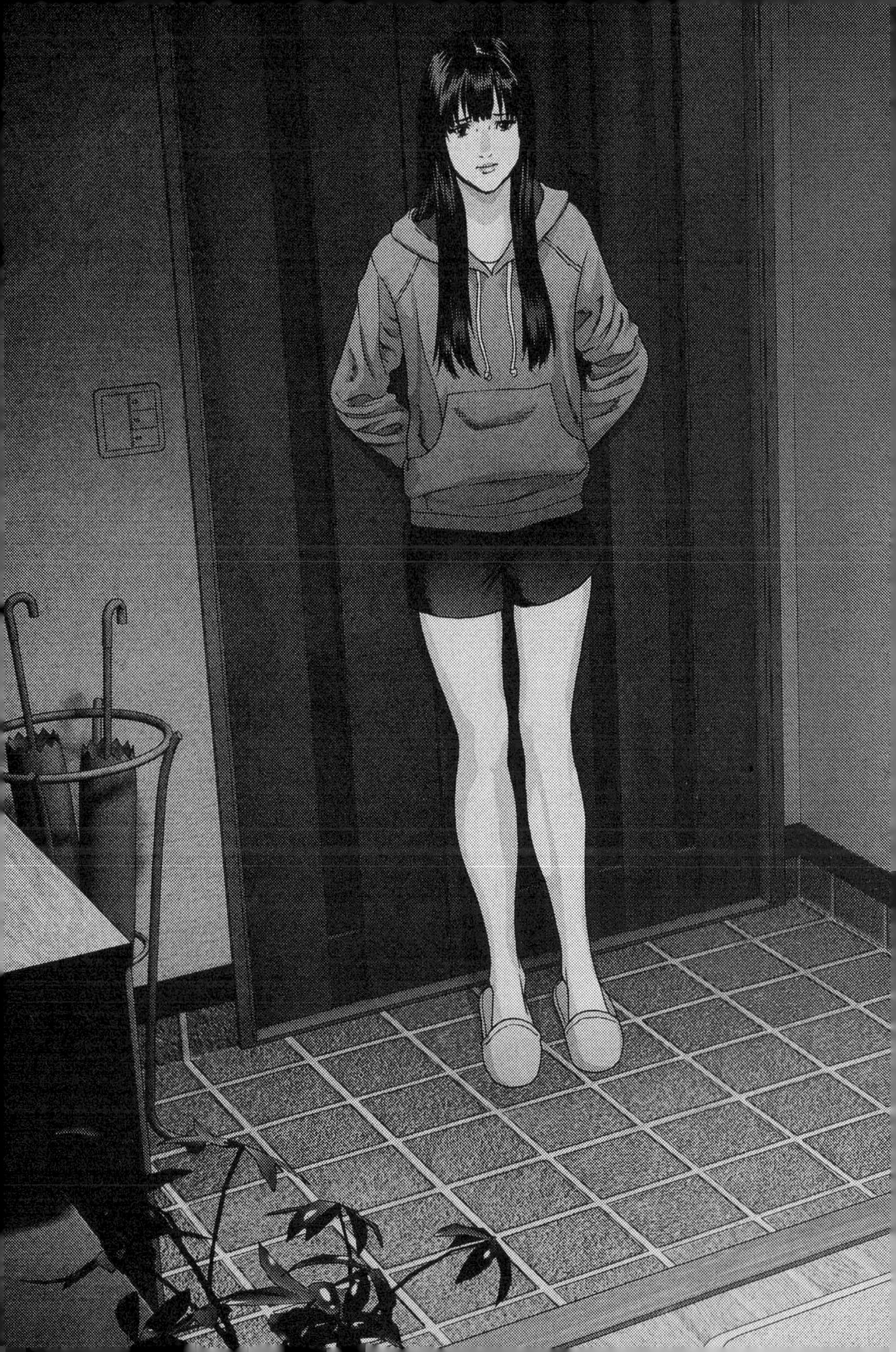

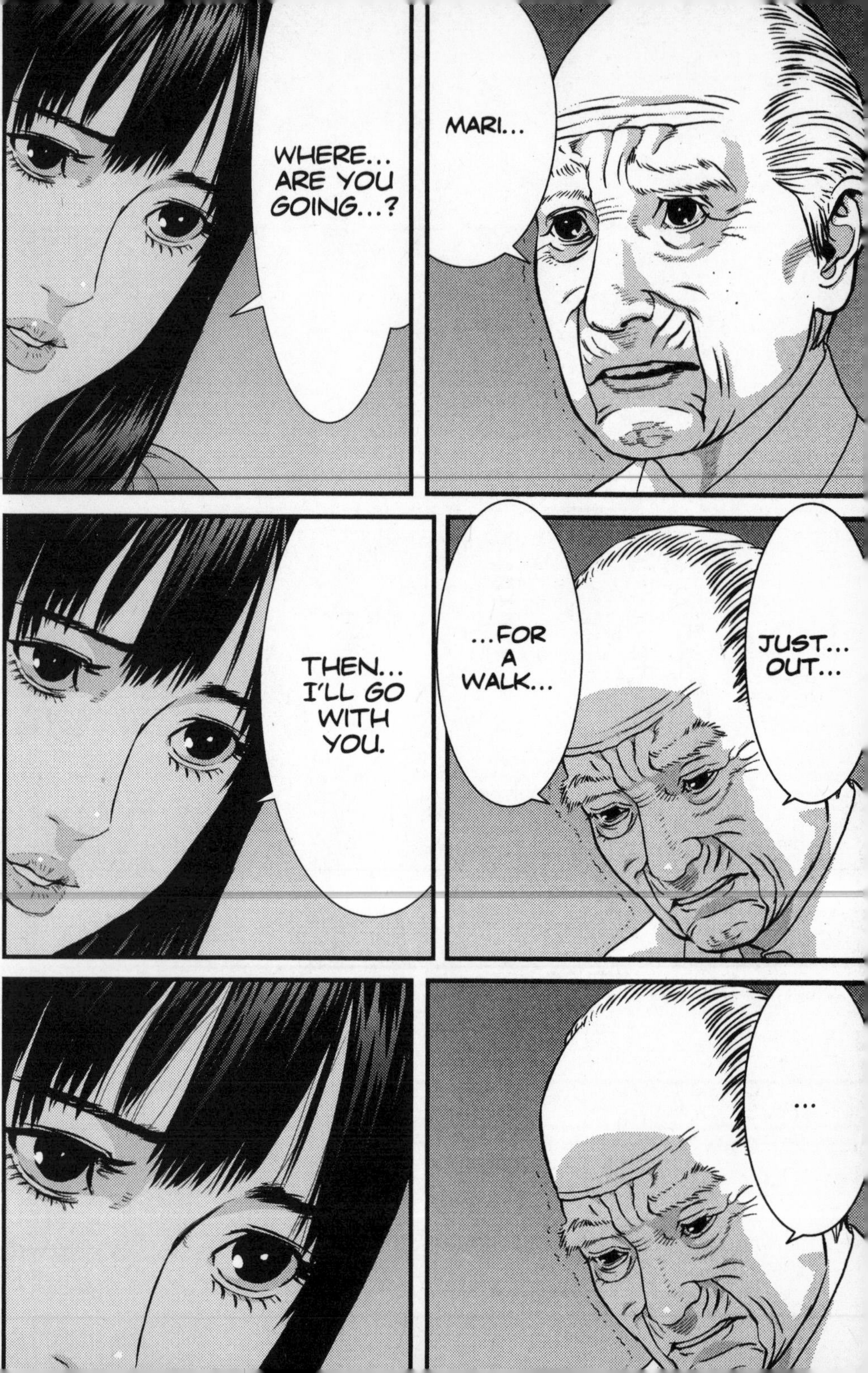
MARI...
WHERE... ARE YOU GOING...?
JUST... OUT...
...FOR A WALK...
THEN... I'LL GO WITH YOU.
...

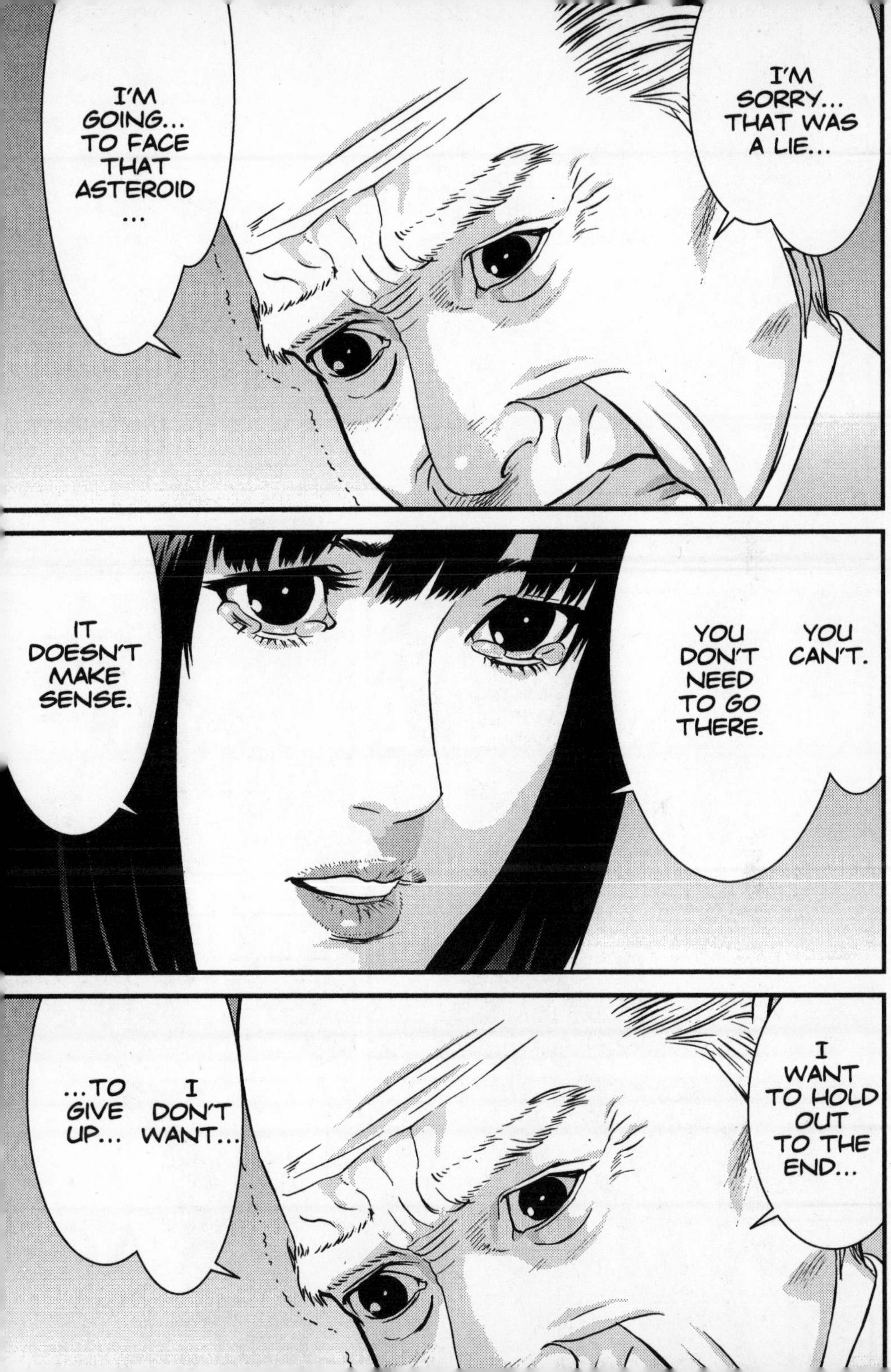
I'M SORRY... THAT WAS A LIE...
I'M GOING... TO FACE THAT ASTEROID ...
YOU CAN'T.
YOU DON'T NEED TO GO THERE.
IT DOESN'T MAKE SENSE.
I WANT TO HOLD OUT TO THE END...
I DON'T WANT...
...TO GIVE UP...

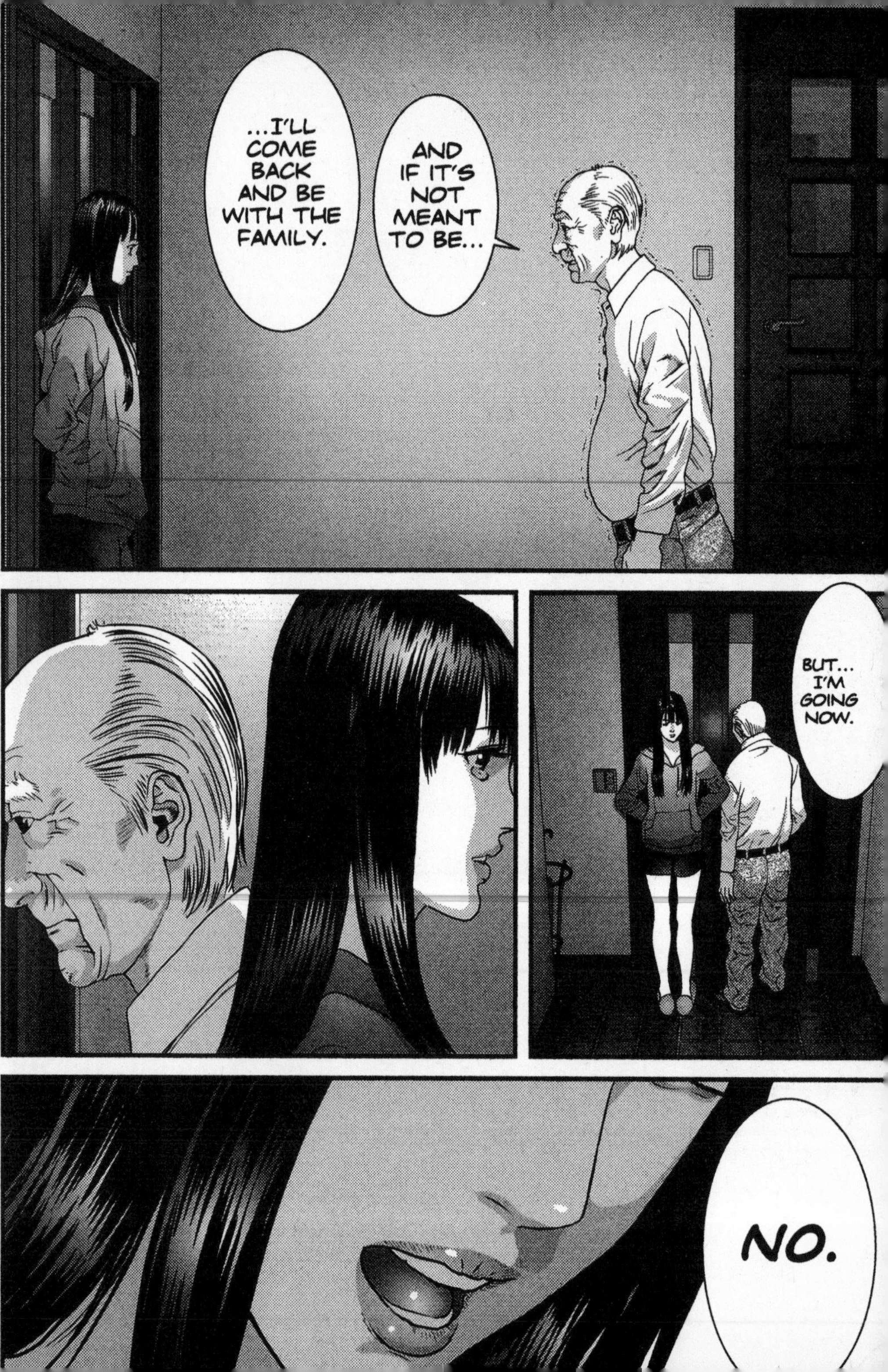
AND IF IT'S NOT MEANT TO BE...
...I'LL COME BACK AND BE WITH THE FAMILY.
BUT... I'M GOING NOW.
NO.

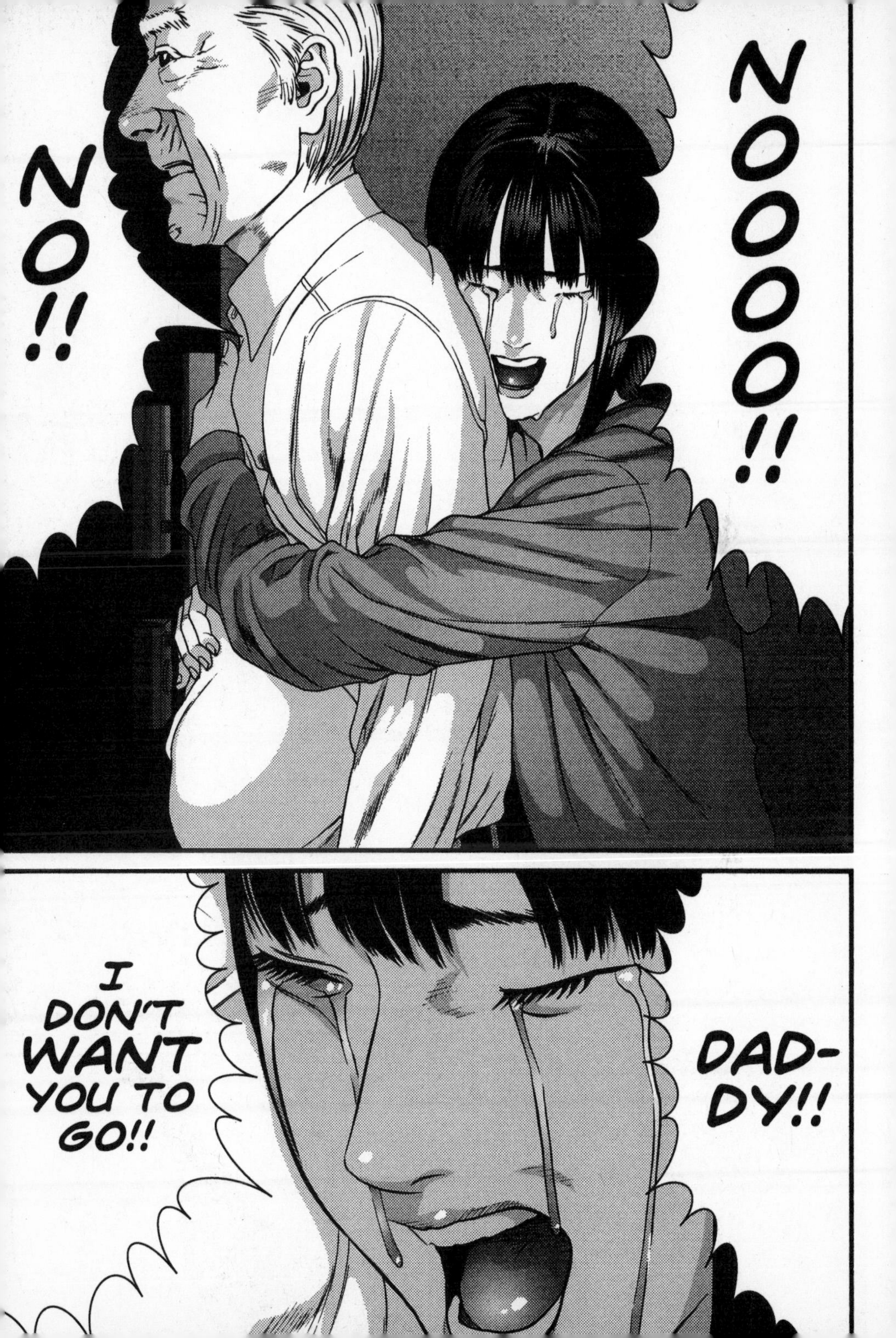
NOOOO!!
NO!!
DAD-DY!!
I DON'T WANT YOU TO GO!!

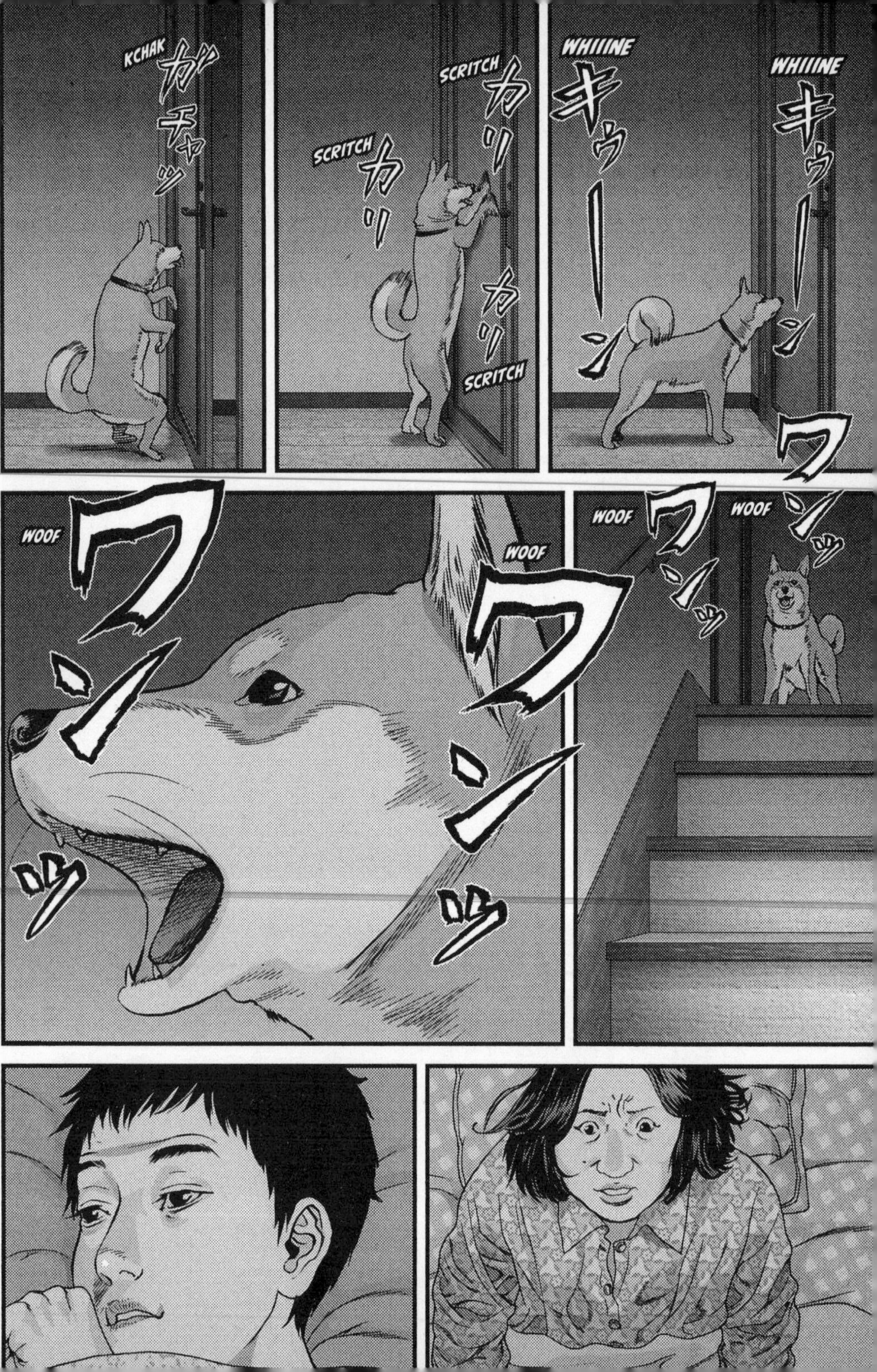
WHIIINE
キューーン
WHIIINE
キューーン
SCRITCH
カリ
SCRITCH
カリ
カリ
SCRITCH
KCHAK
ガチャッ
WOOF
ワンッ
WOOF
ワンッ
WOOF
ワンッ
WOOF
ワンッ

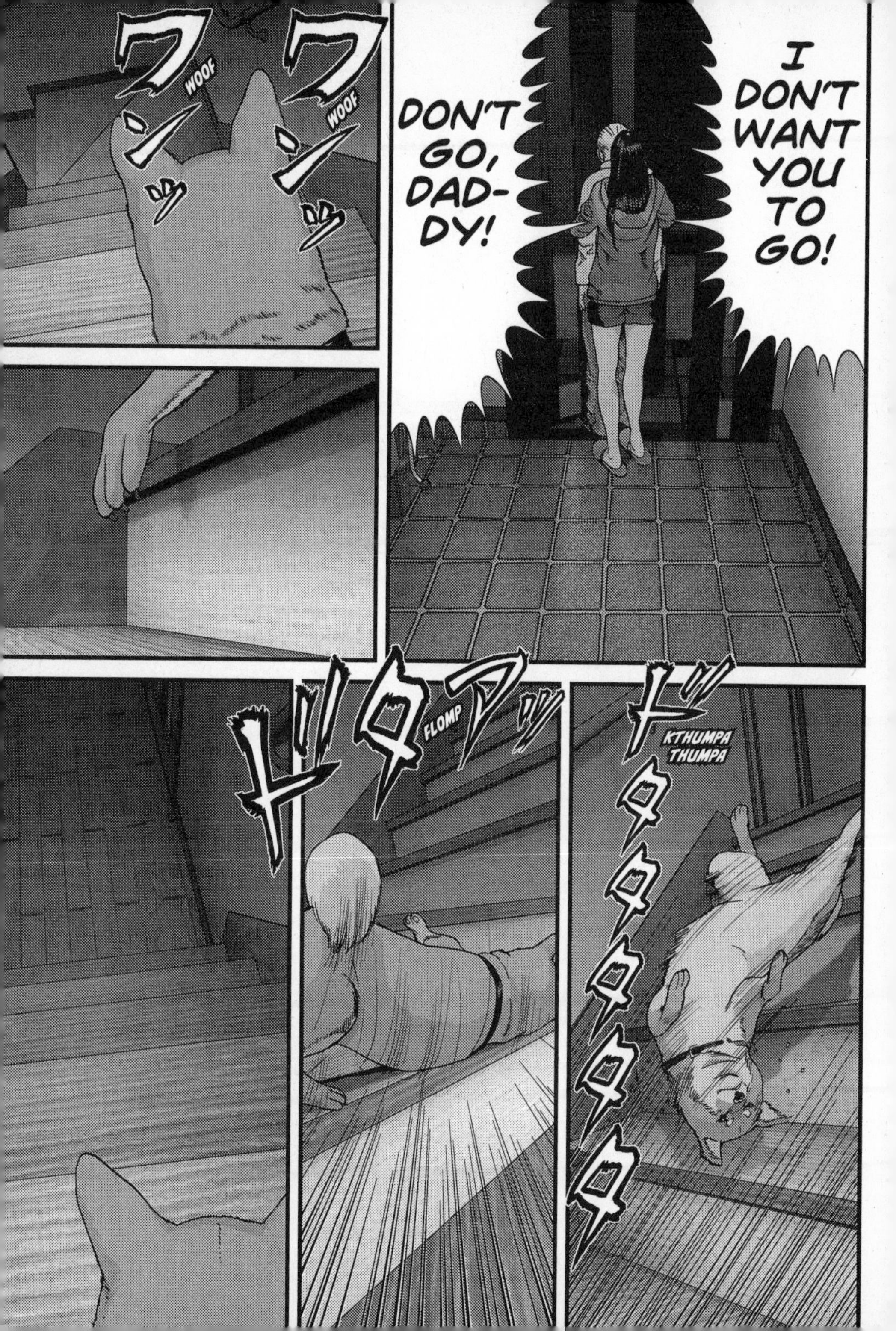
I DON'T WANT YOU TO GO!
DON'T GO, DADDY!
WOOF
WOOF
KTHUMPA THUMPA
FLOMP

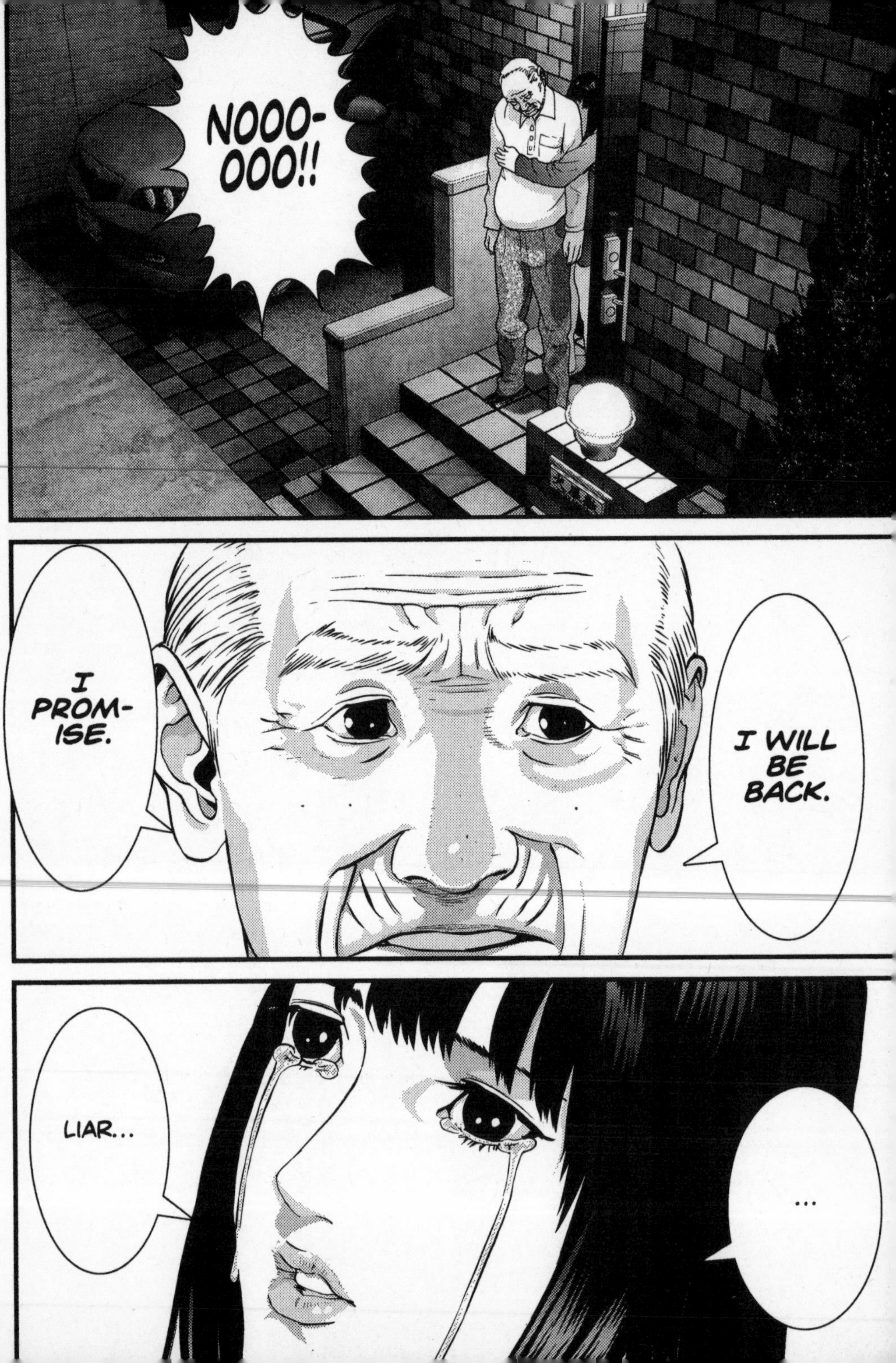
NOOO-
OOO!!
I WILL BE BACK.
I PROMISE.
...
LIAR...

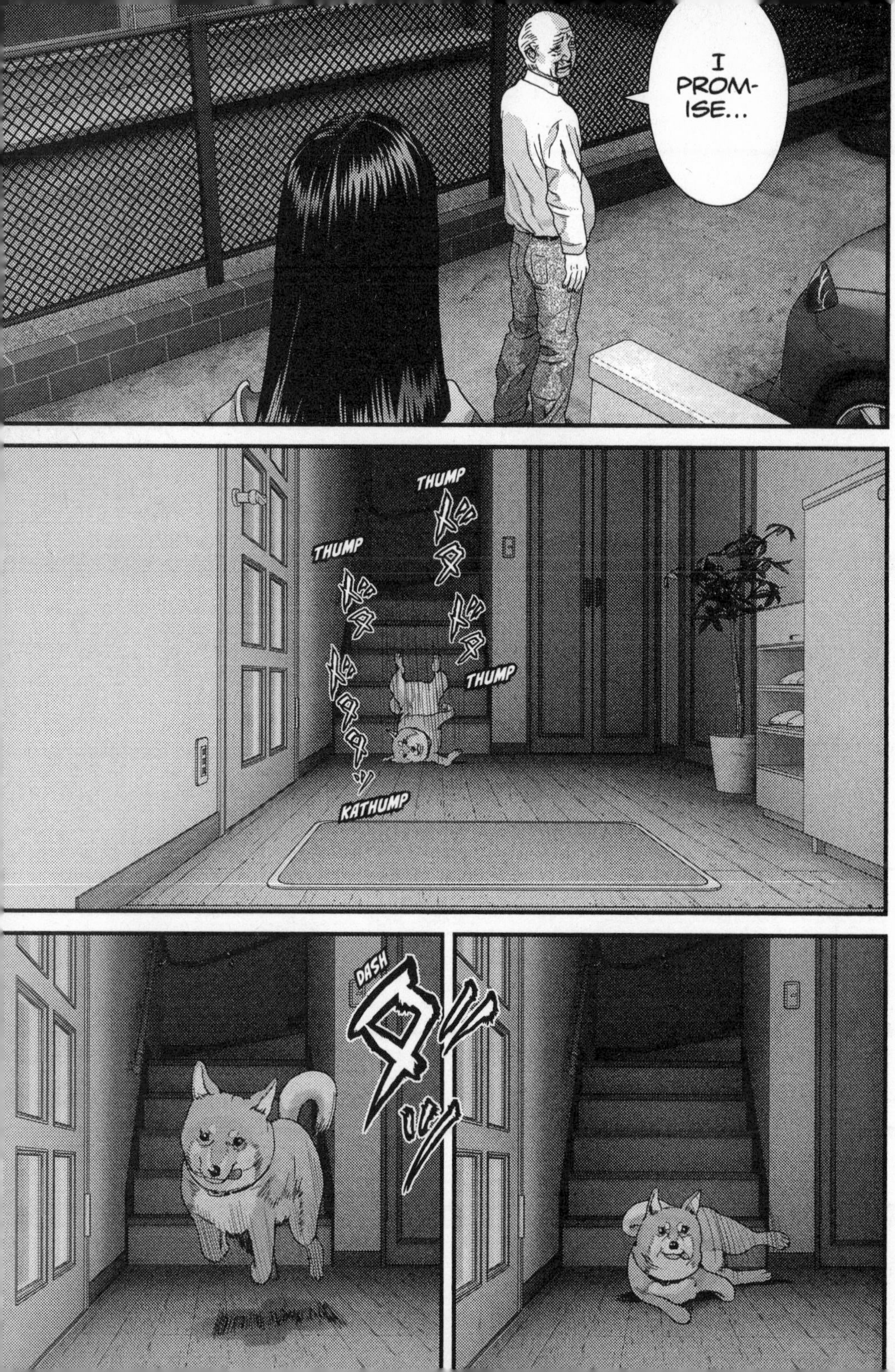
I PROM-
ISE...
THUMP
THUMP
THUMP
KATHUMP
DASH

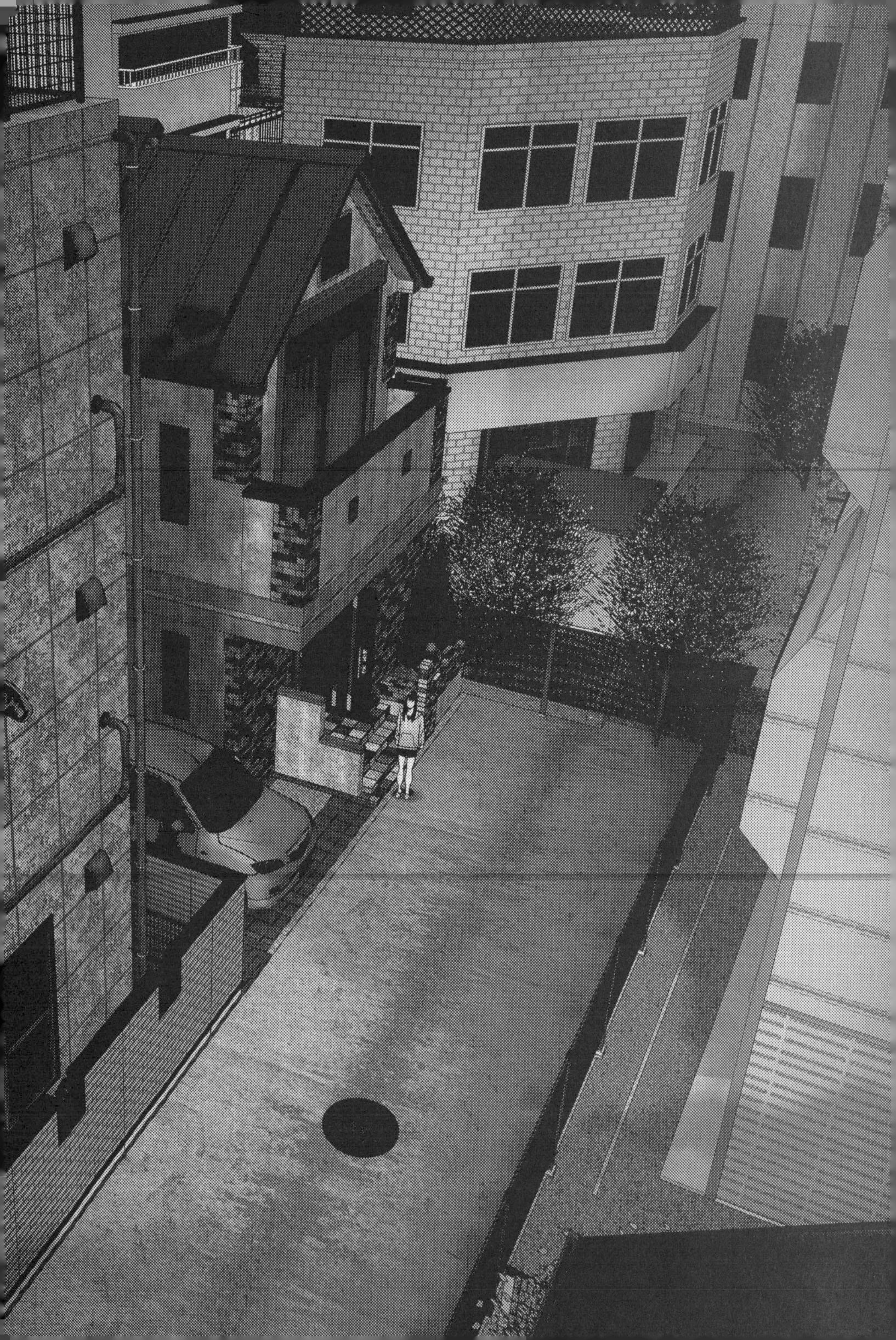

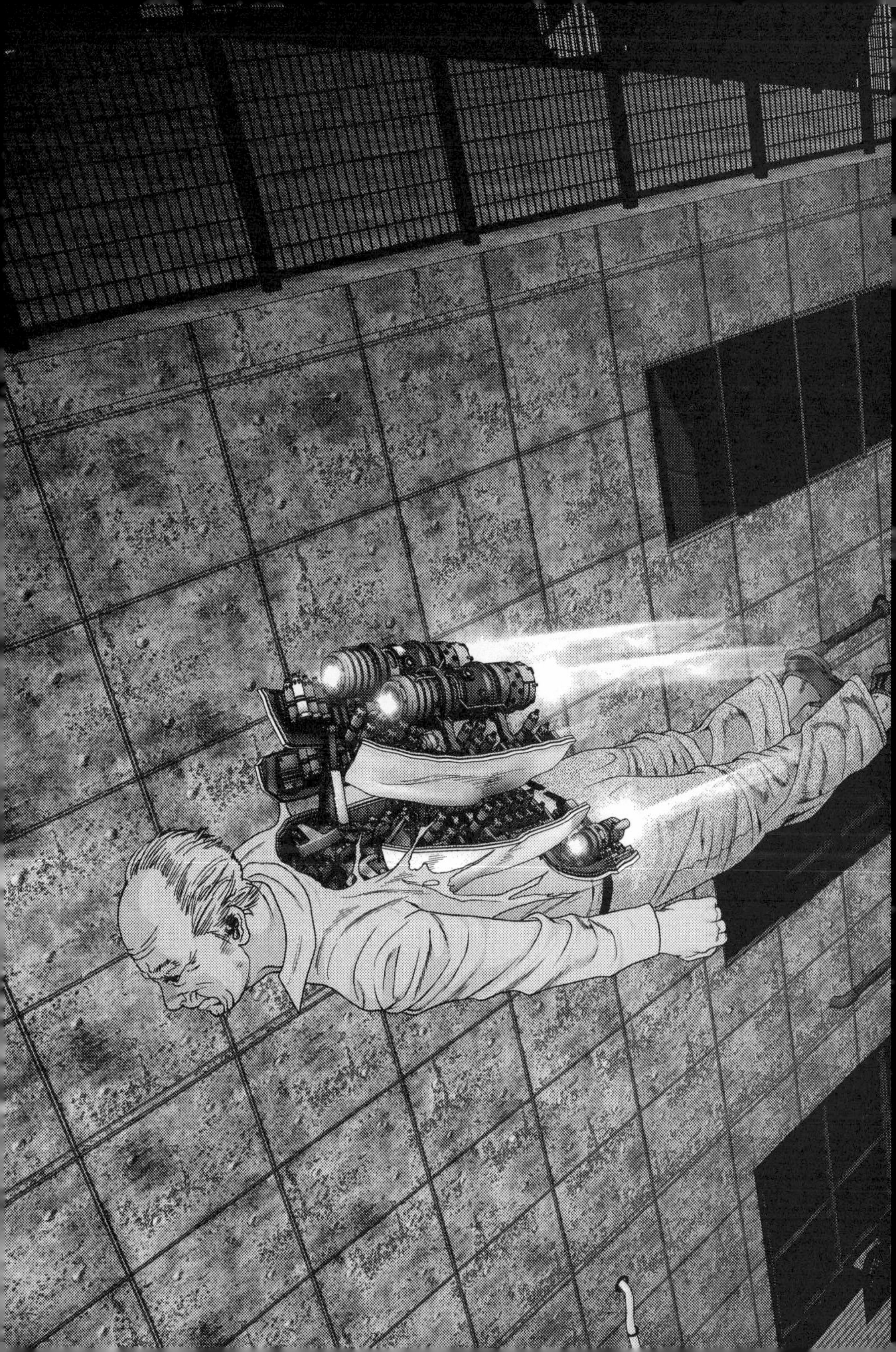

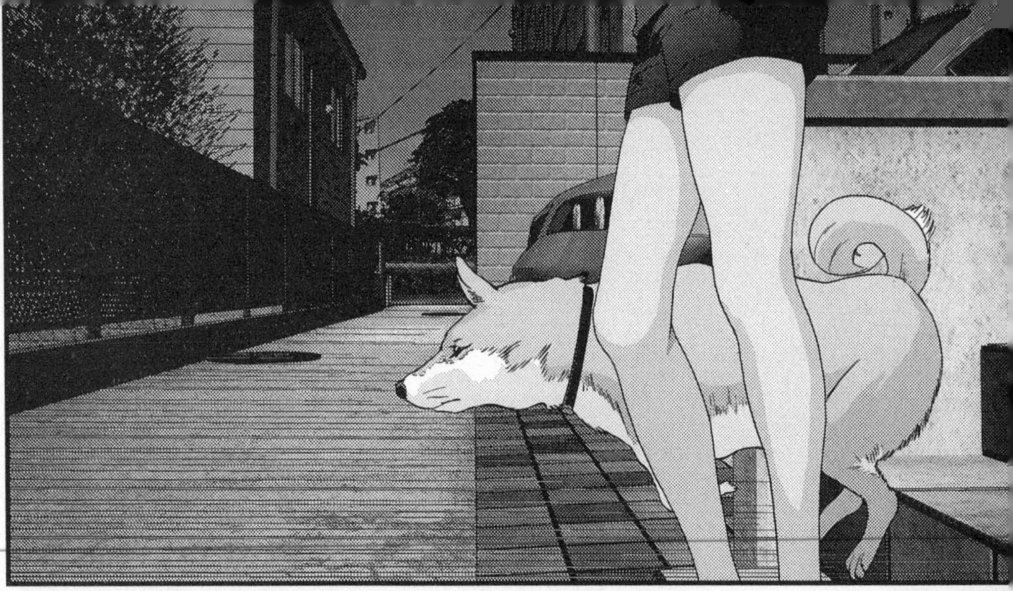

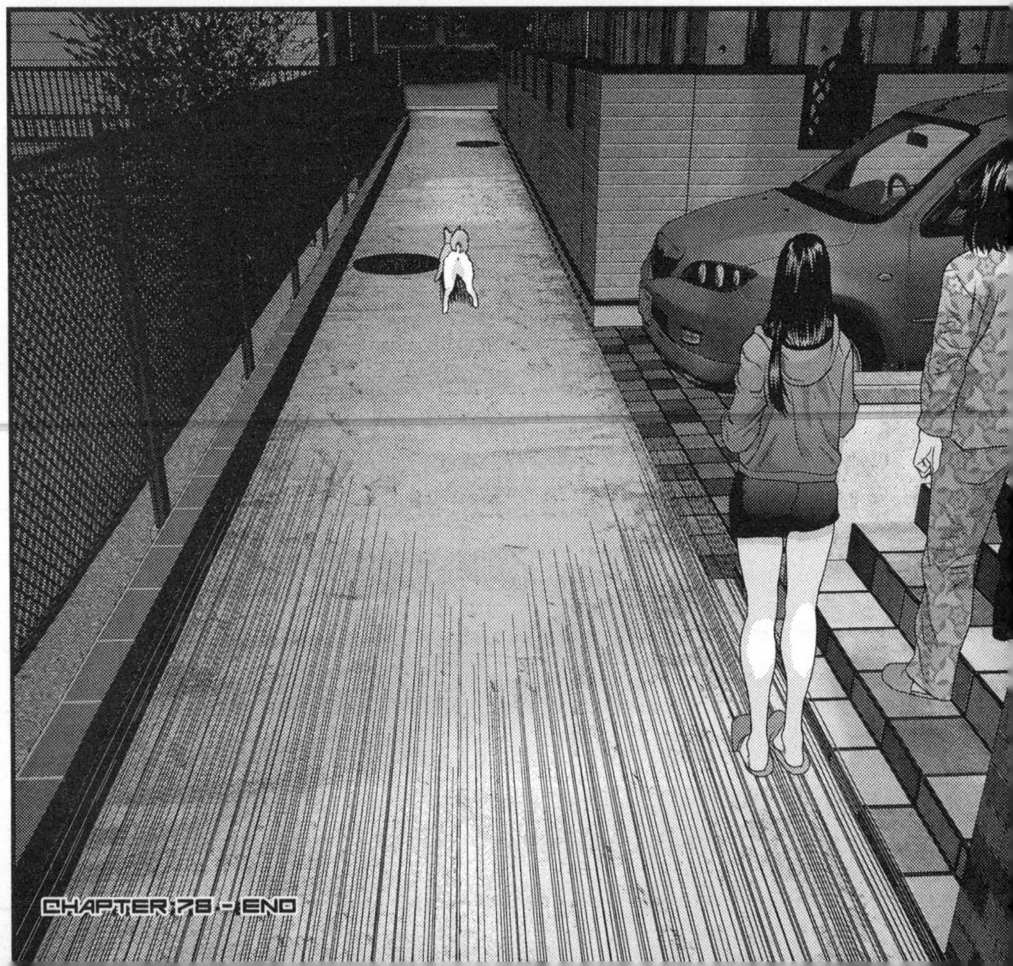
CHAPTER 78 - END

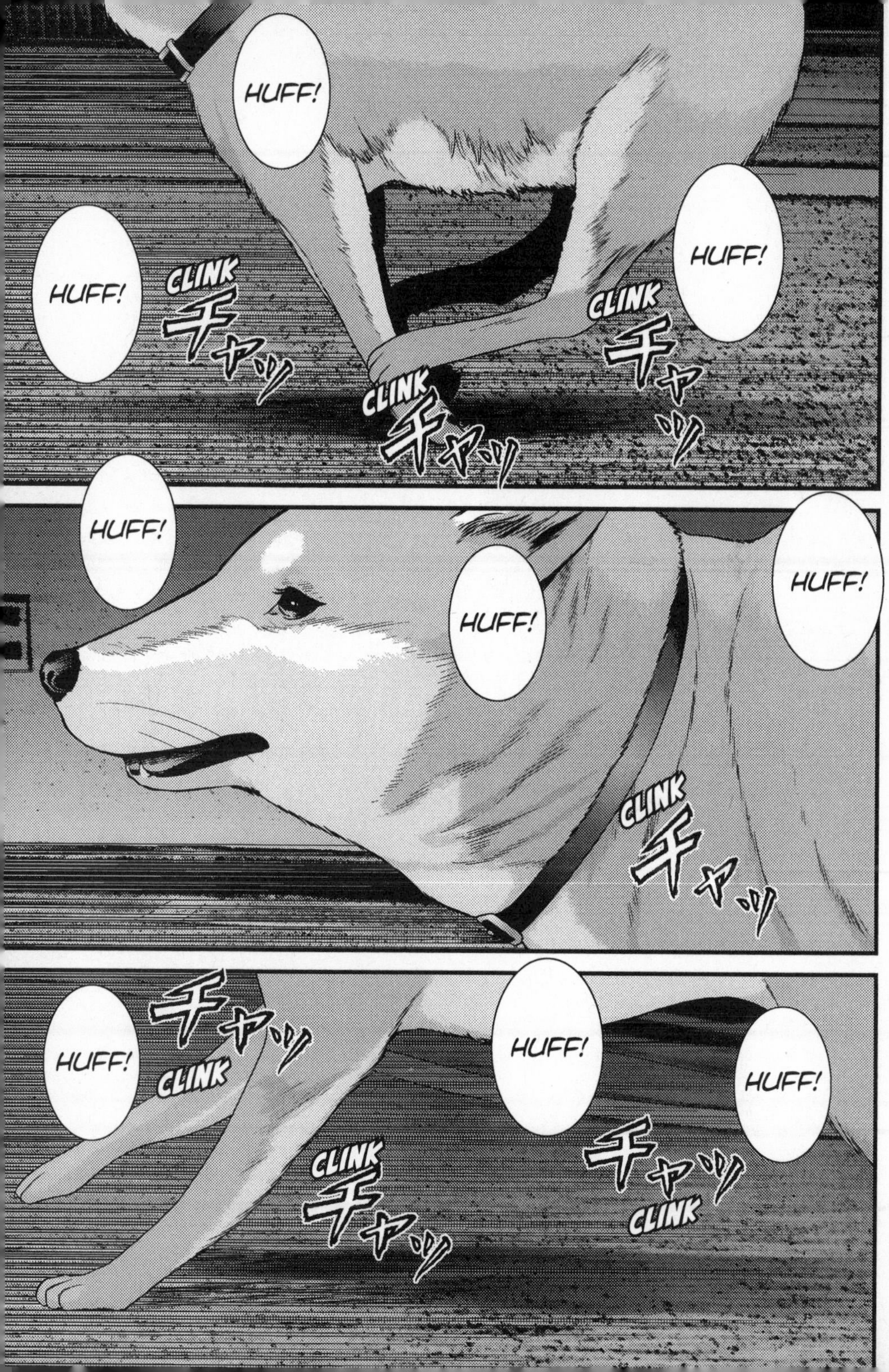
HUFF!
HUFF!
CLINK
チャッ
HUFF!
CLINK
チャッ
CLINK
チャッ
HUFF!
HUFF!
HUFF!
CLINK
チャッ
HUFF!
HUFF!
チャッ
CLINK
CLINK
チャッ
HUFF!
チャッ
CLINK

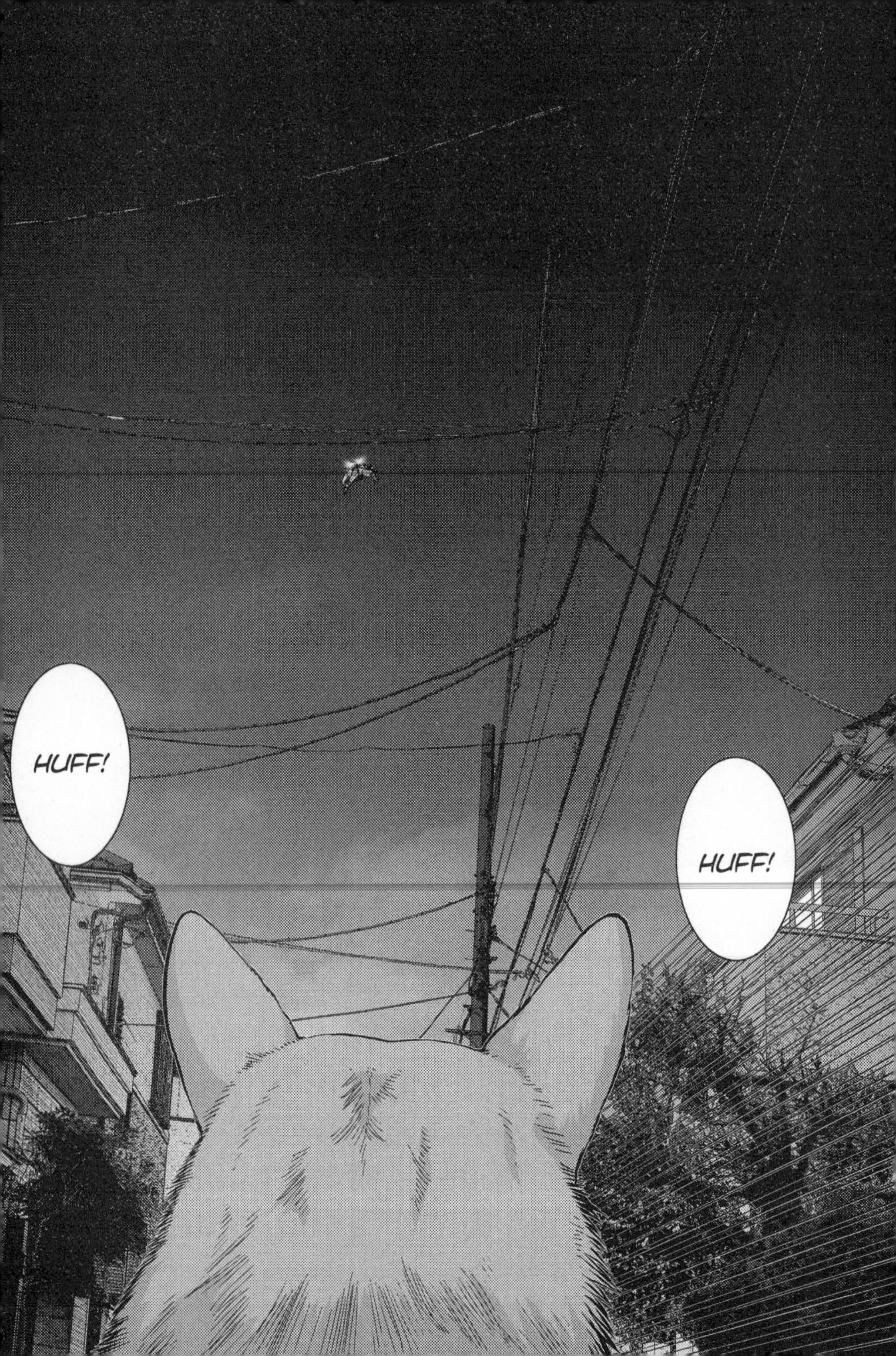
HUFF!
HUFF!

CHAPTER 79: FATHER, THOU SHALT NOT DIE

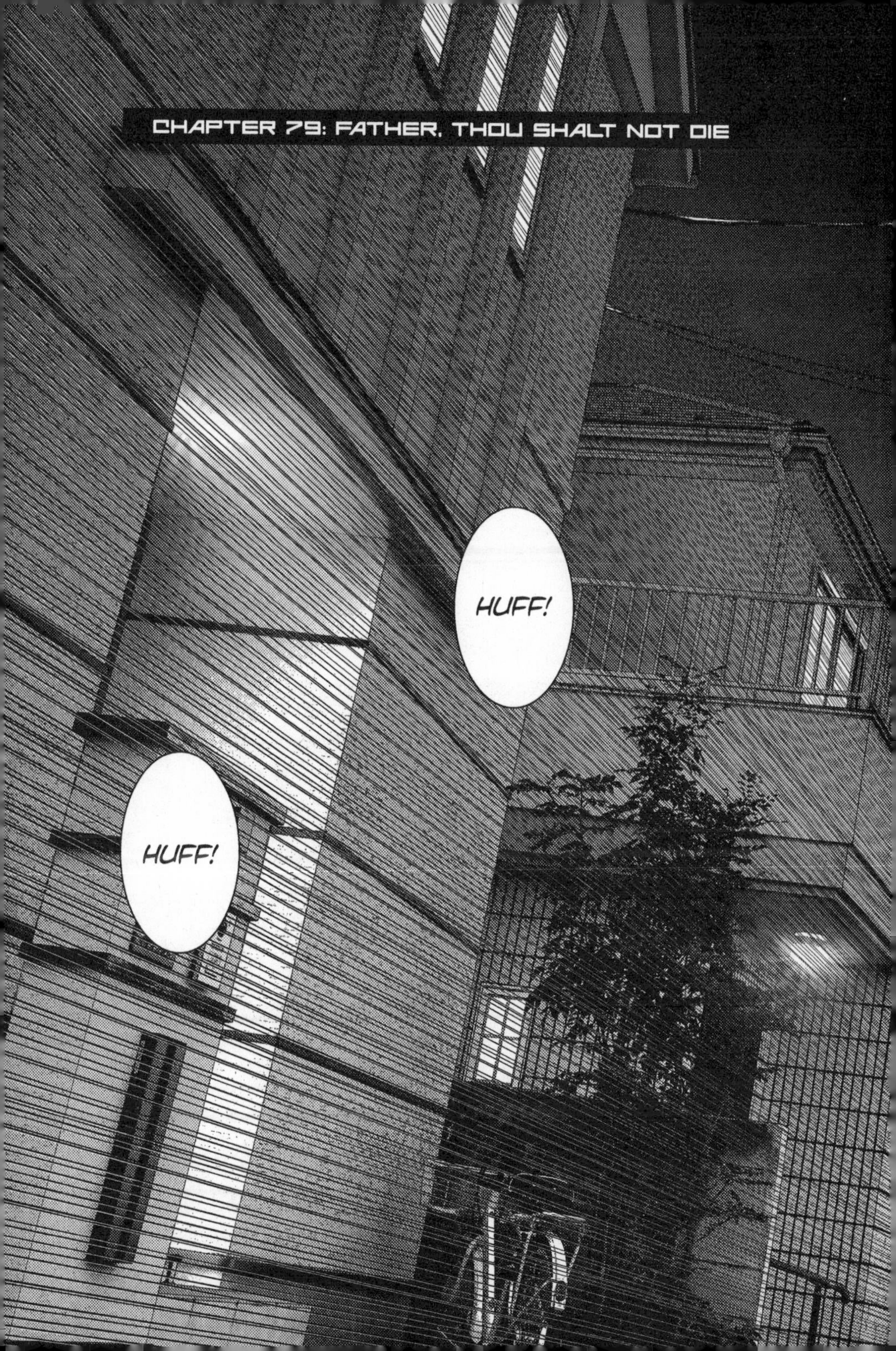
HUFF!
HUFF!

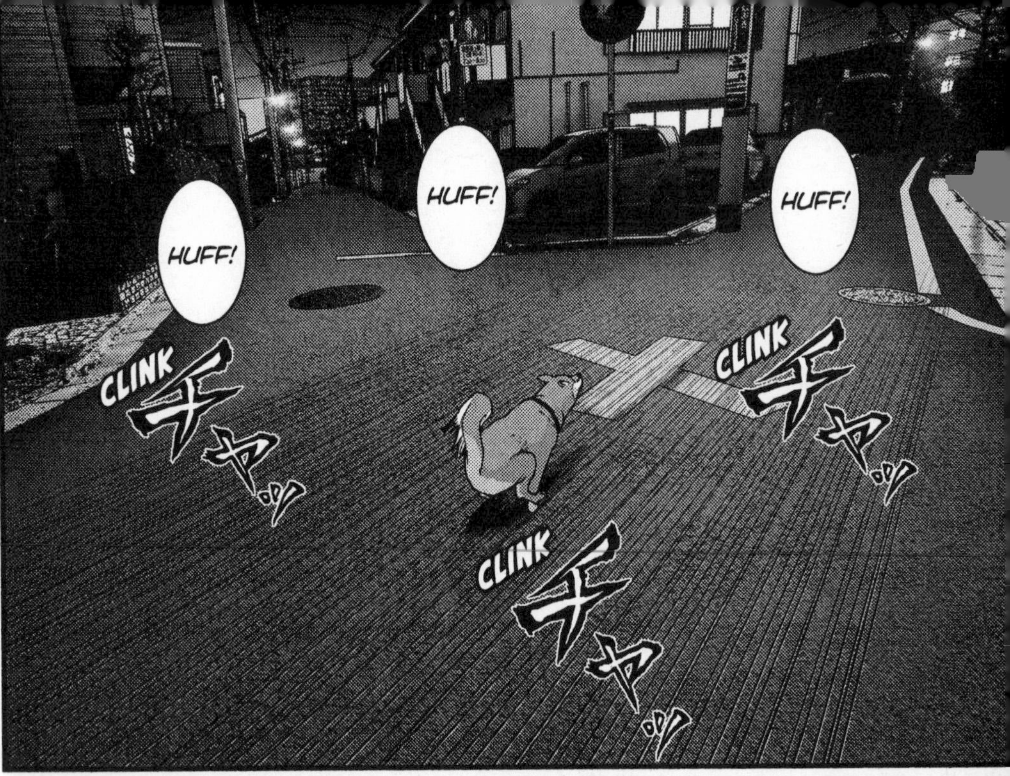
HUFF!
HUFF!
HUFF!
CLINK チャッ
CLINK チャッ
CLINK チャッ
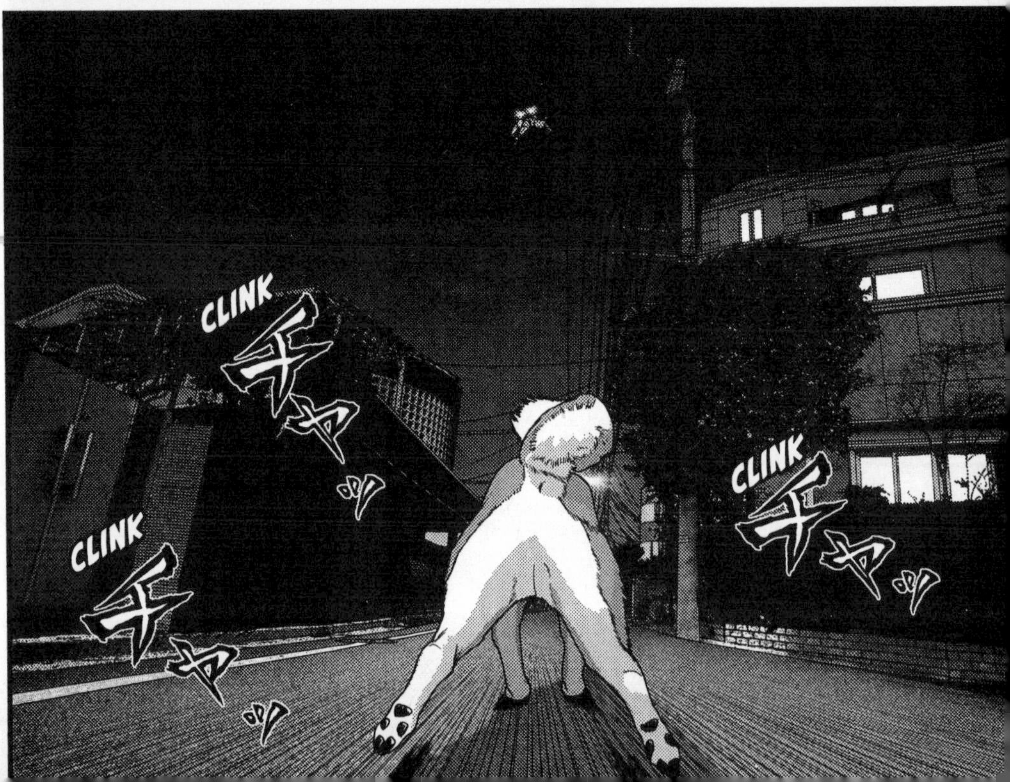
CLINK チャッ
CLINK チャッ
CLINK チャッ

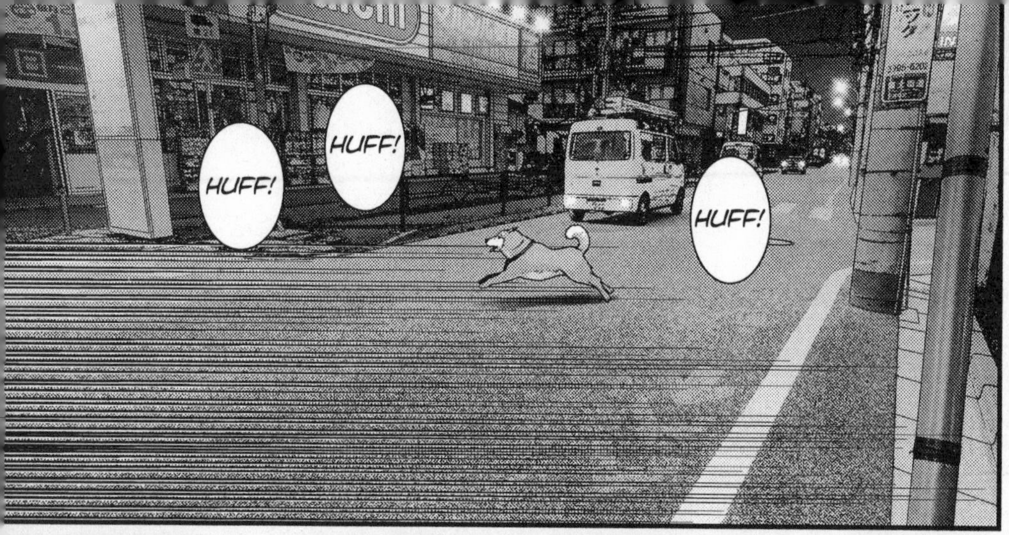
HUFF!
HUFF!
HUFF!

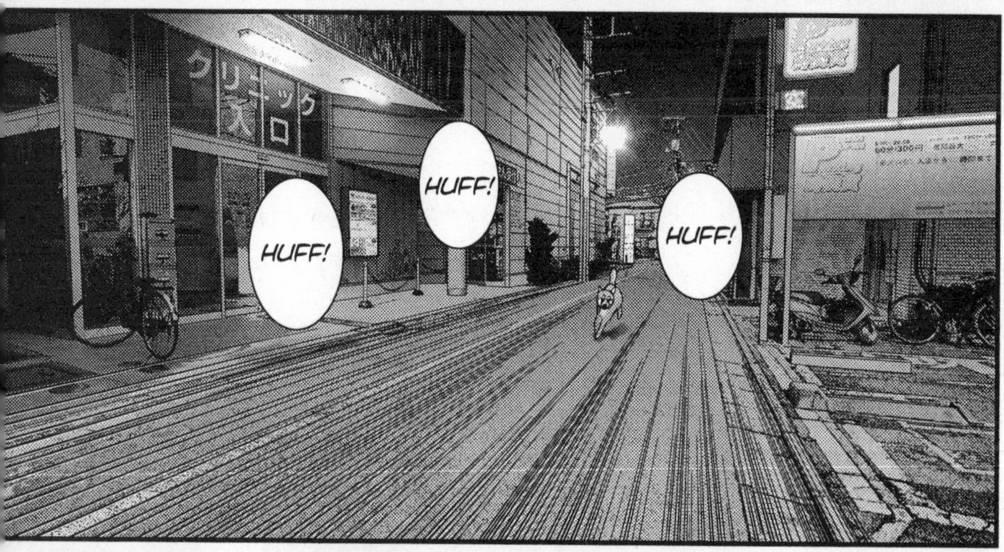
HUFF!
HUFF!
クリニック
入口
HUFF!

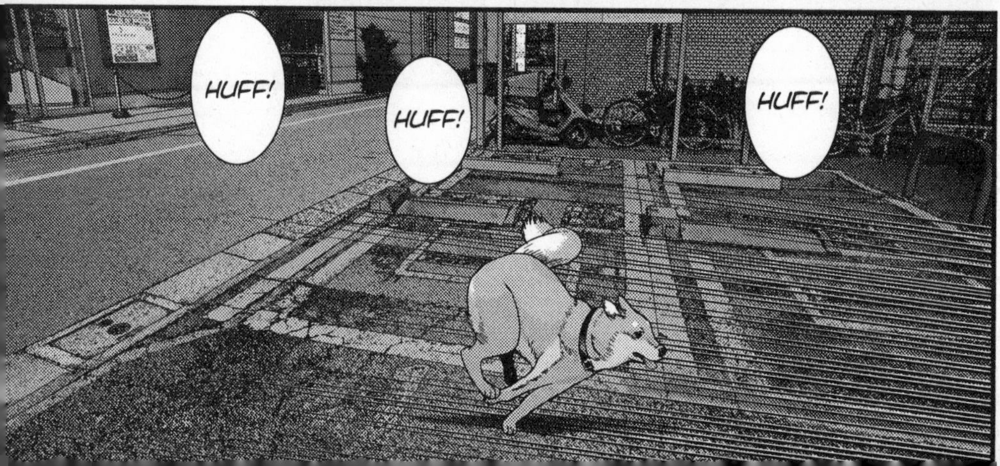
HUFF!
HUFF!
HUFF!

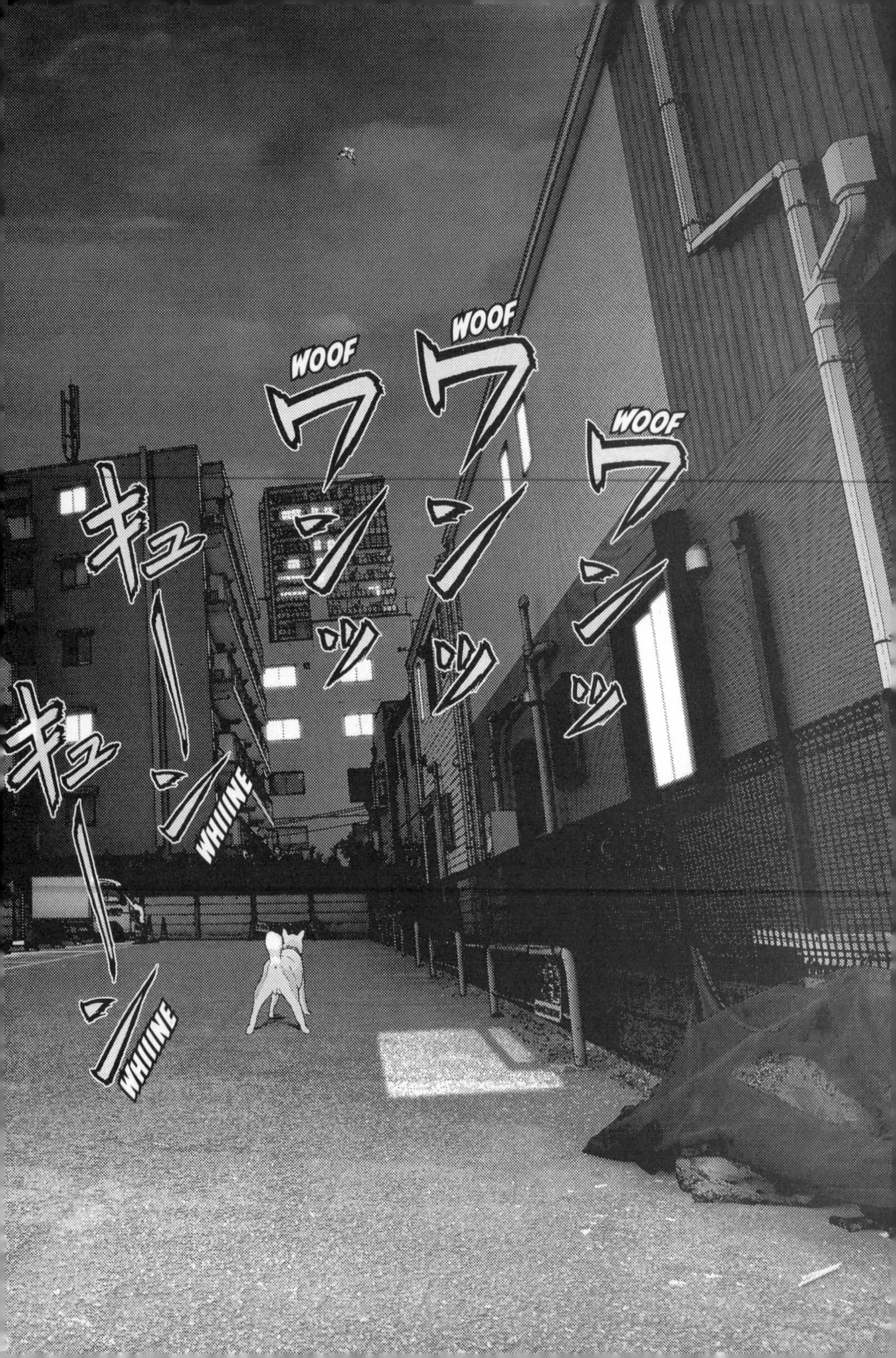
WOOF
ワンッ
WOOF
ワンッ
WOOF
ワンッ
キューン
WHIINE
キューン
WHIINE

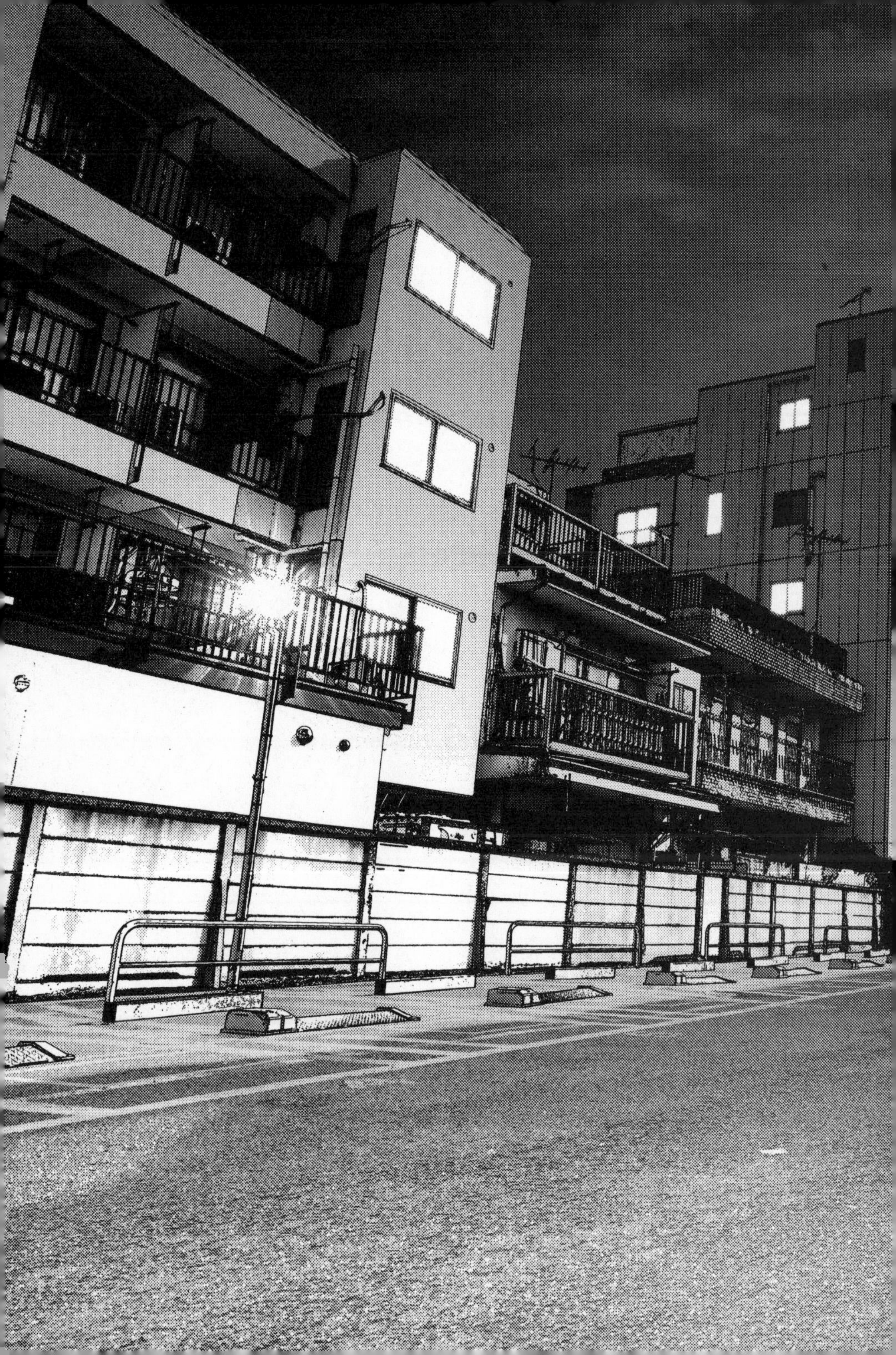

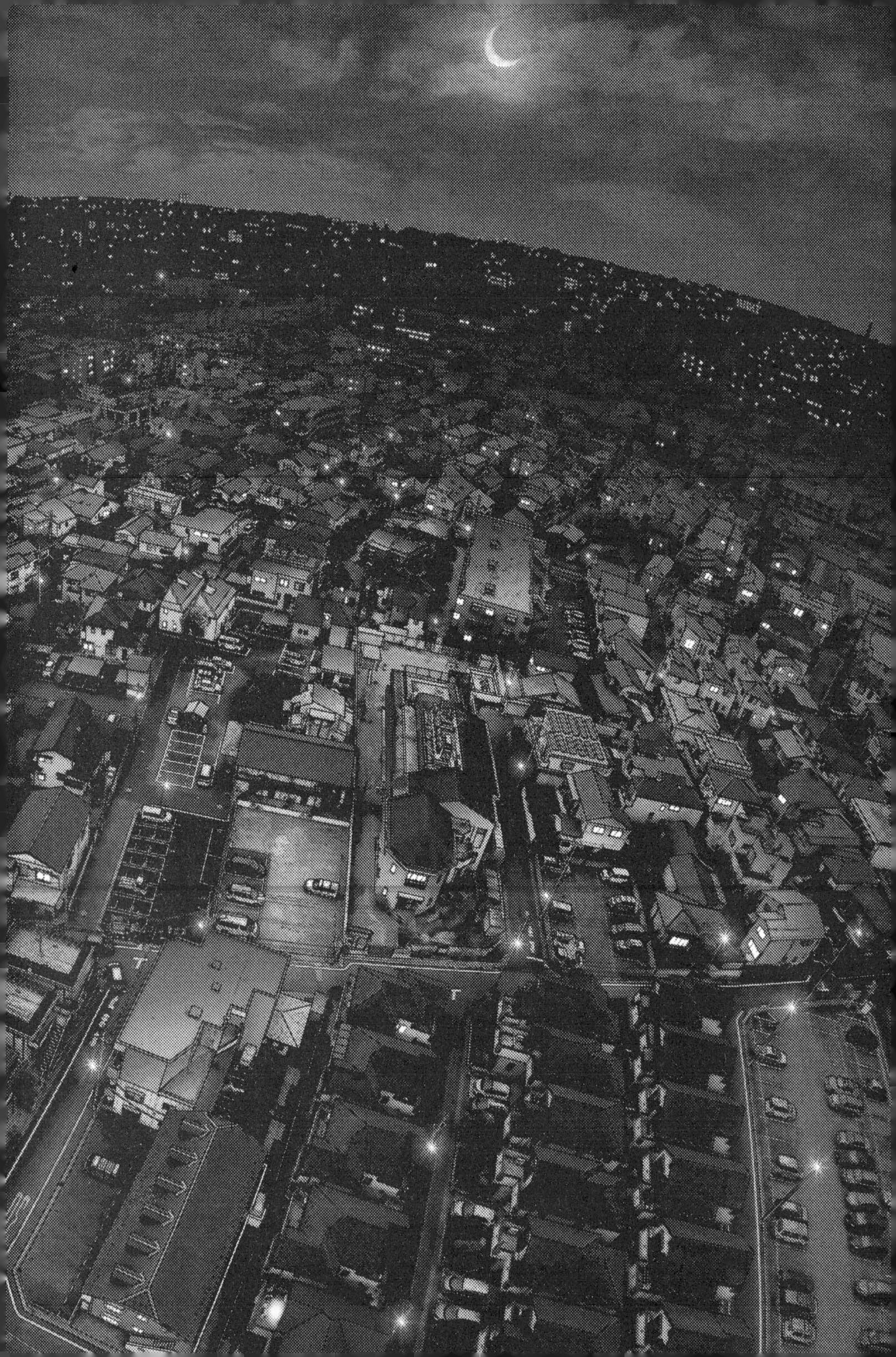

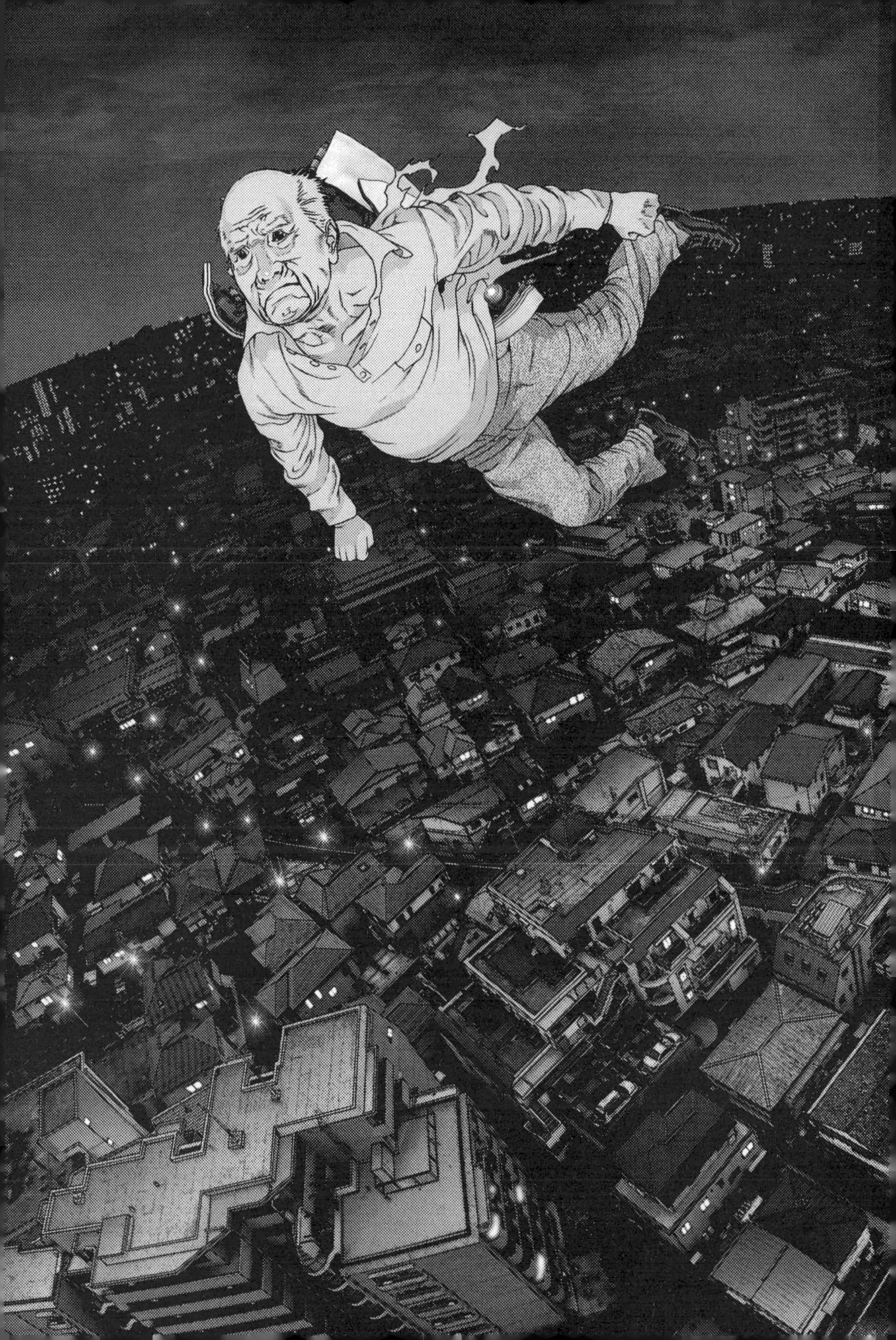

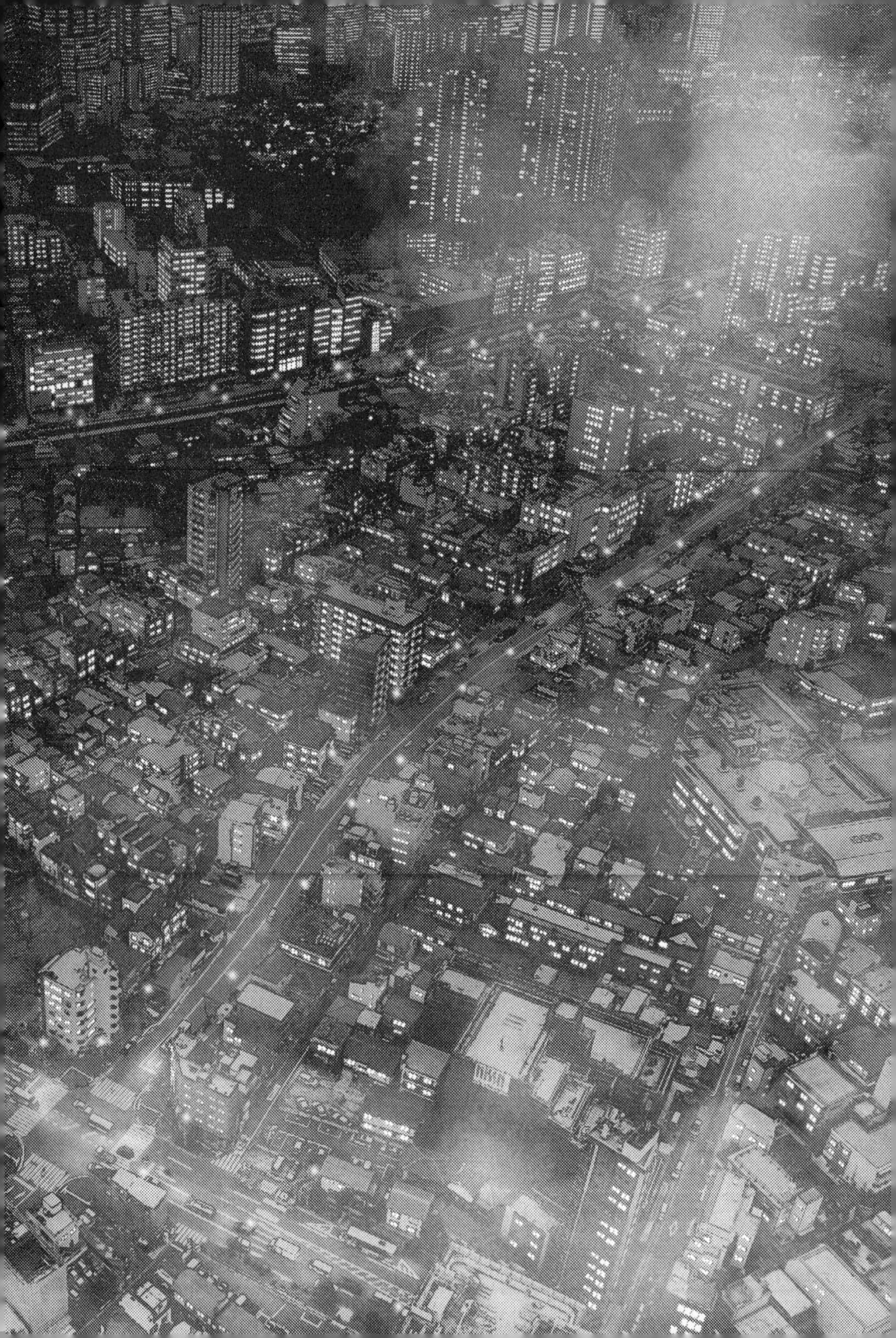

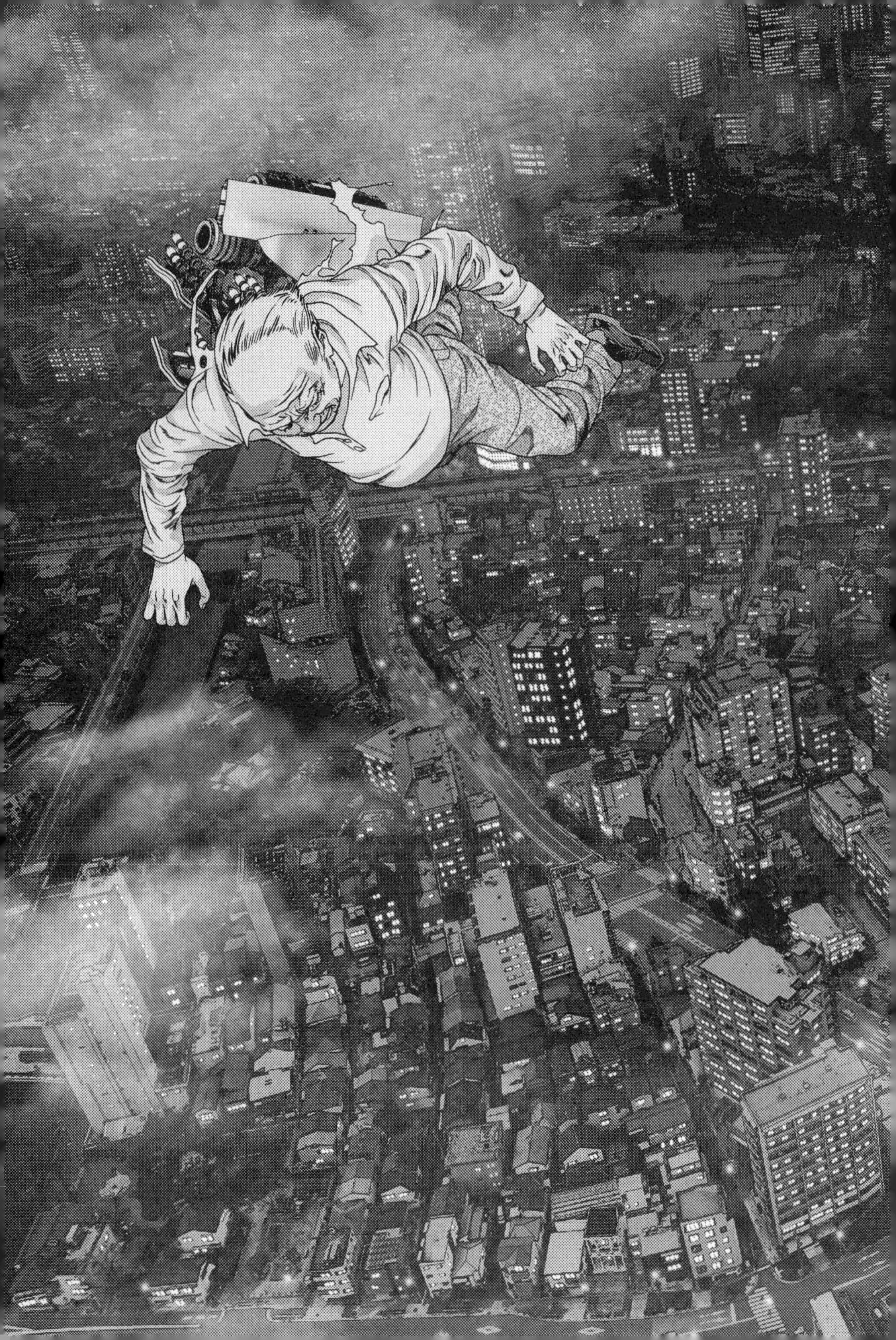

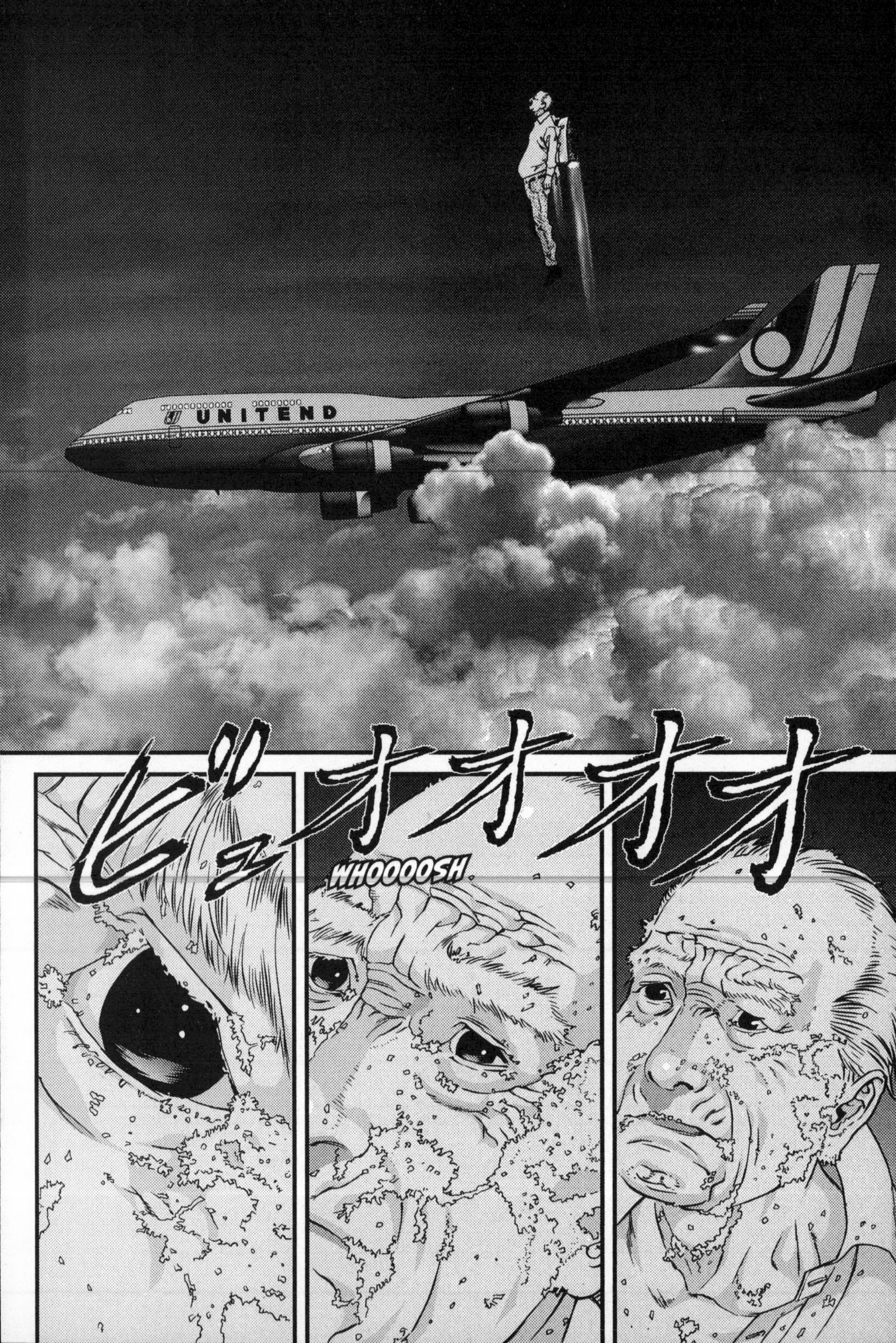
UNITEND
ビュオオオオ
WHOOOOSH

フッ
FFT

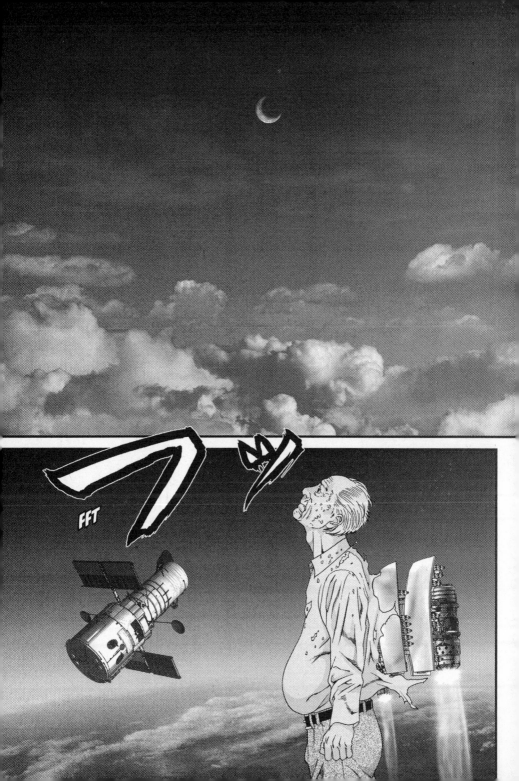

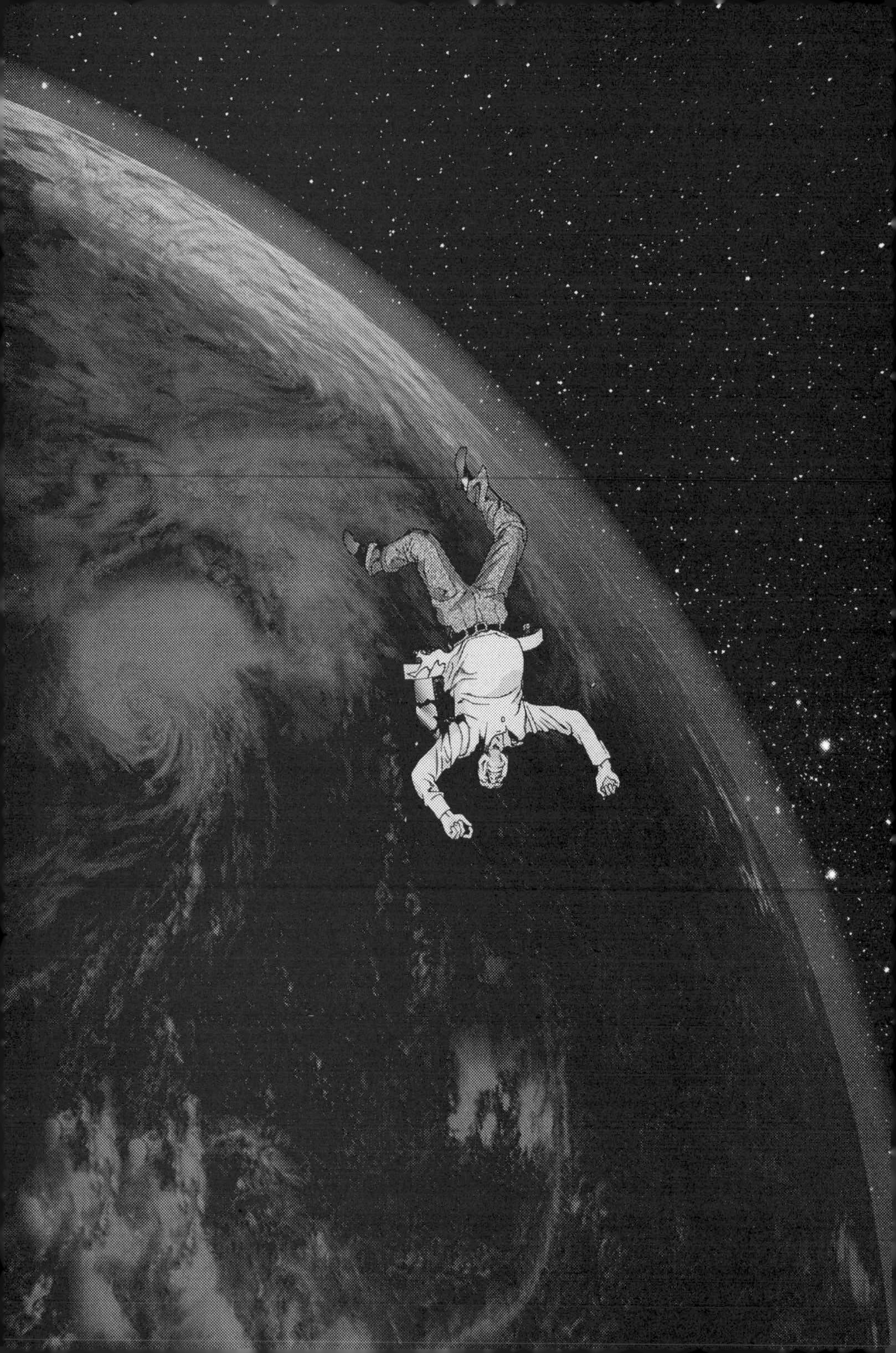

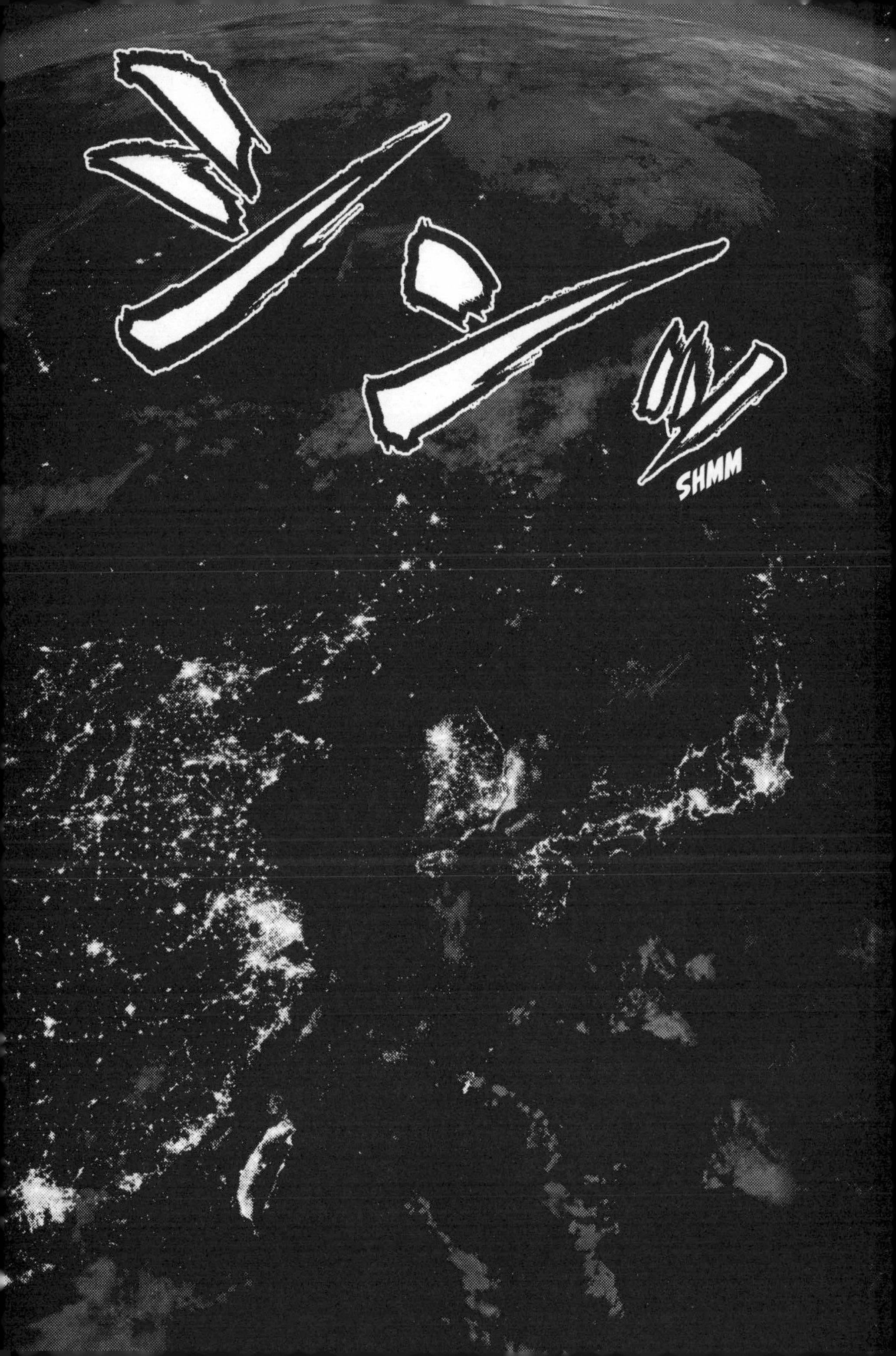
SHMM

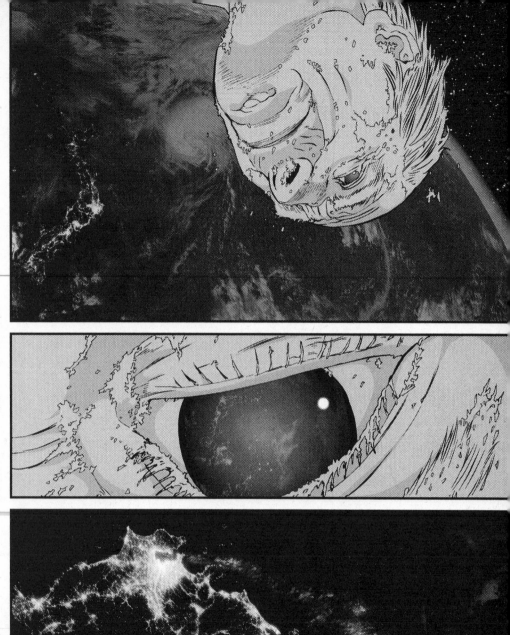
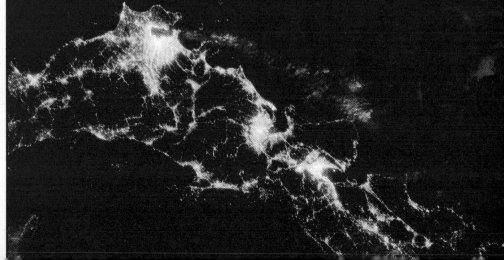

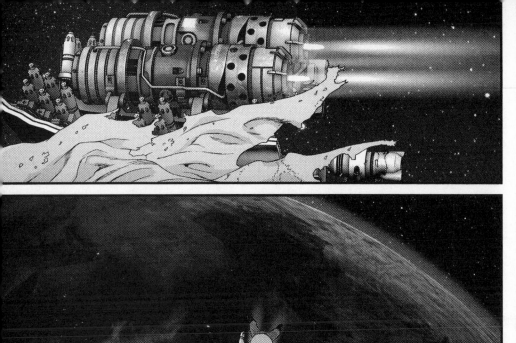

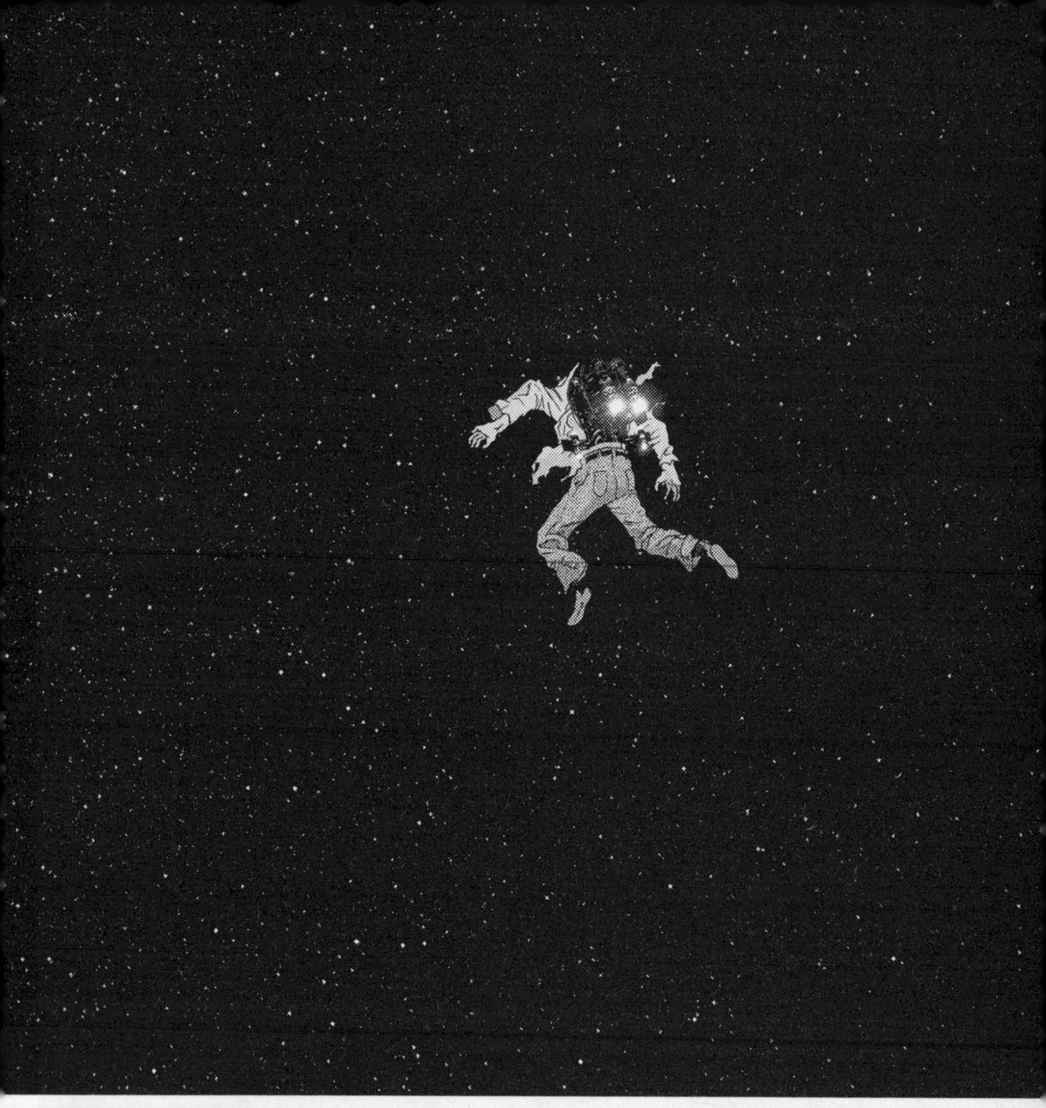
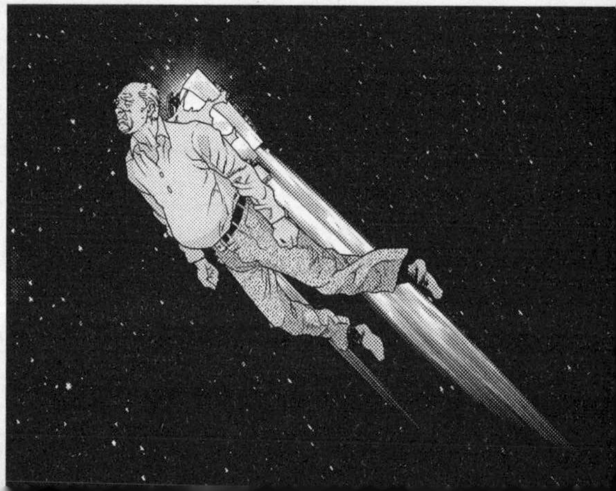
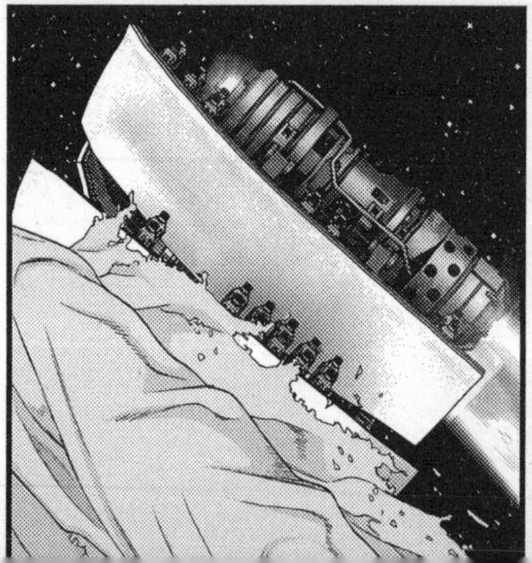

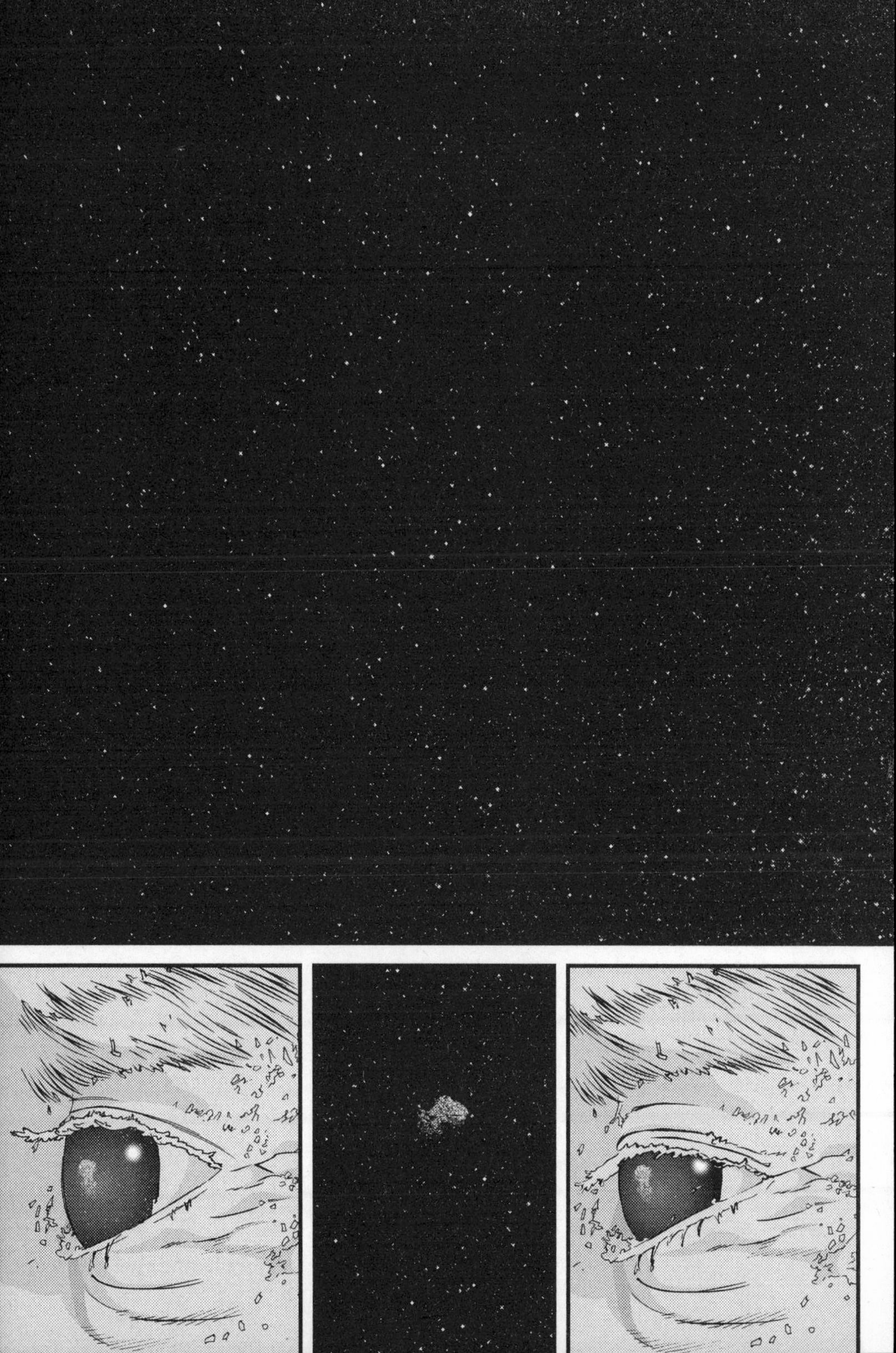

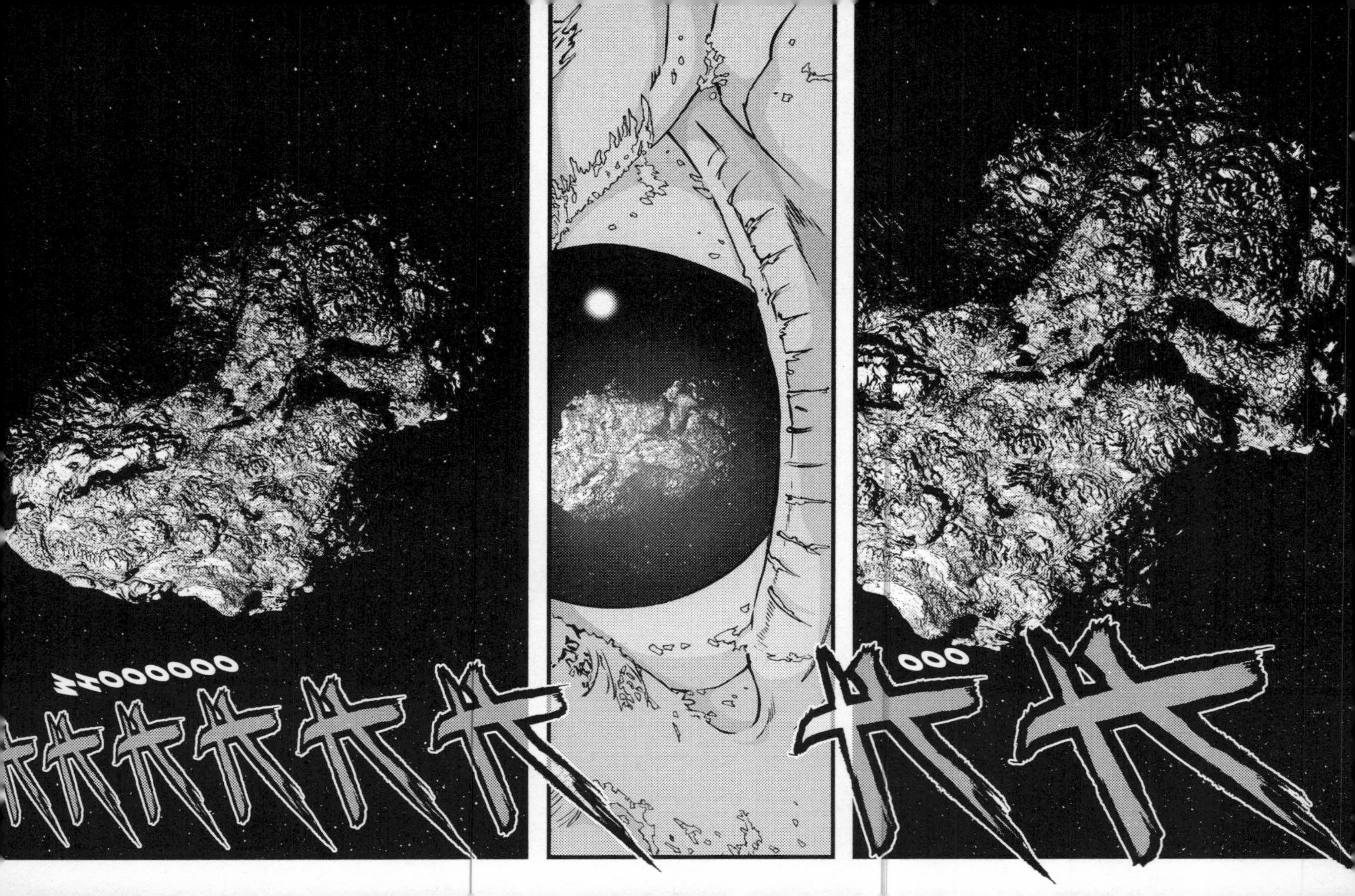
WHOOOOOO
OOO

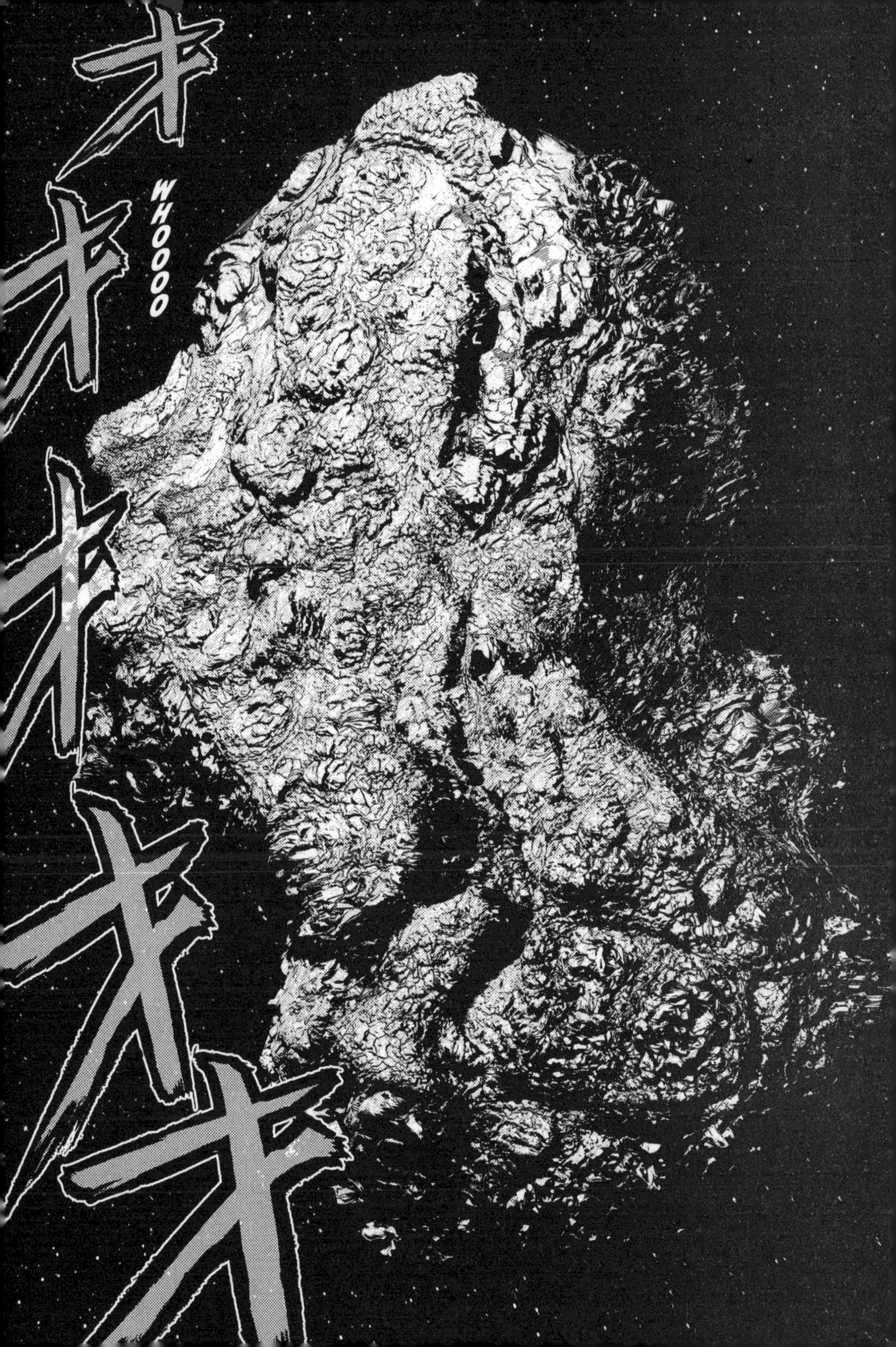
オオオオオ
WHOOOO

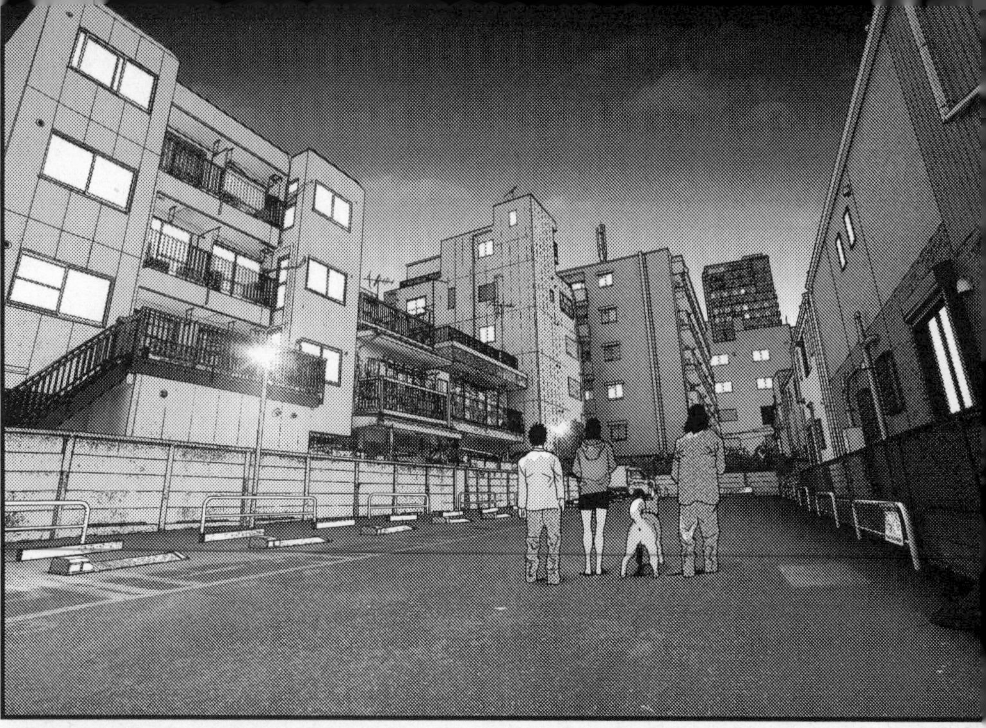
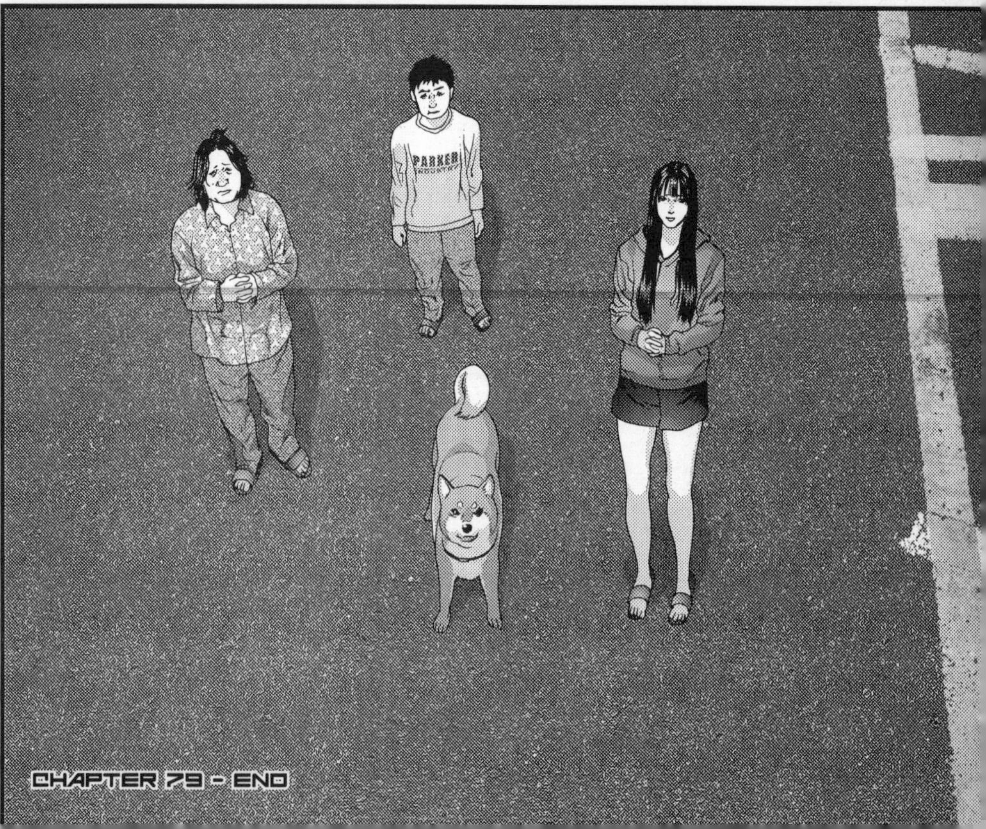
PARKER
CHAPTER 79 - END

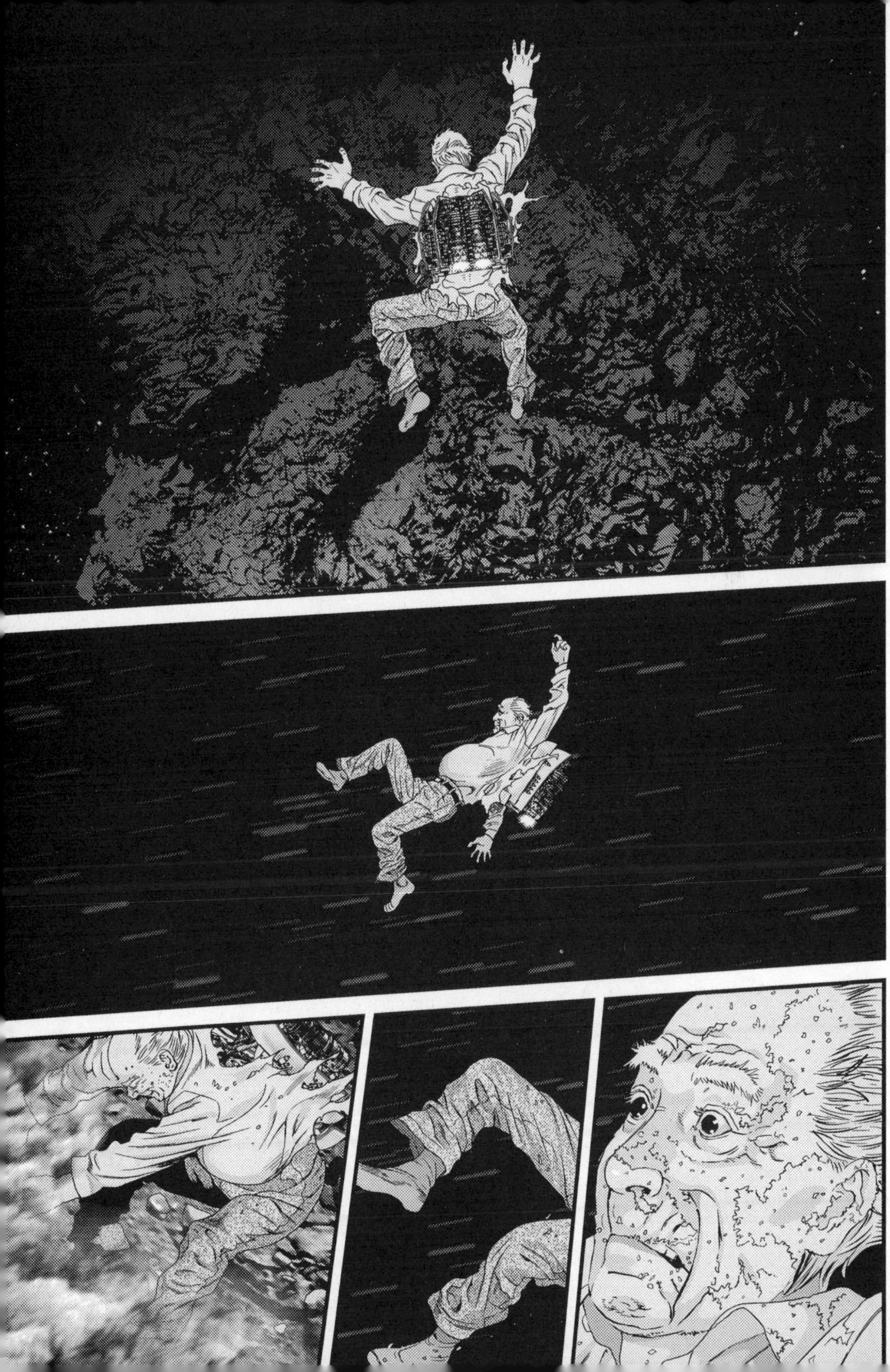

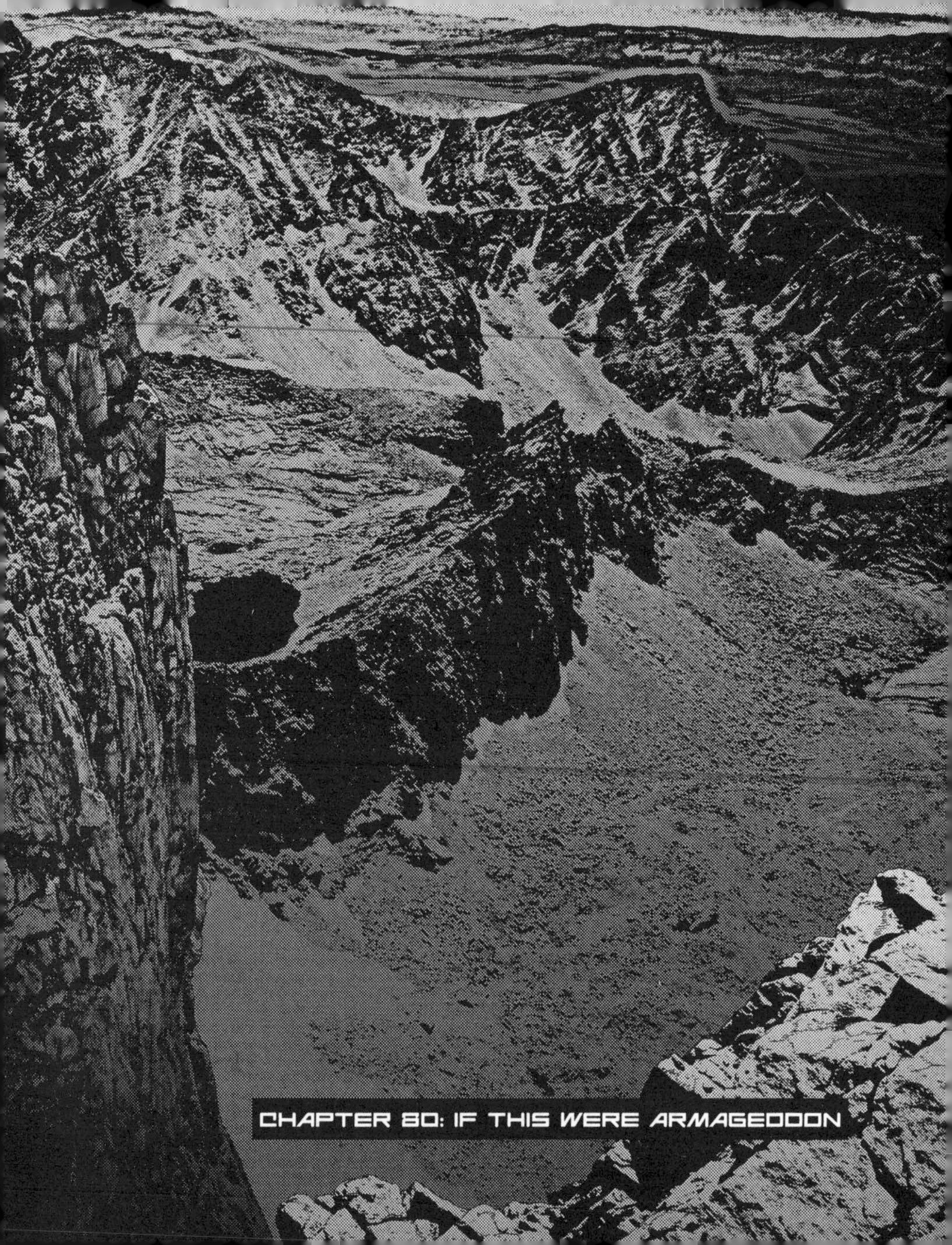
CHAPTER 80: IF THIS WERE ARMAGEDDON

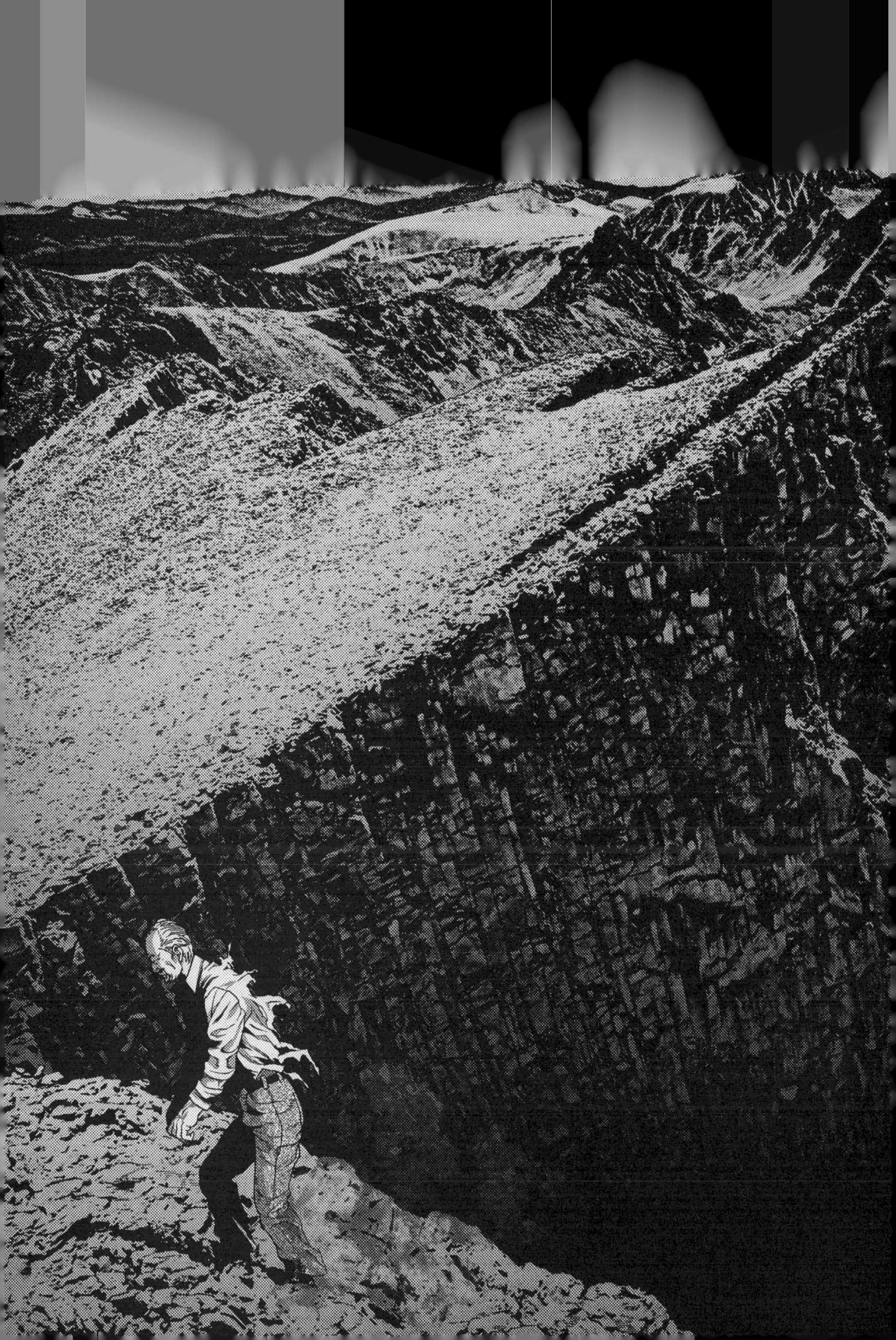

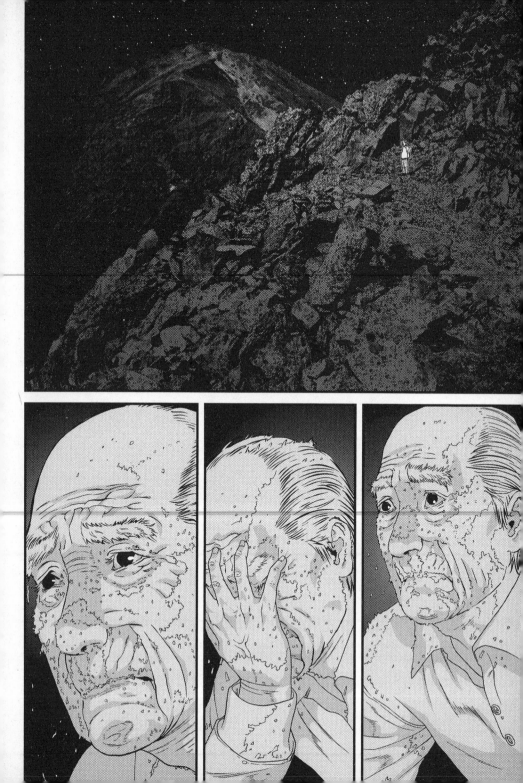

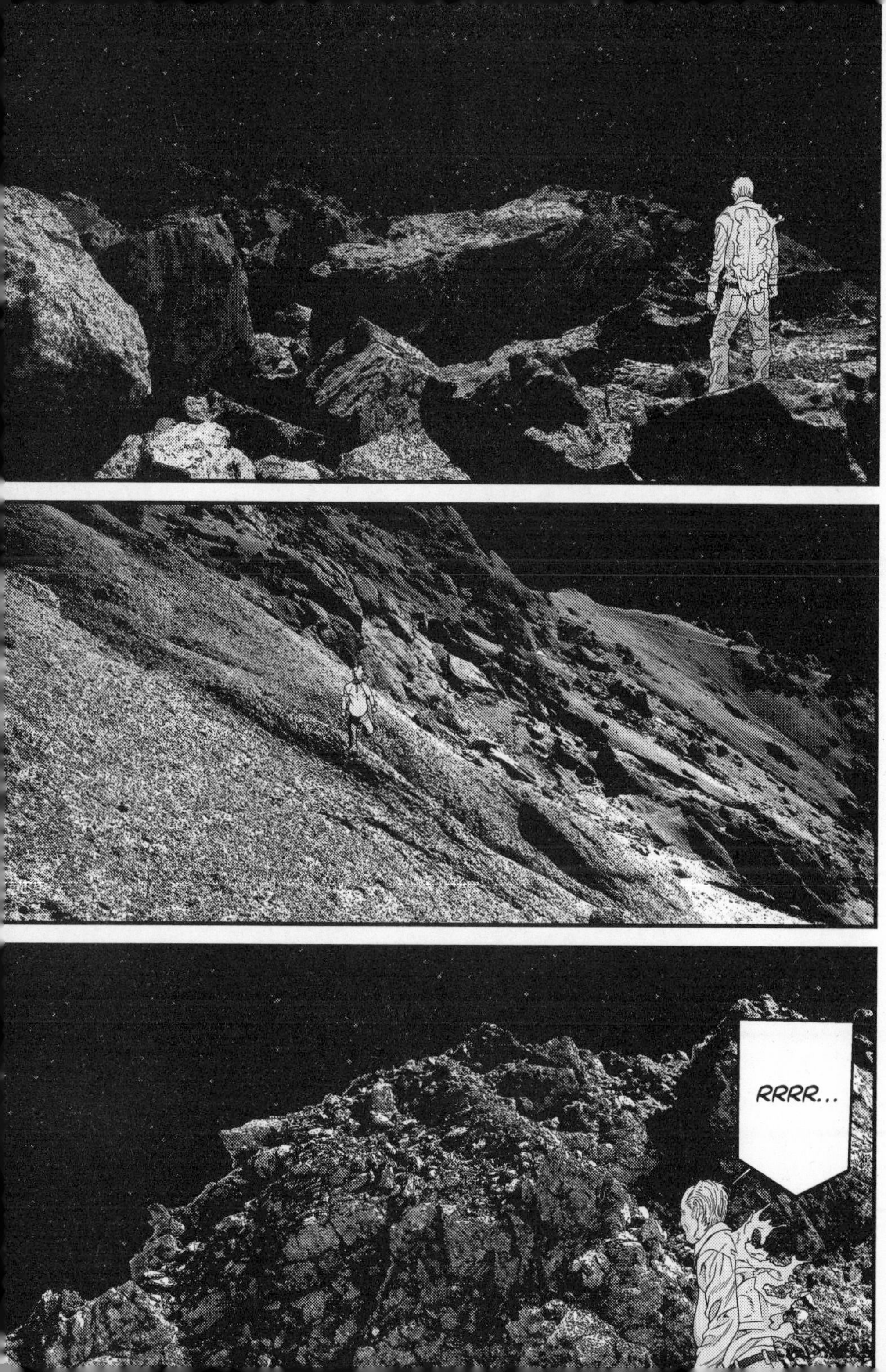
RRRR...

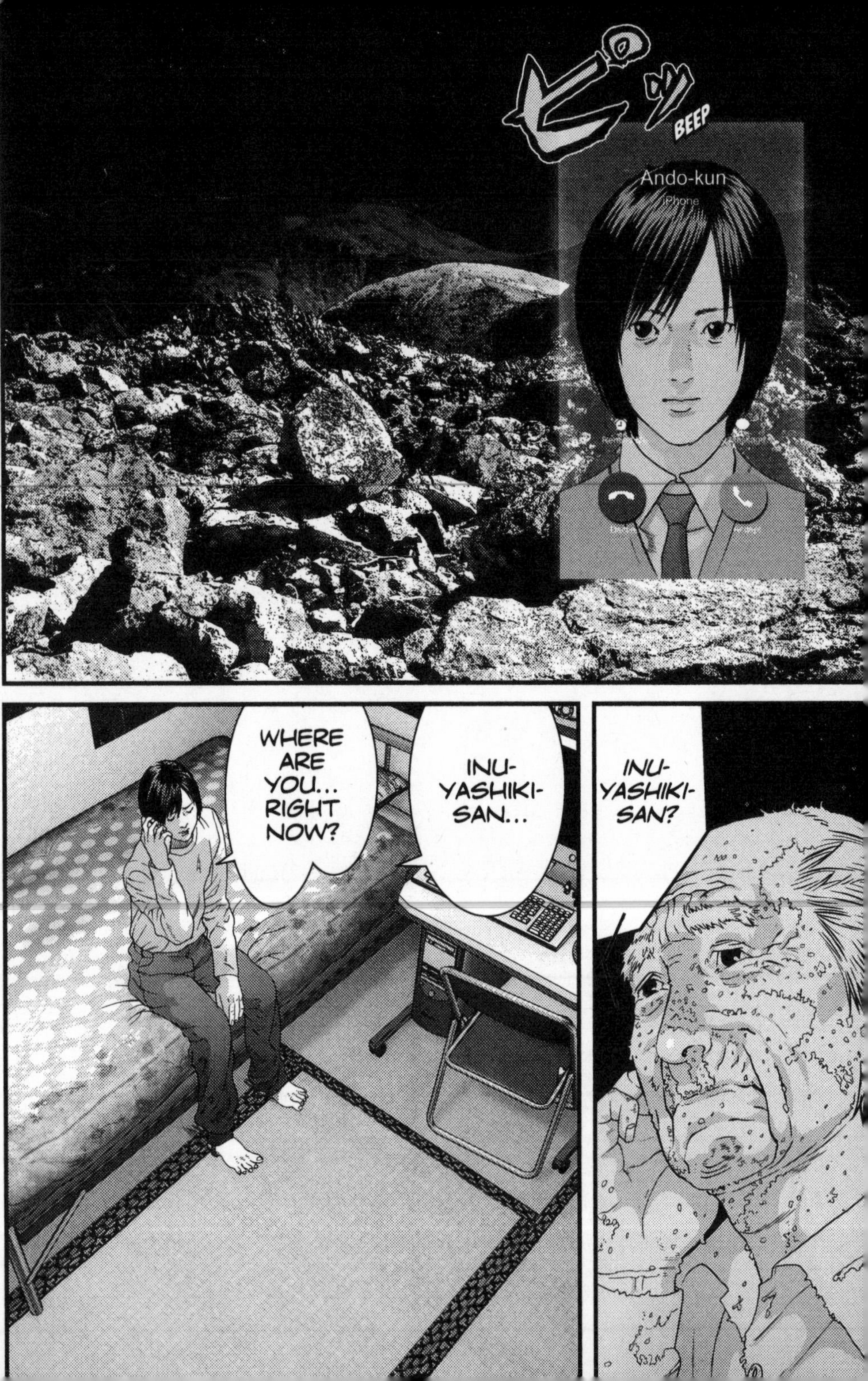
ピッ
BEEP
Ando-kun
iPhone
INU-YASHIKI-SAN?
INU-YASHIKI-SAN...
WHERE ARE YOU... RIGHT NOW?

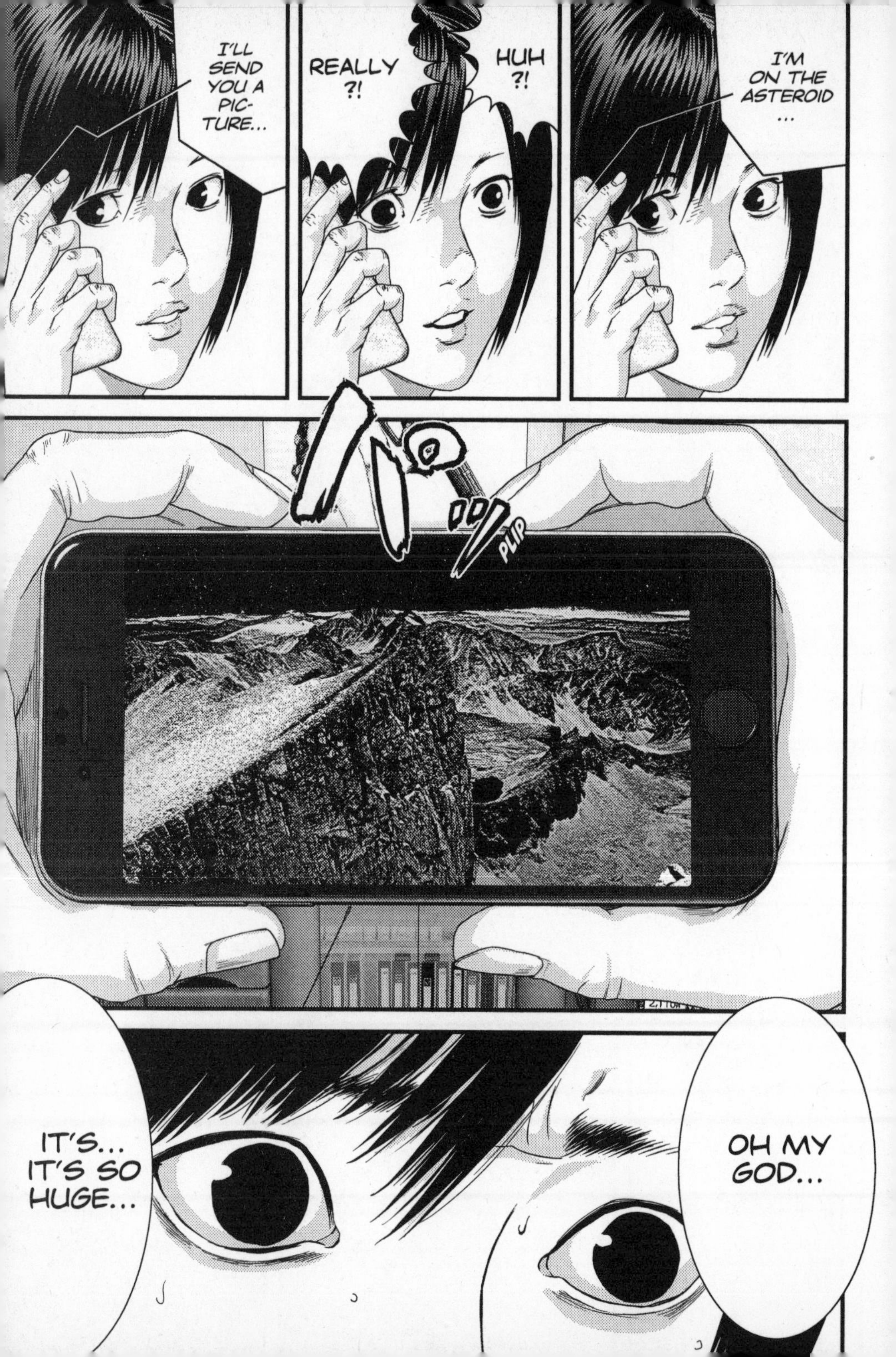
I'M ON THE ASTEROID ...
HUH ?!
REALLY ?!
I'LL SEND YOU A PIC-TURE...
PLIP
OH MY GOD...
IT'S... IT'S SO HUGE...

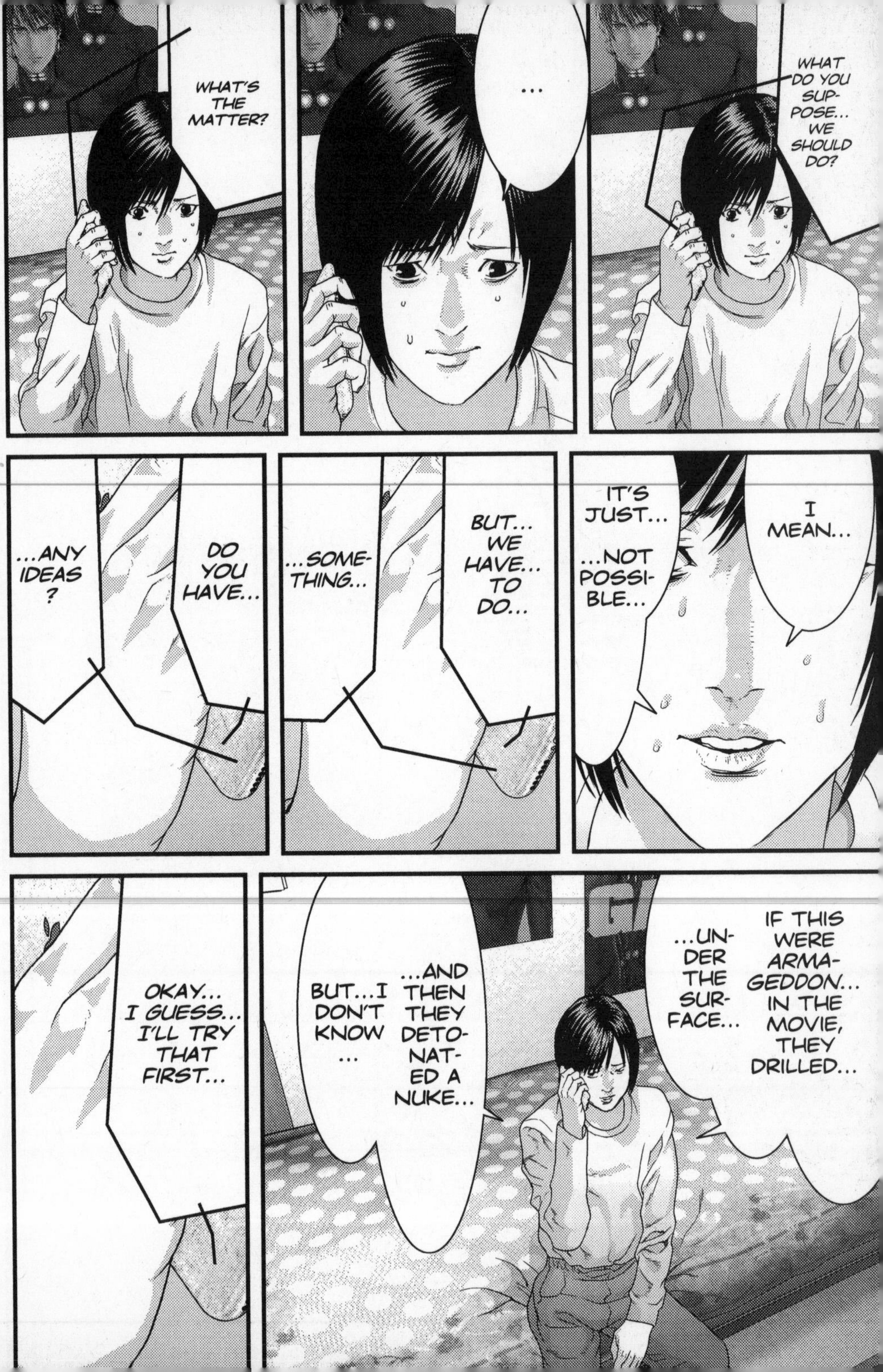
WHAT DO YOU SUP-POSE... WE SHOULD DO?
...
WHAT'S THE MATTER?
I MEAN...
IT'S JUST... ...NOT POSSI-BLE...
BUT... WE HAVE... TO DO...
...SOME-THING...
DO YOU HAVE...
...ANY IDEAS ?
IF THIS WERE ARMA-GEDDON... IN THE MOVIE, THEY DRILLED...
...UN-DER THE SUR-FACE...
...AND THEN THEY DETO-NAT-ED A NUKE...
BUT...I DON'T KNOW ...
OKAY... I GUESS... I'LL TRY THAT FIRST...

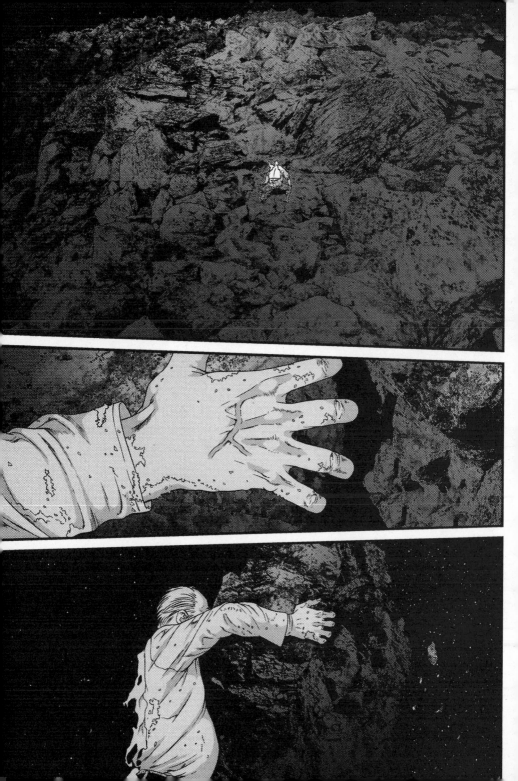

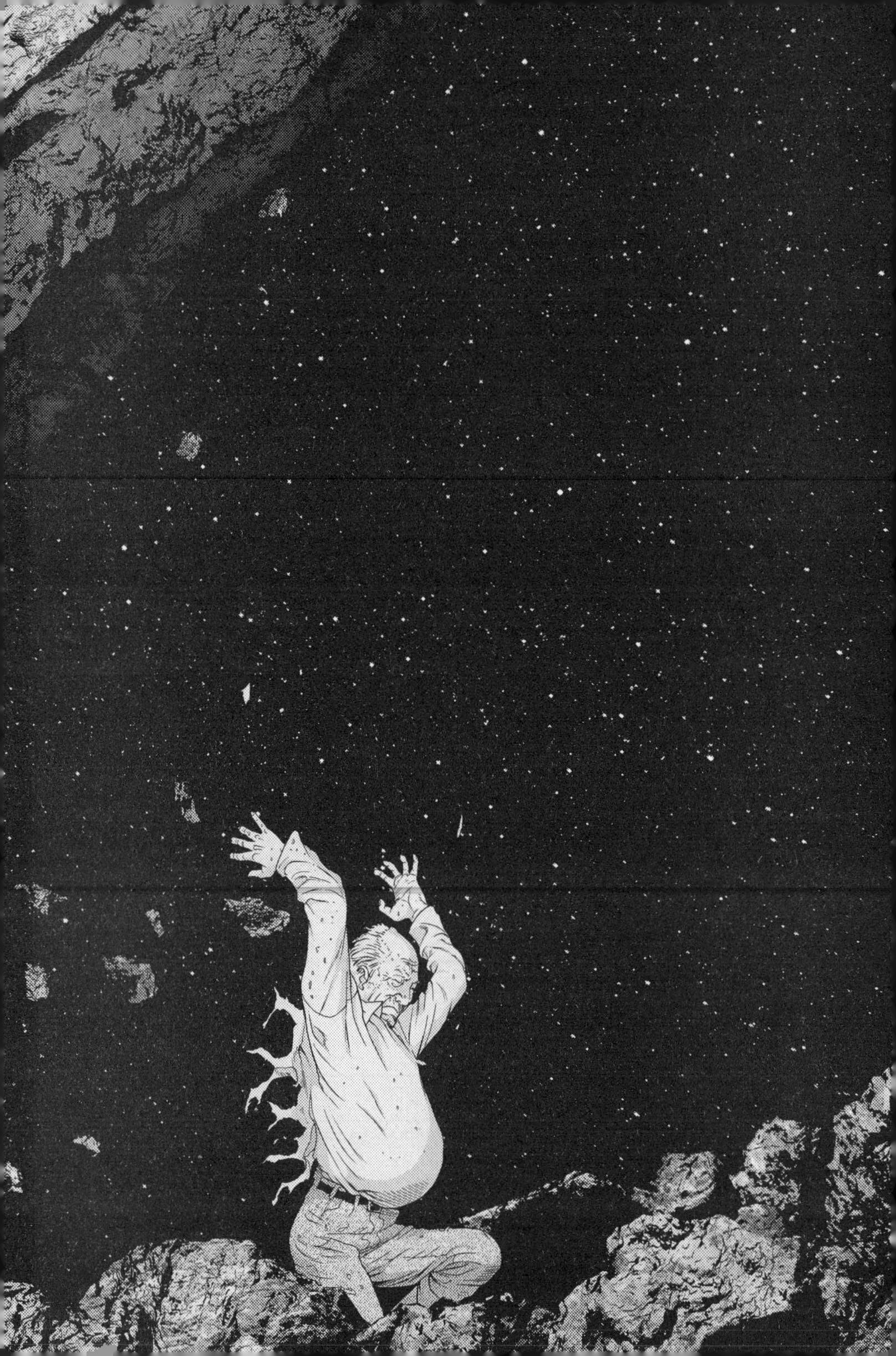

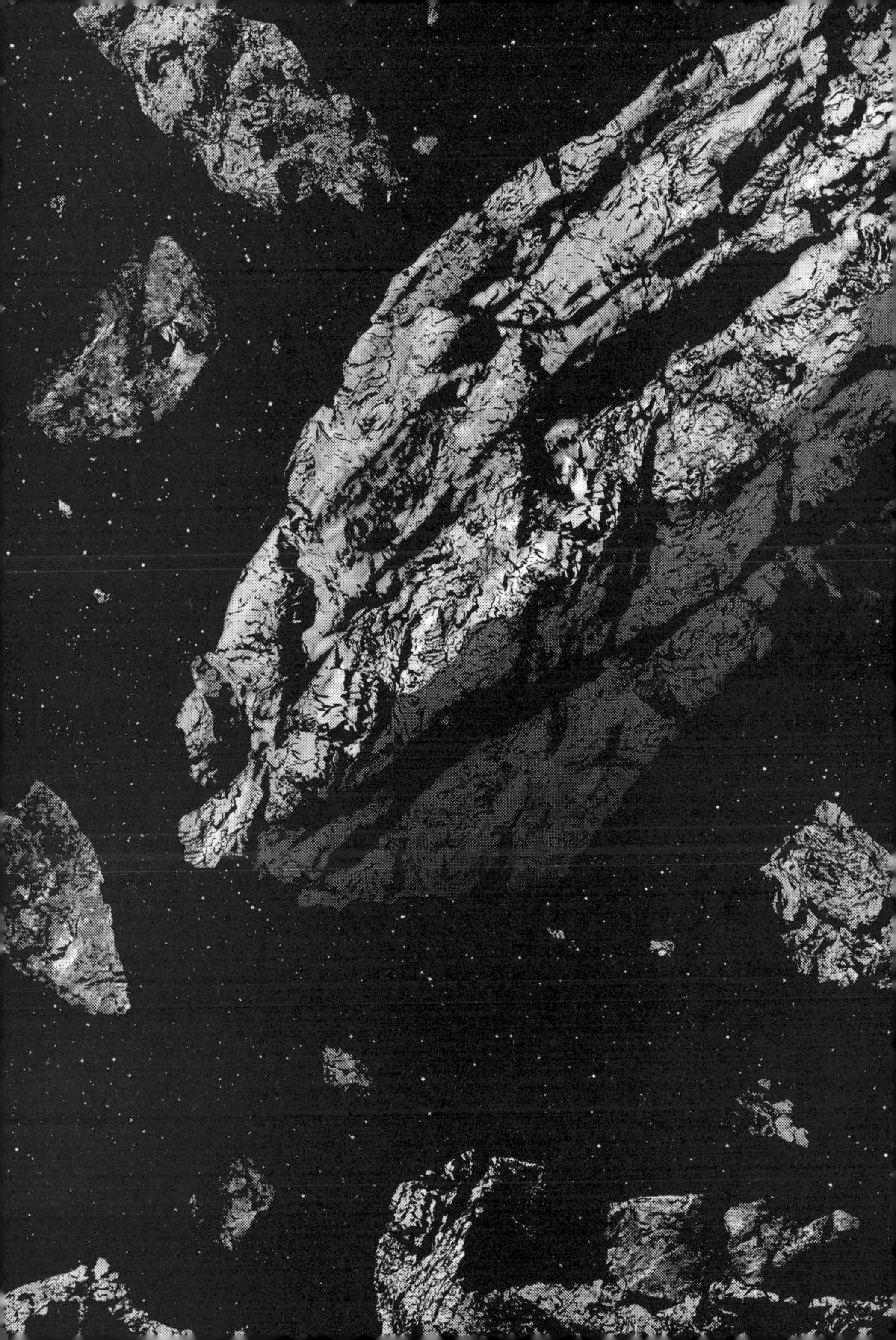

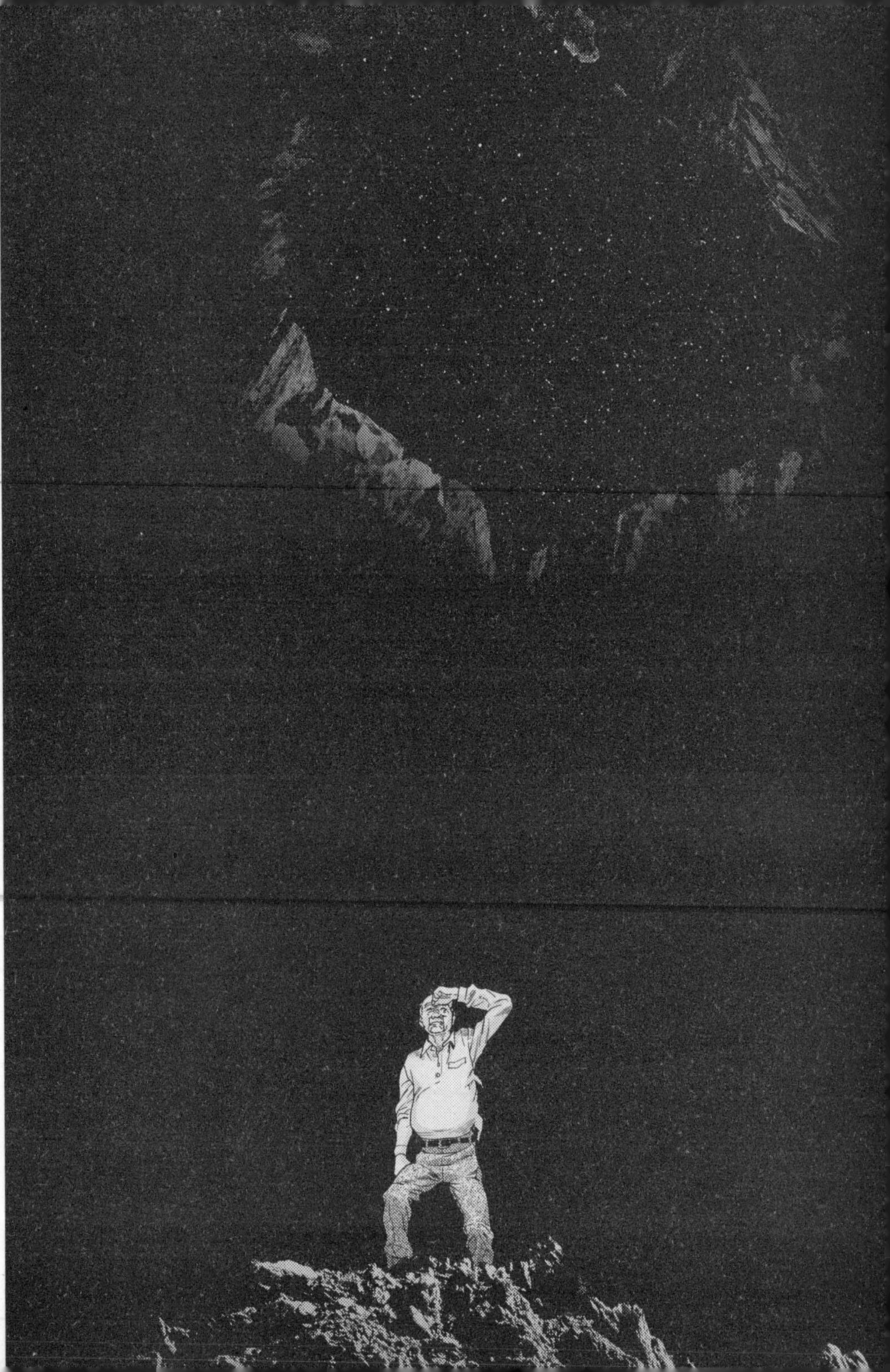

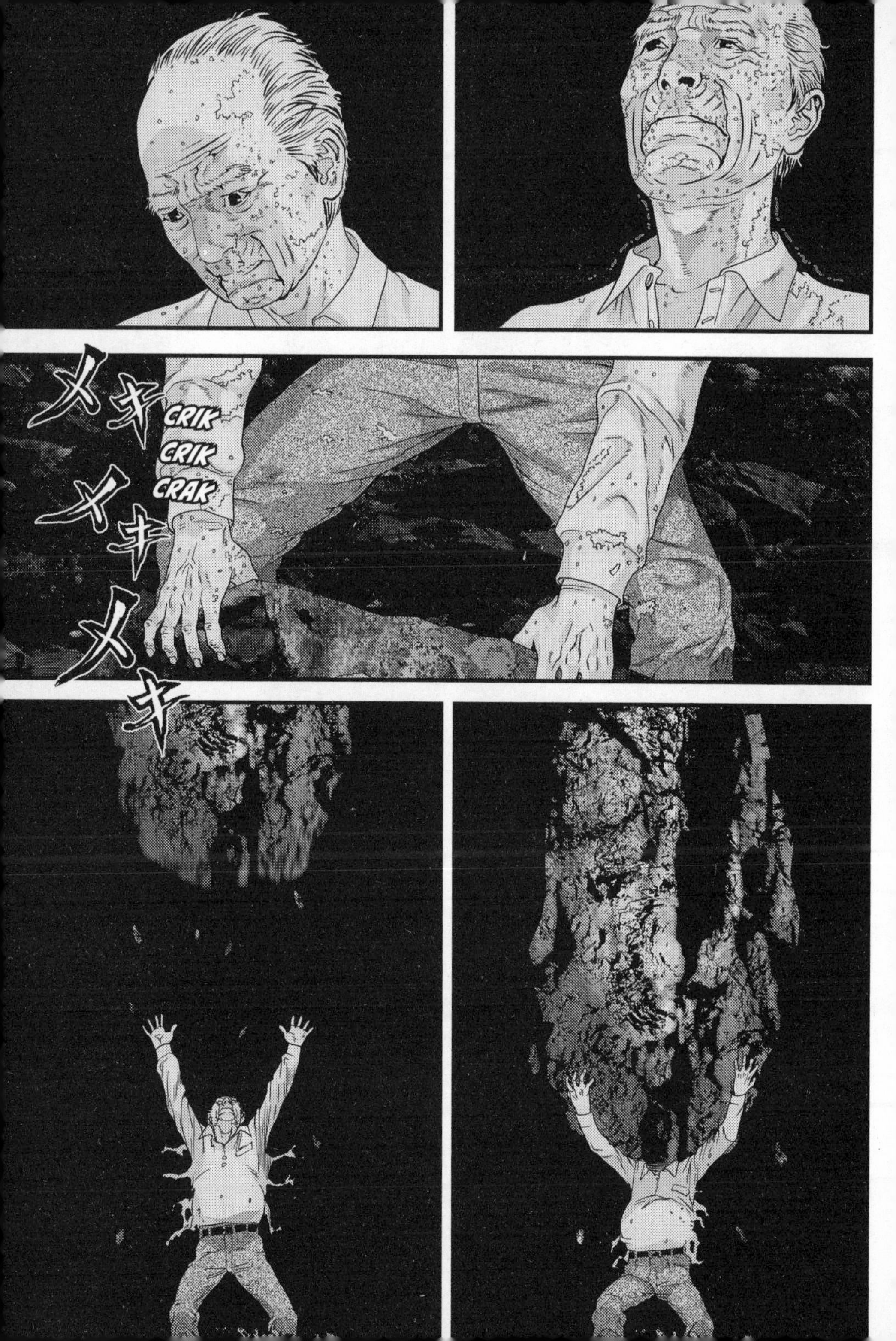
メキメキメキ
CRIK
CRIK
CRAK

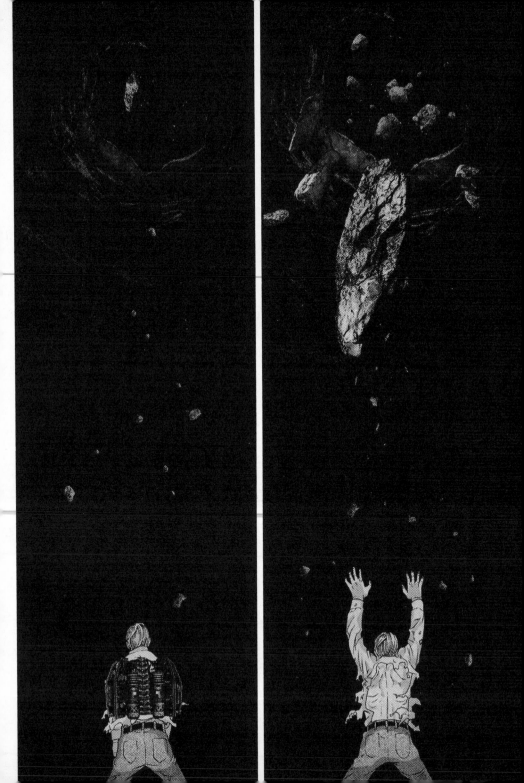

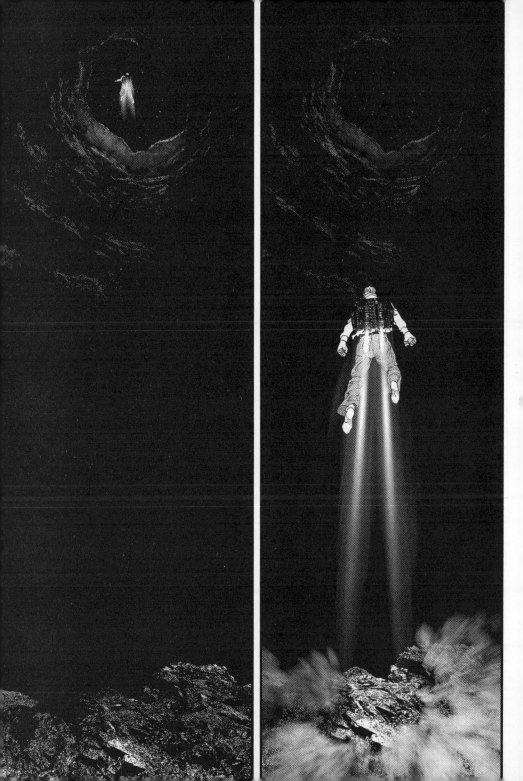

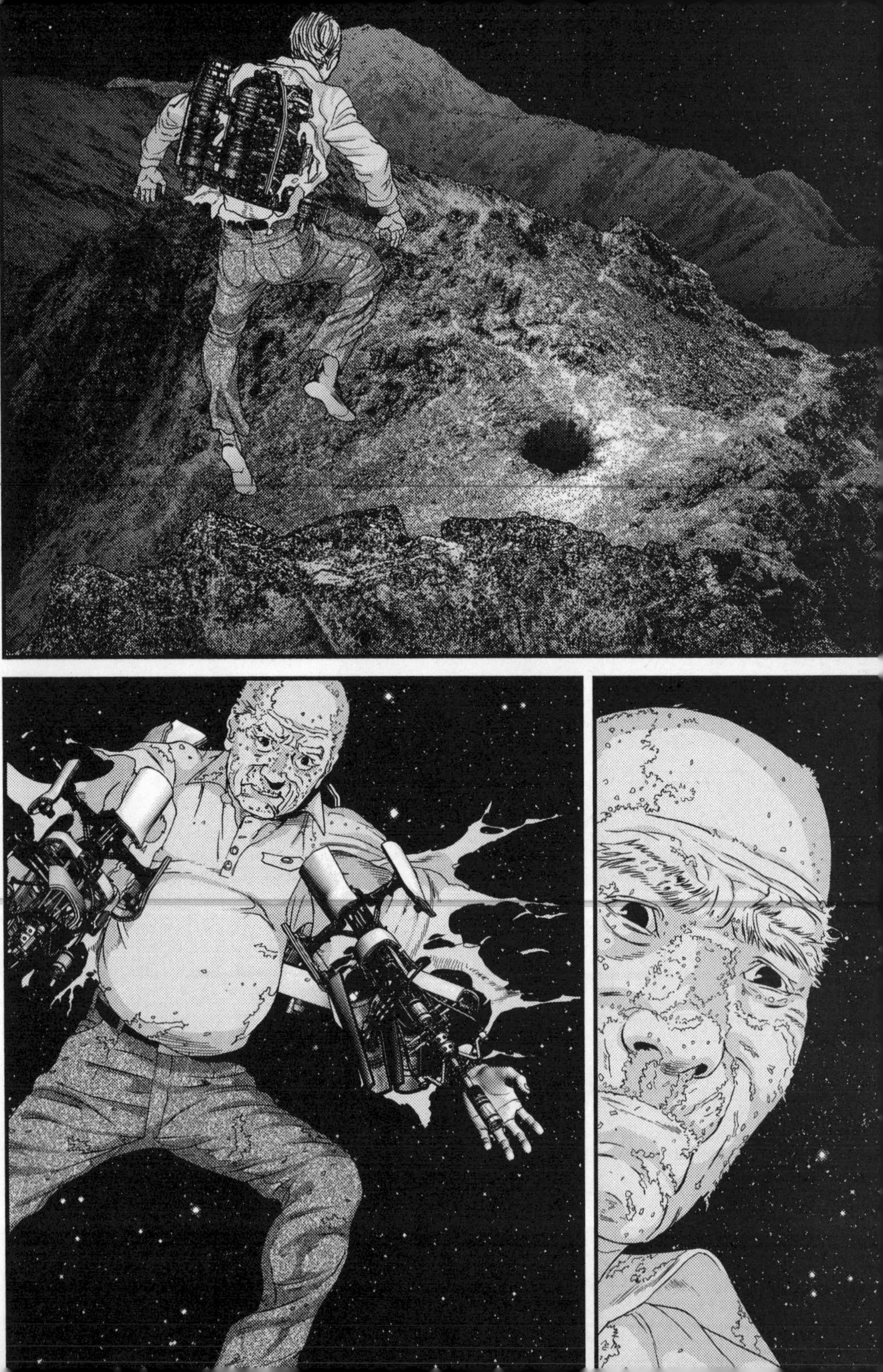

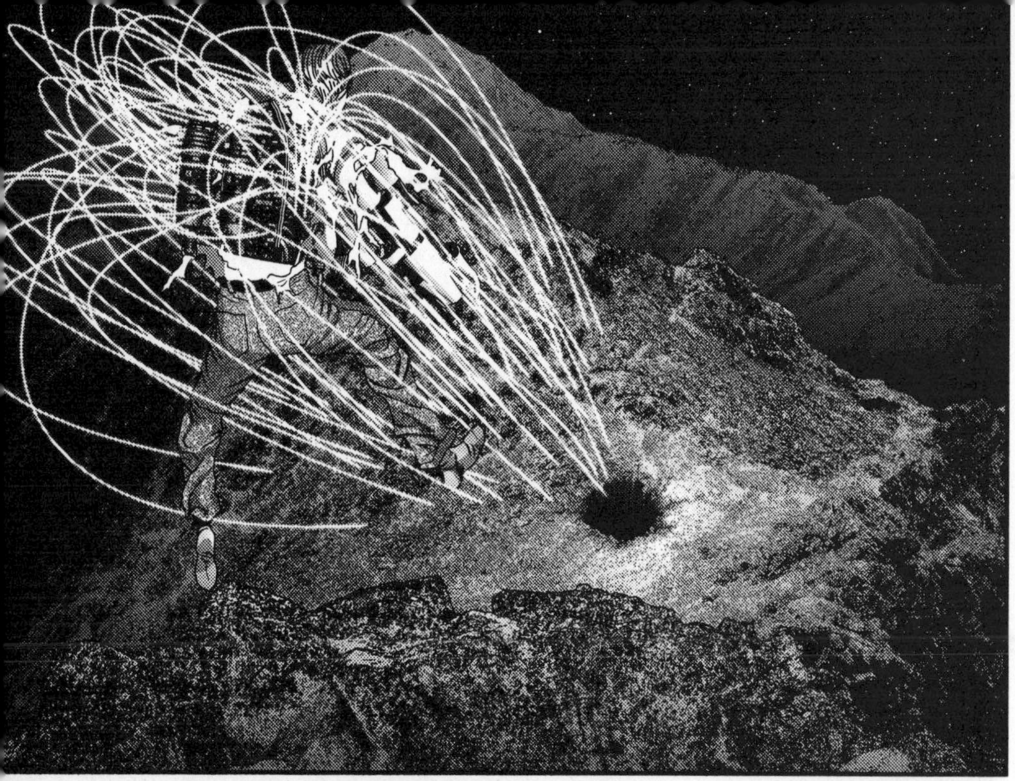
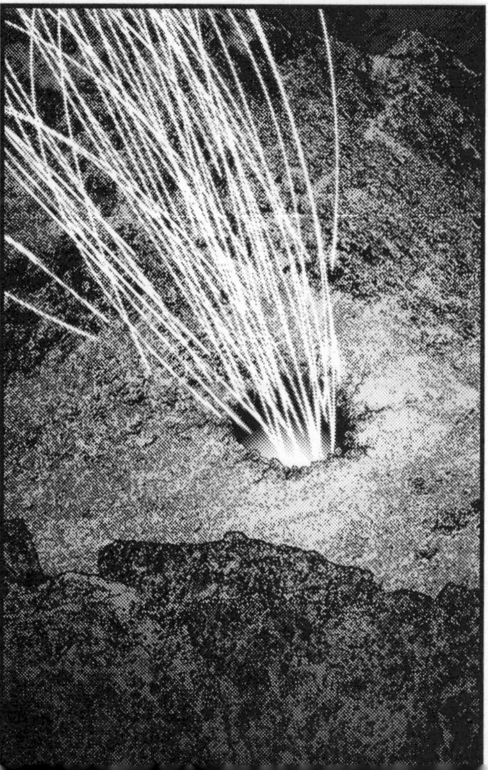
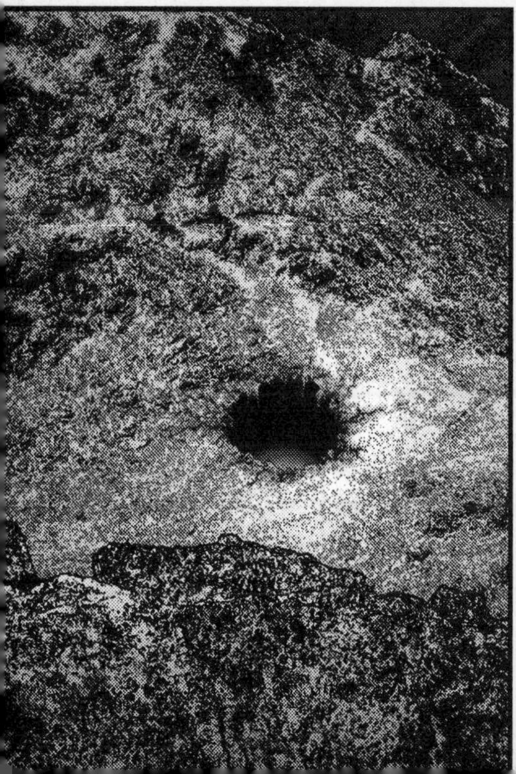

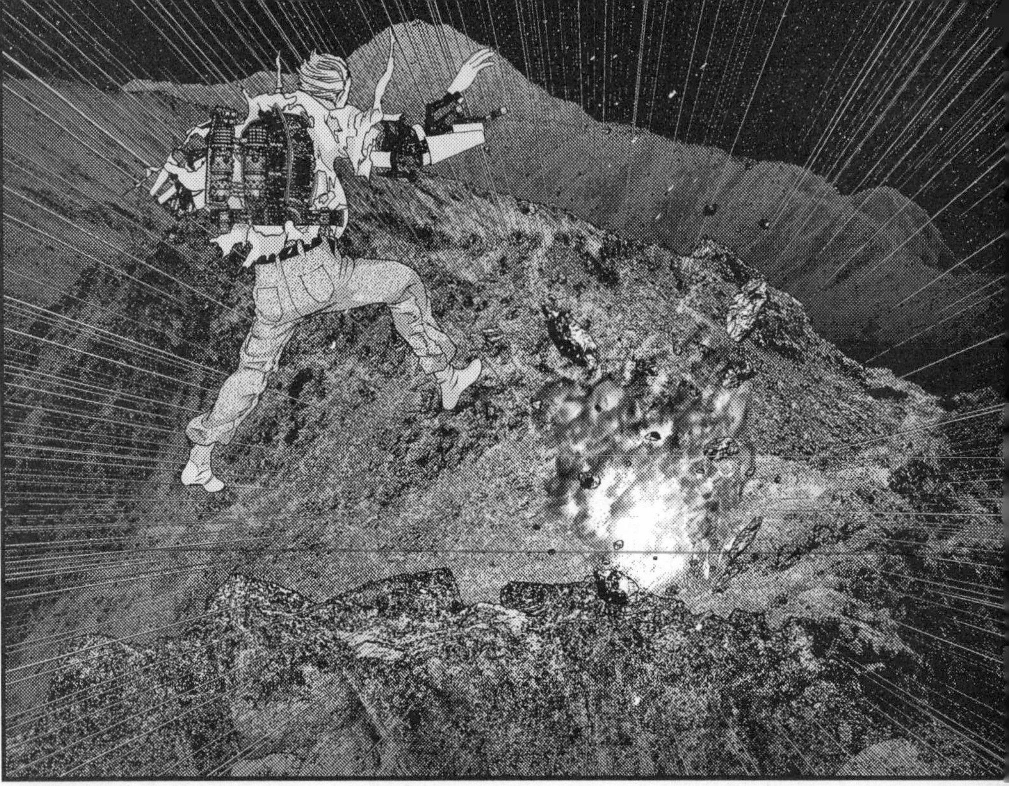
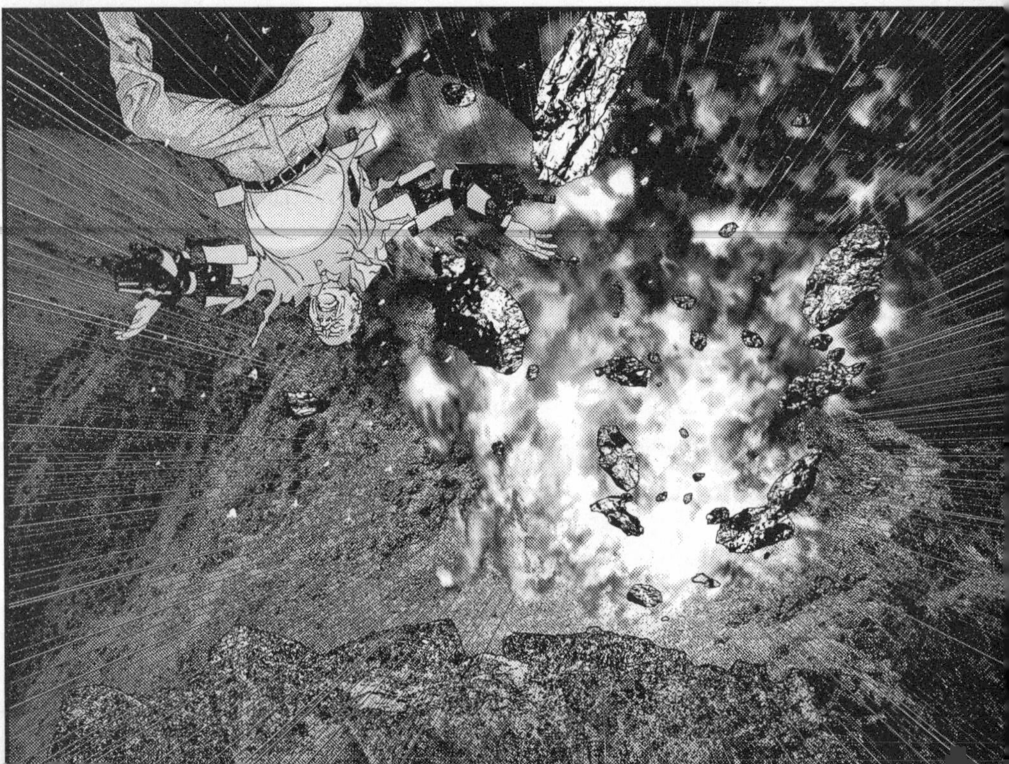

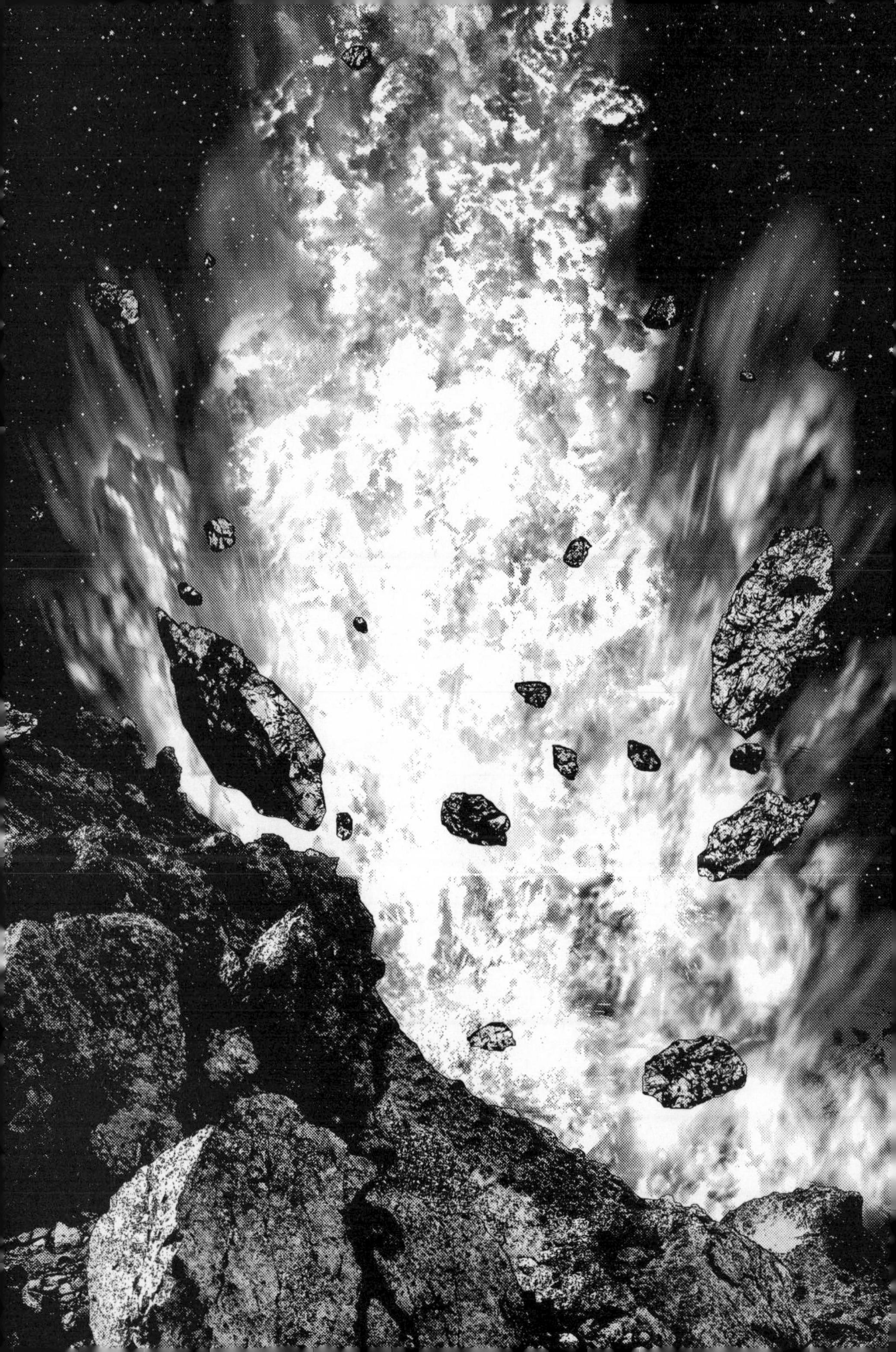

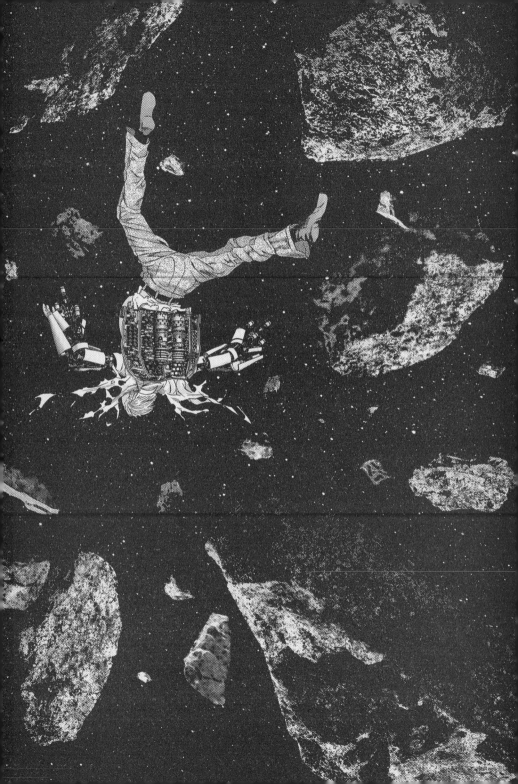

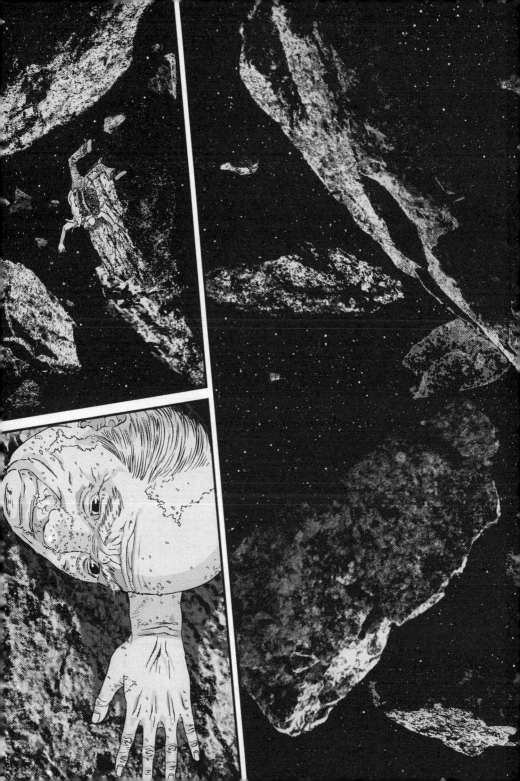

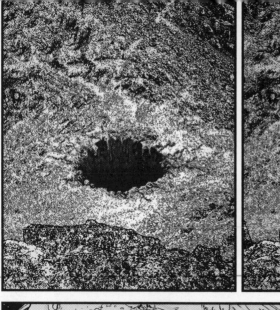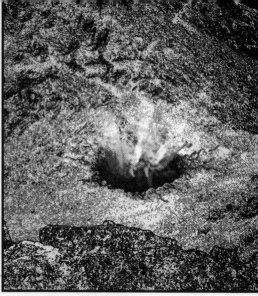

INUYASHIKI-SAN, DID IT WORK? HOW'S IT GOING?!

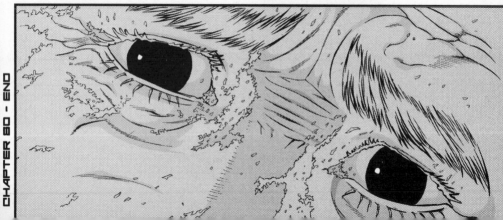

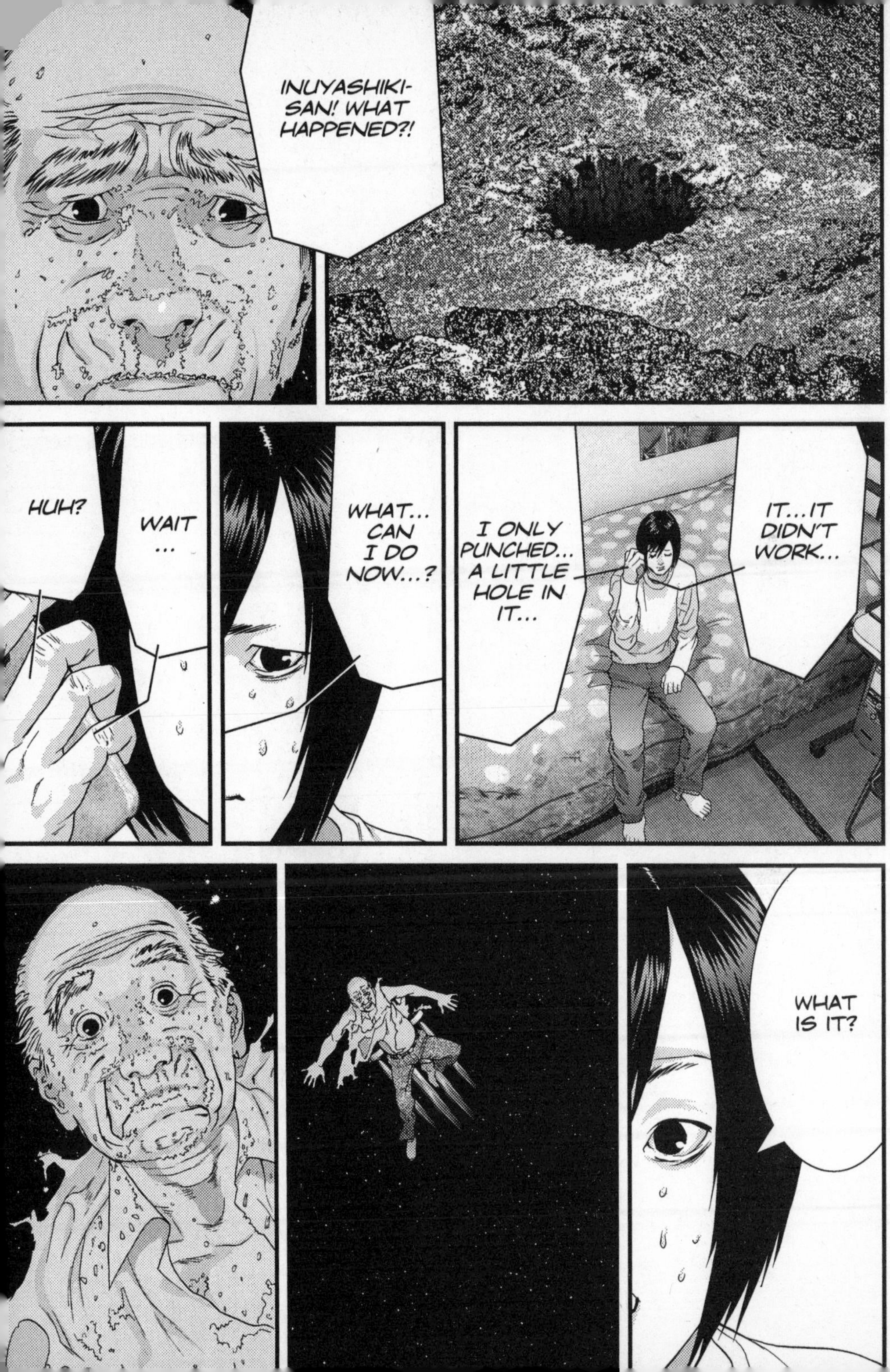
INUYASHIKI-SAN! WHAT HAPPENED?!
IT...IT DIDN'T WORK...
I ONLY PUNCHED... A LITTLE HOLE IN IT...
WHAT... CAN I DO NOW...?
WAIT ...
HUH?
WHAT IS IT?

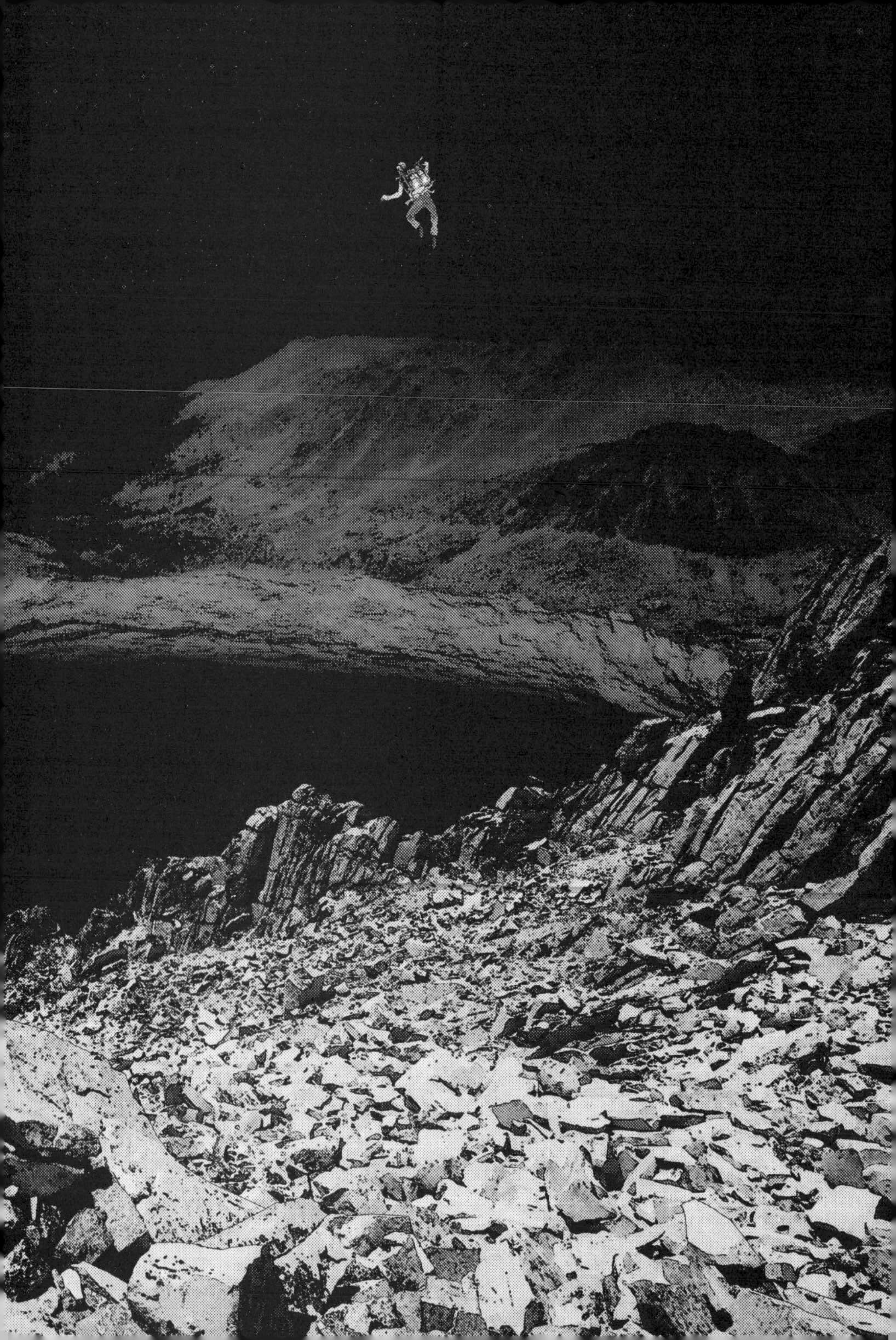

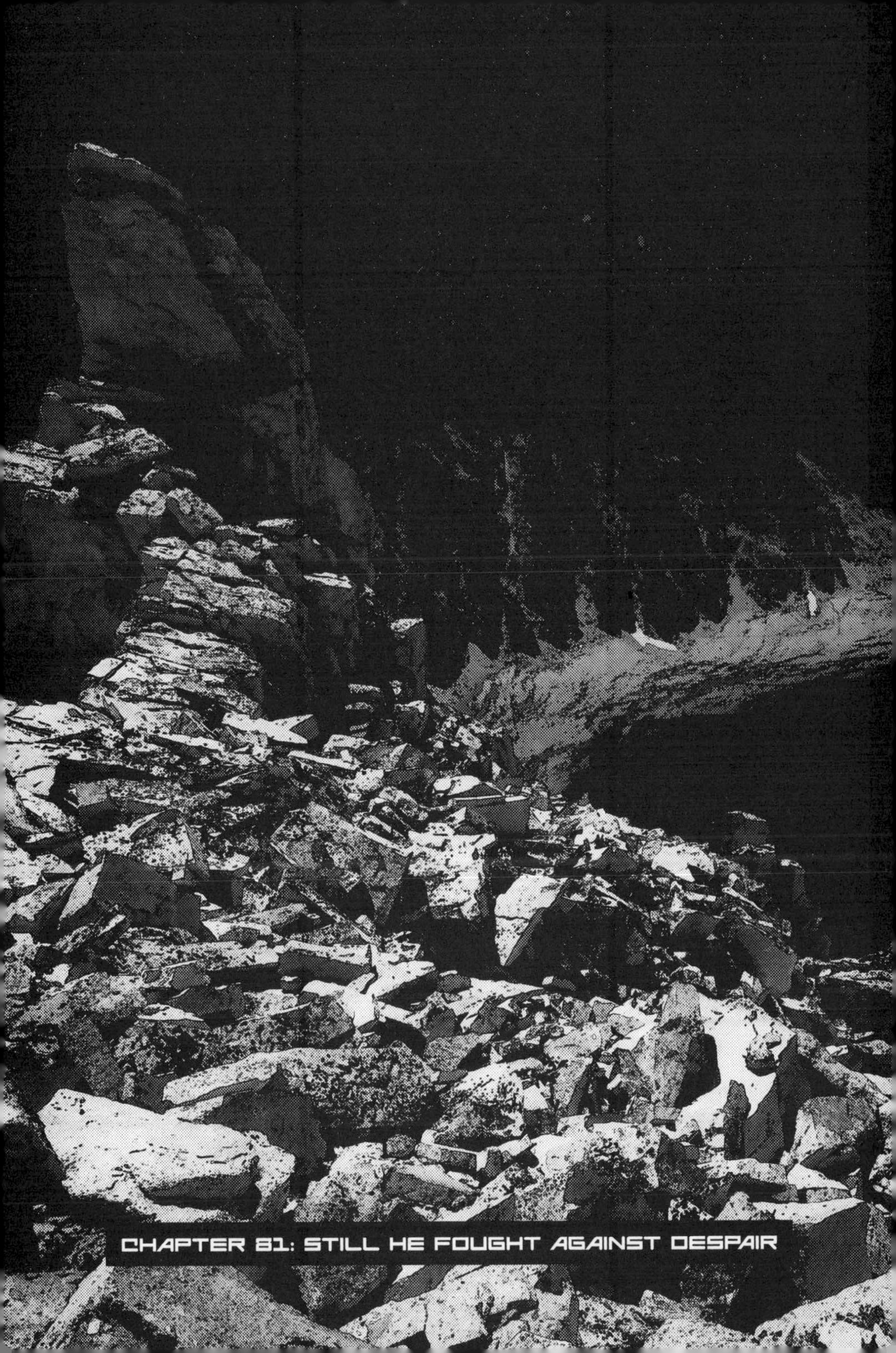
CHAPTER 81: STILL HE FOUGHT AGAINST DESPAIR

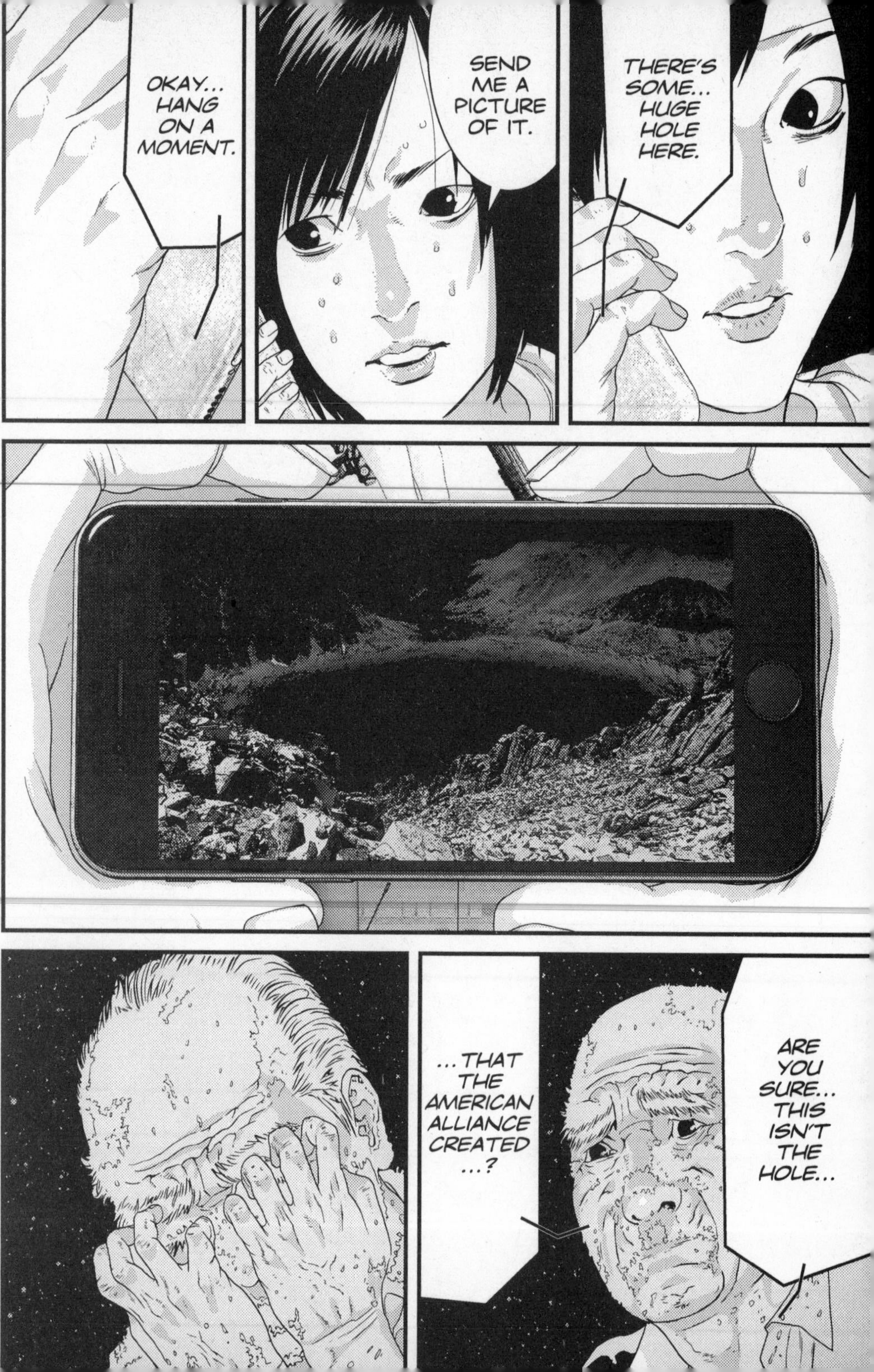
THERE'S SOME... HUGE HOLE HERE.
SEND ME A PICTURE OF IT.
OKAY... HANG ON A MOMENT.
ARE YOU SURE... THIS ISN'T THE HOLE...
...THAT THE AMERICAN ALLIANCE CREATED ...?

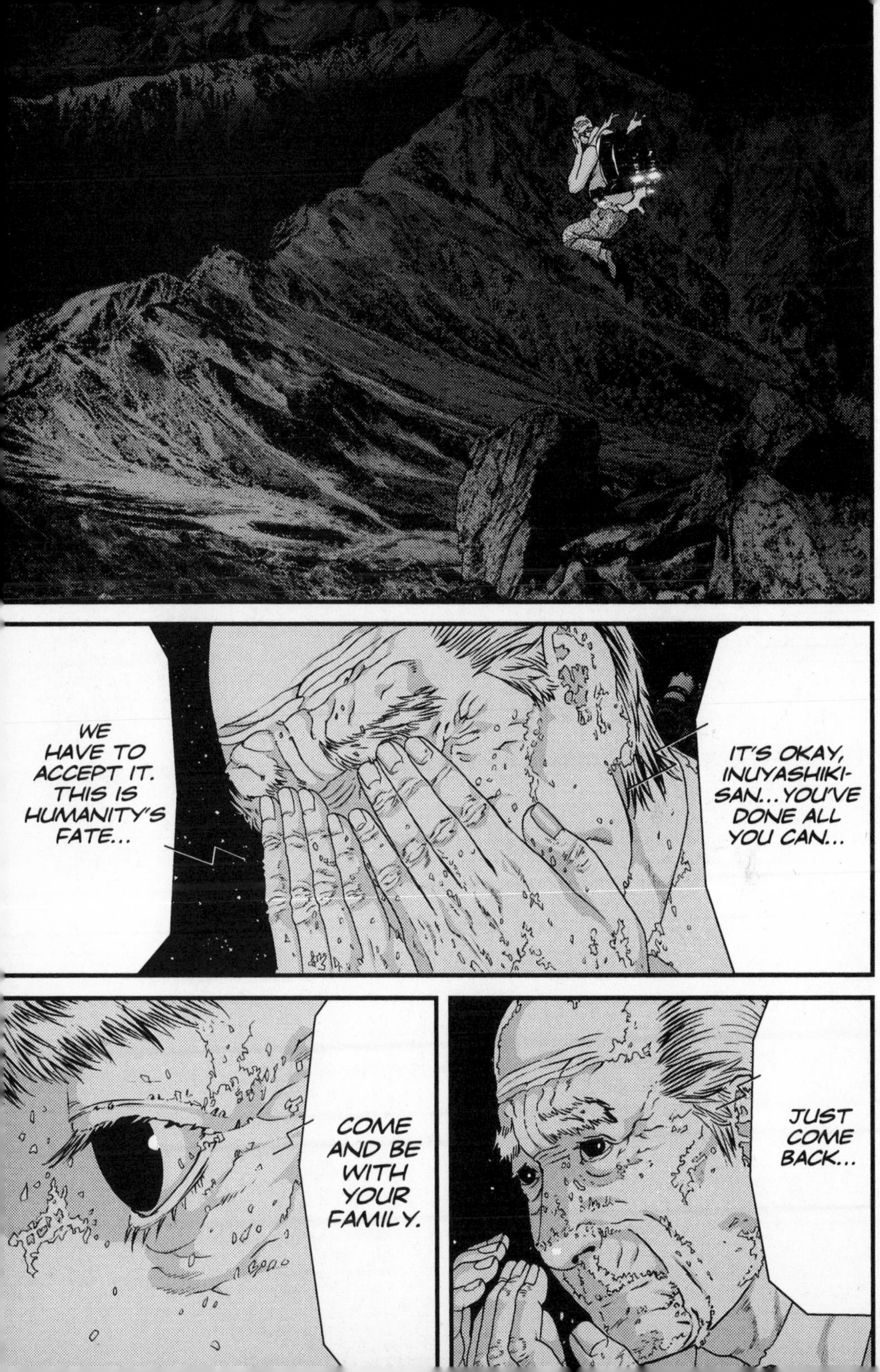
IT'S OKAY, INUYASHIKI-SAN... YOU'VE DONE ALL YOU CAN...
WE HAVE TO ACCEPT IT. THIS IS HUMANITY'S FATE...
JUST COME BACK...
COME AND BE WITH YOUR FAMILY.

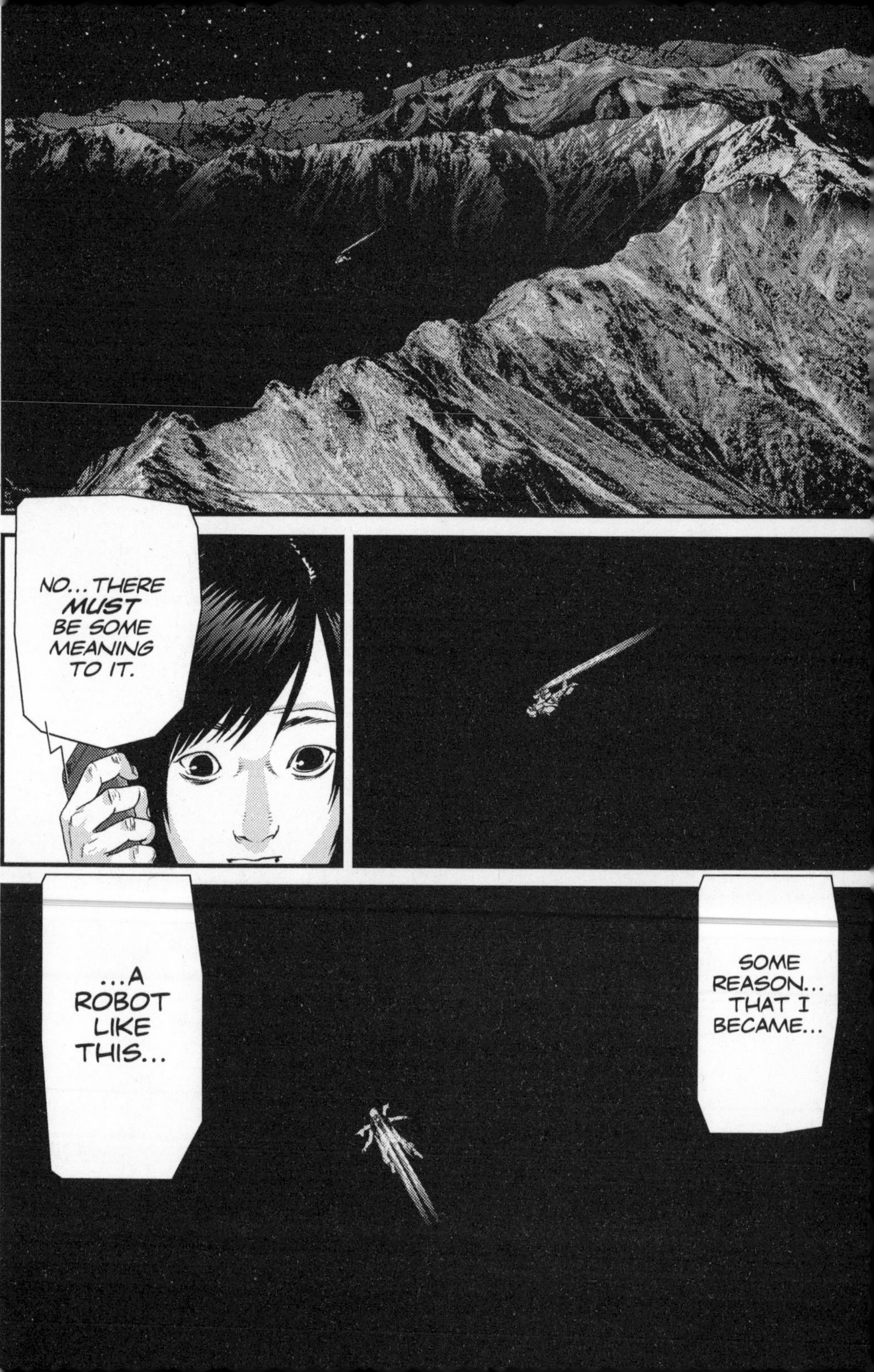
NO... THERE MUST BE SOME MEANING TO IT.
SOME REASON... THAT I BECAME...
...A ROBOT LIKE THIS...

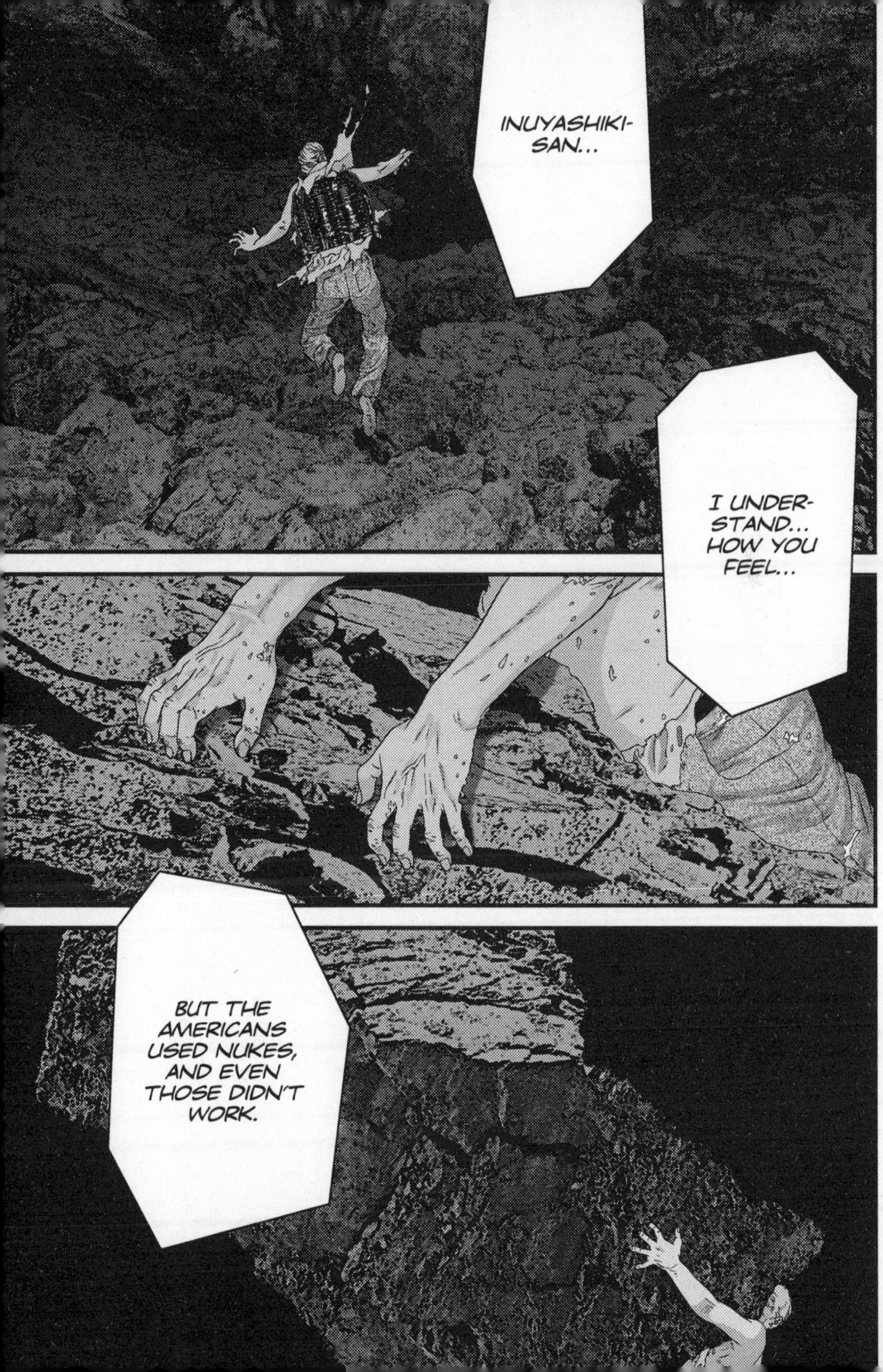
INUYASHIKI-SAN...
I UNDER-STAND... HOW YOU FEEL...
BUT THE AMERICANS USED NUKES, AND EVEN THOSE DIDN'T WORK.

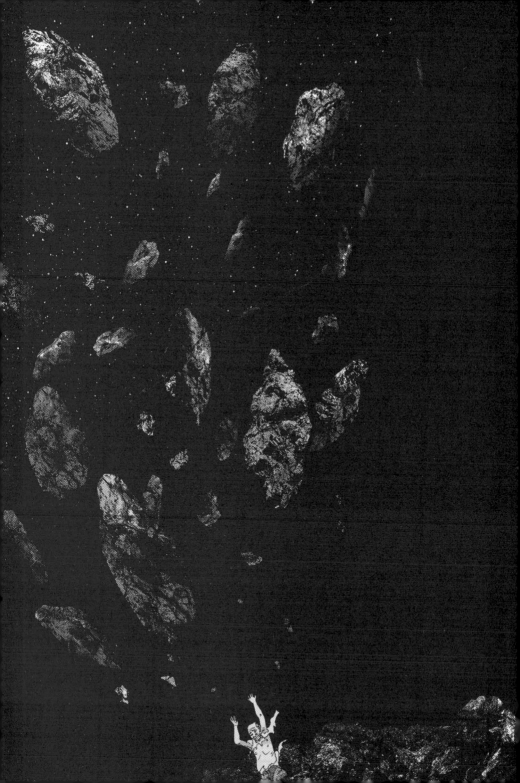

INUYASHIKI-
SAN...

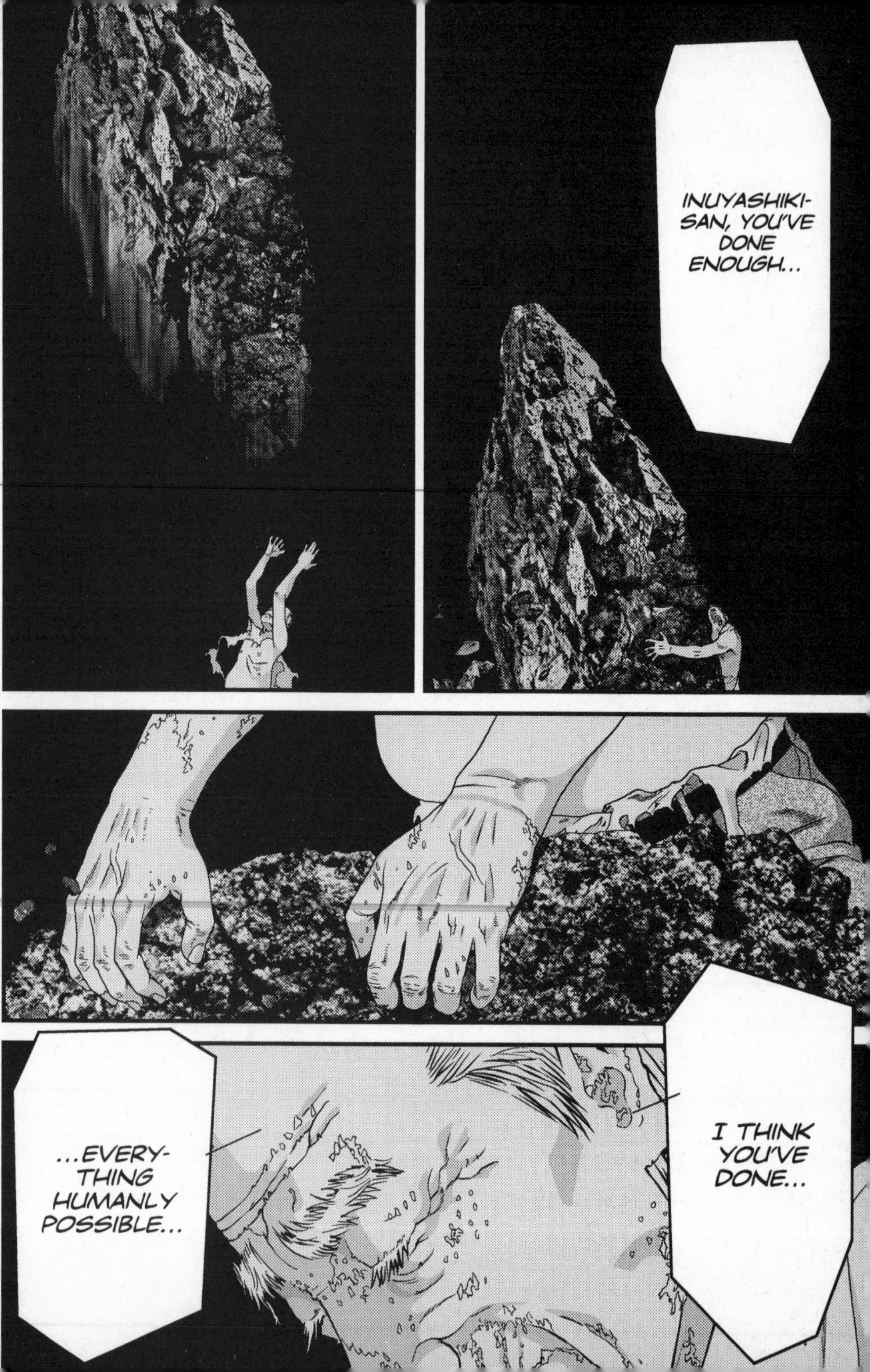
INUYASHIKI-SAN, YOU'VE DONE ENOUGH...
I THINK YOU'VE DONE...
...EVERY-THING HUMANLY POSSIBLE...

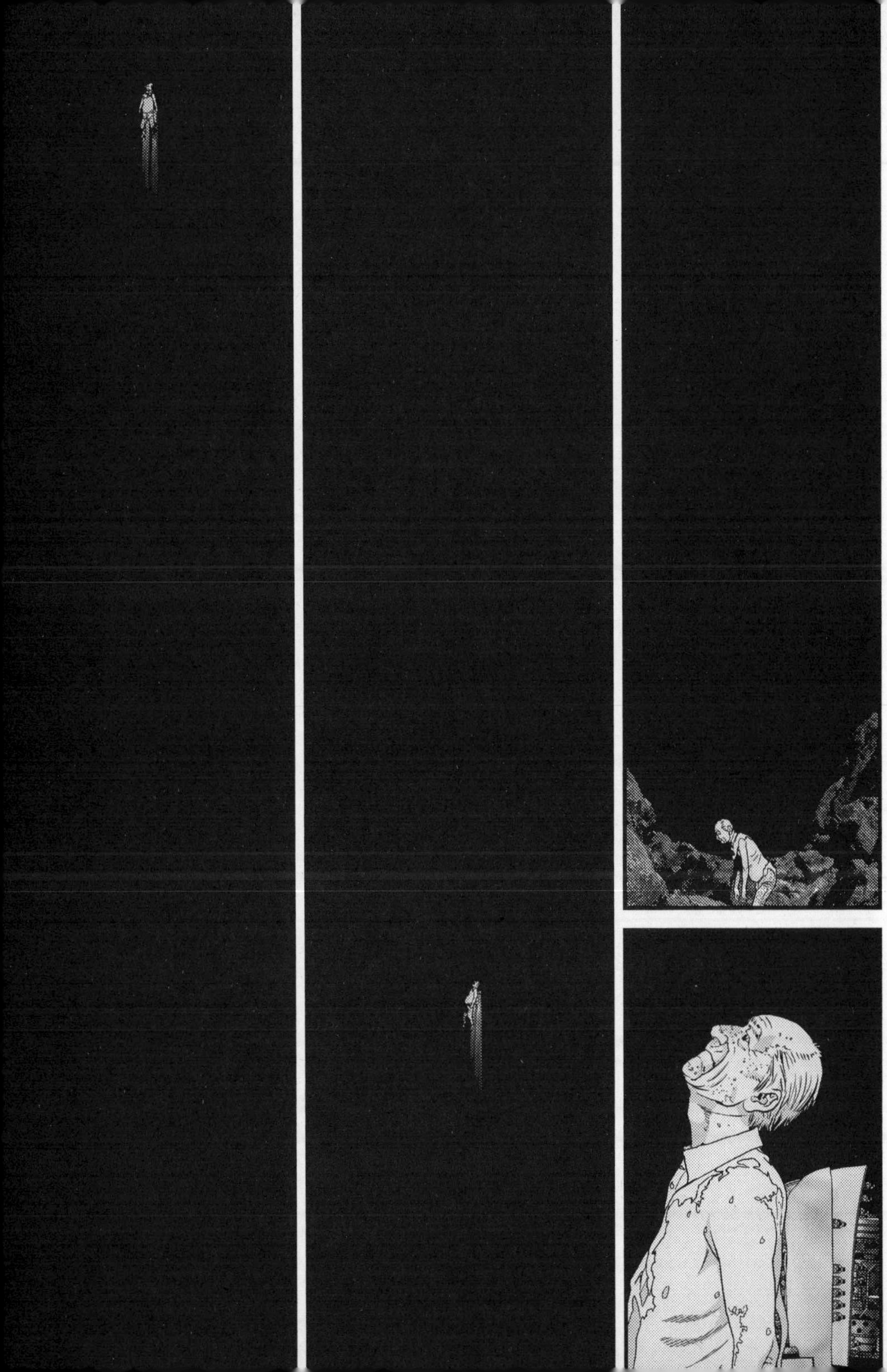

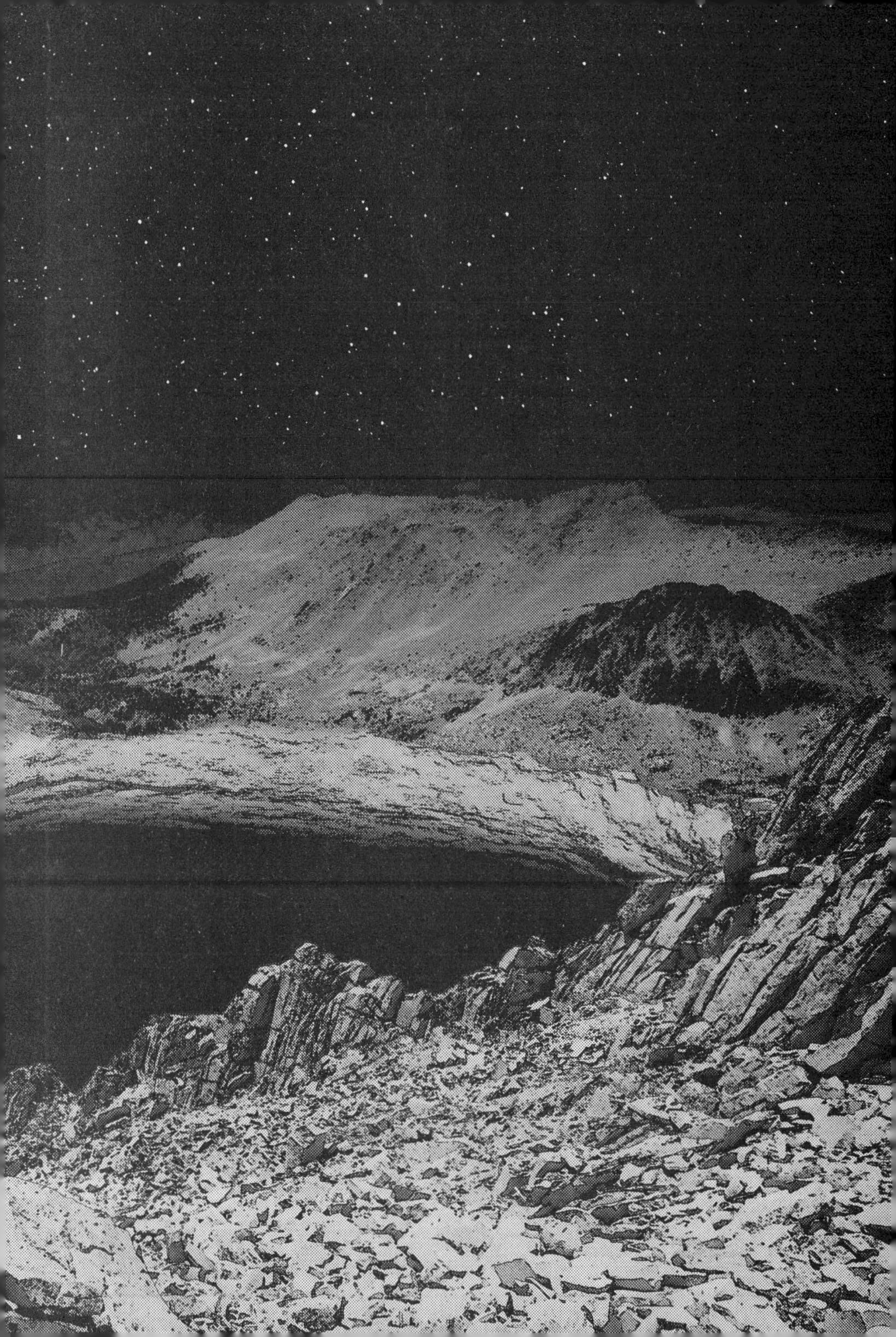

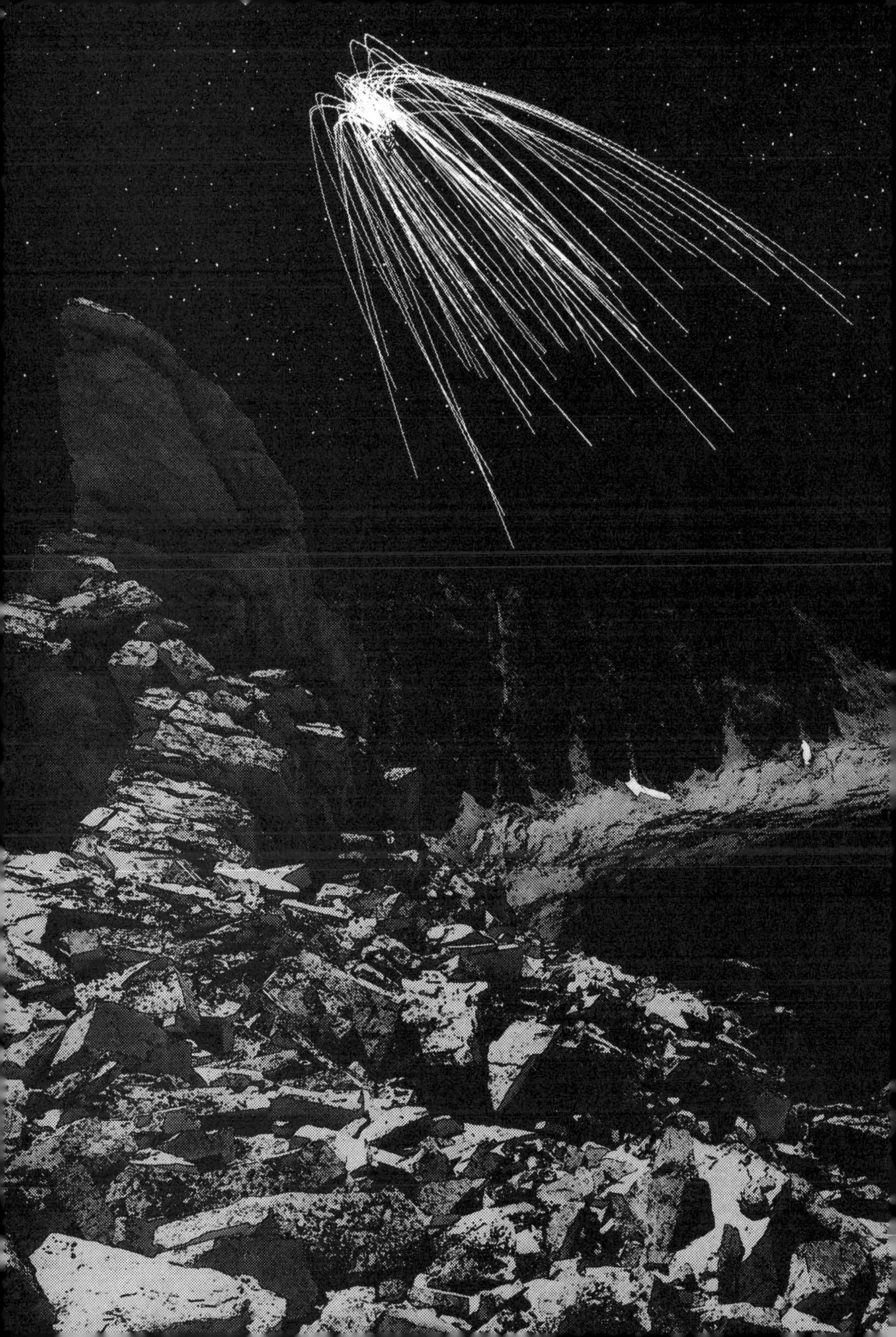

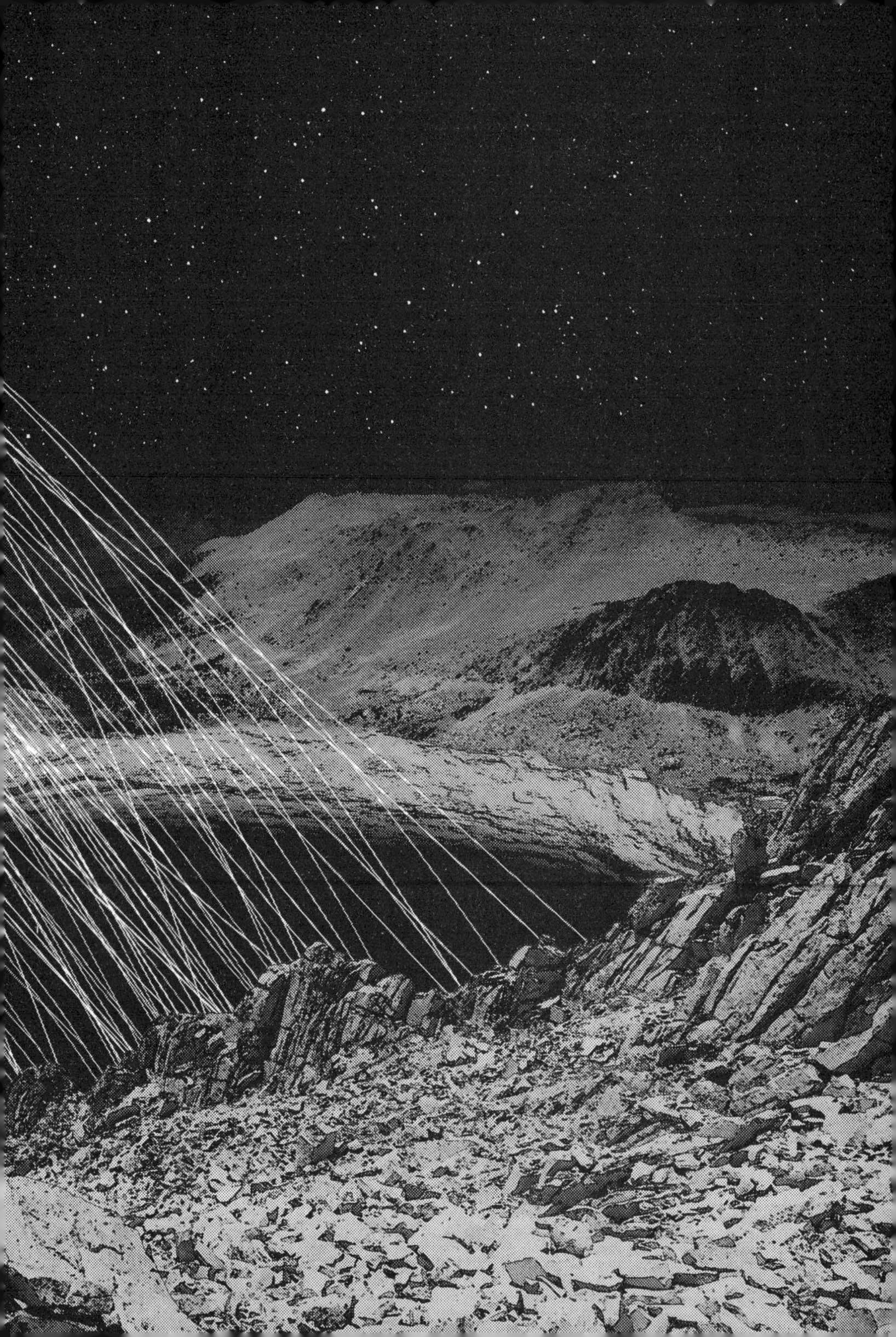

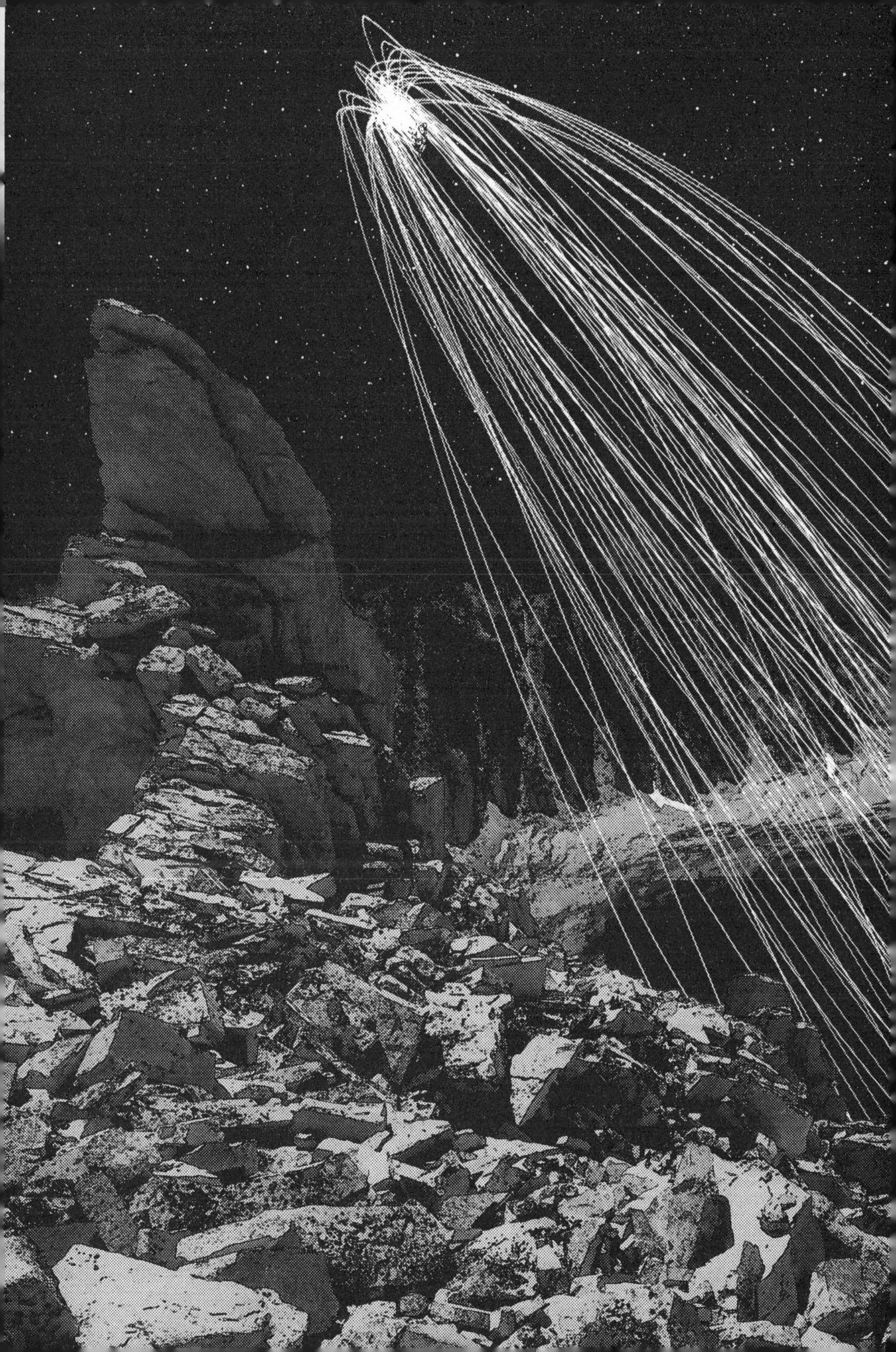

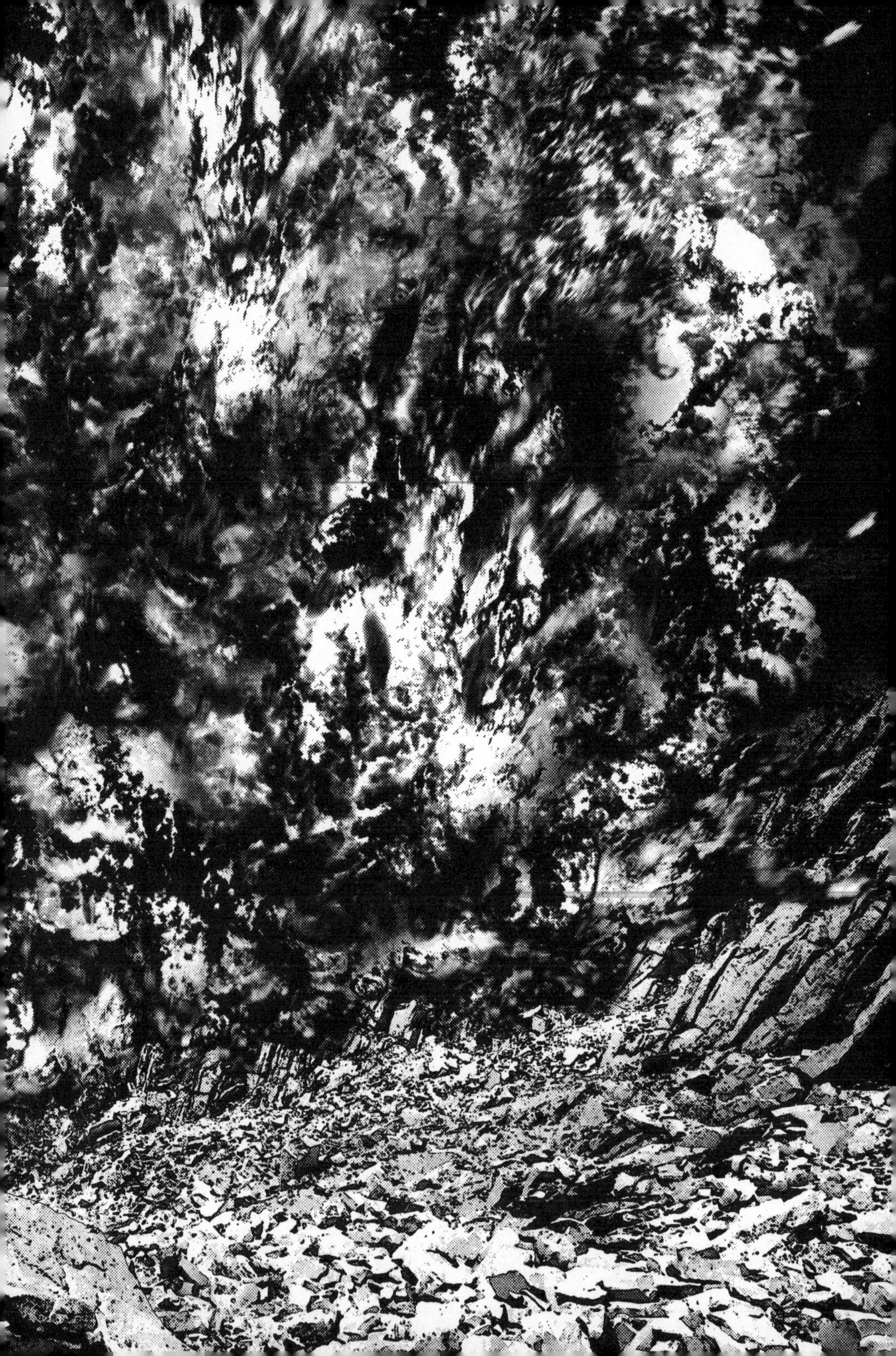

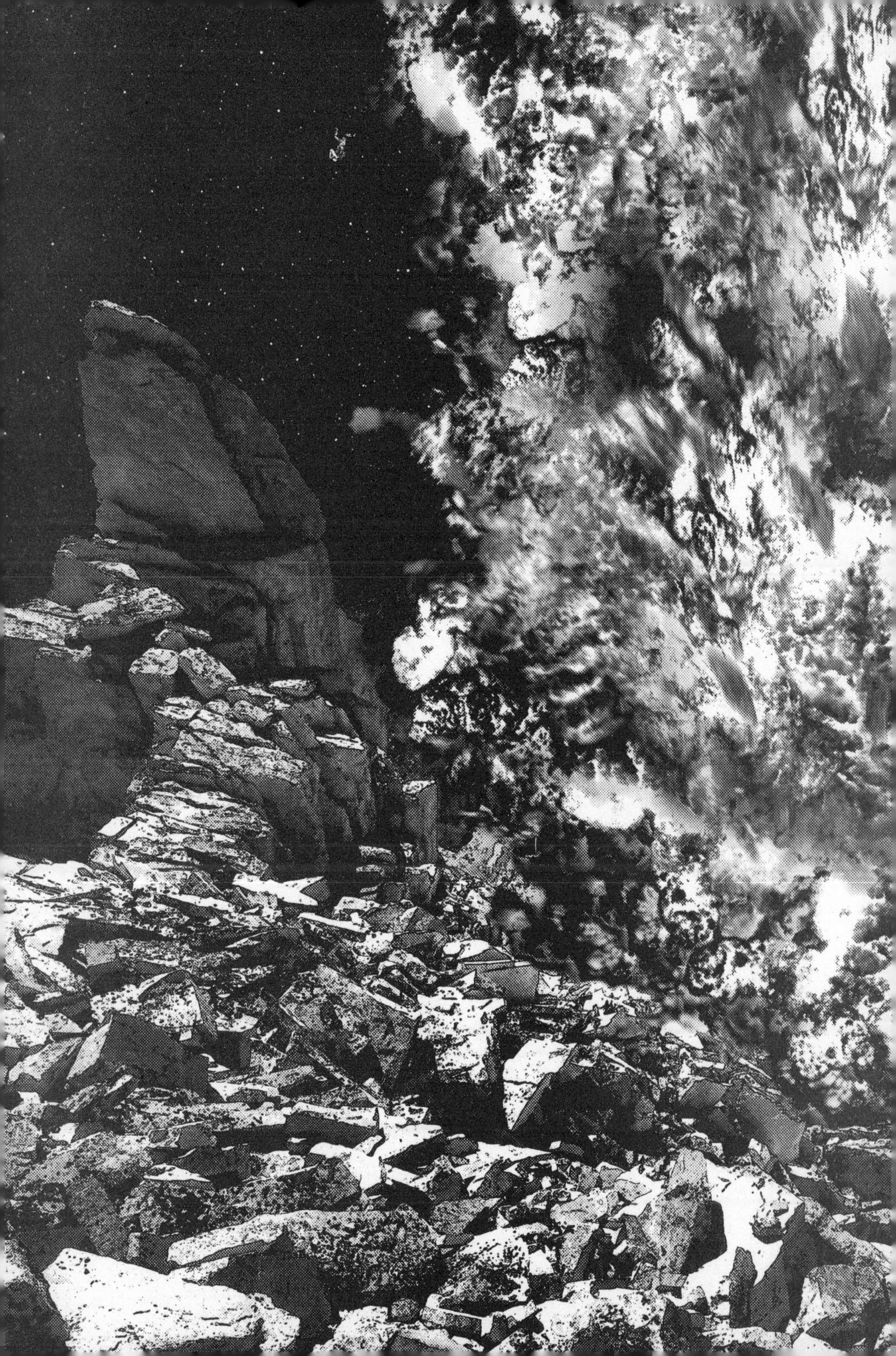

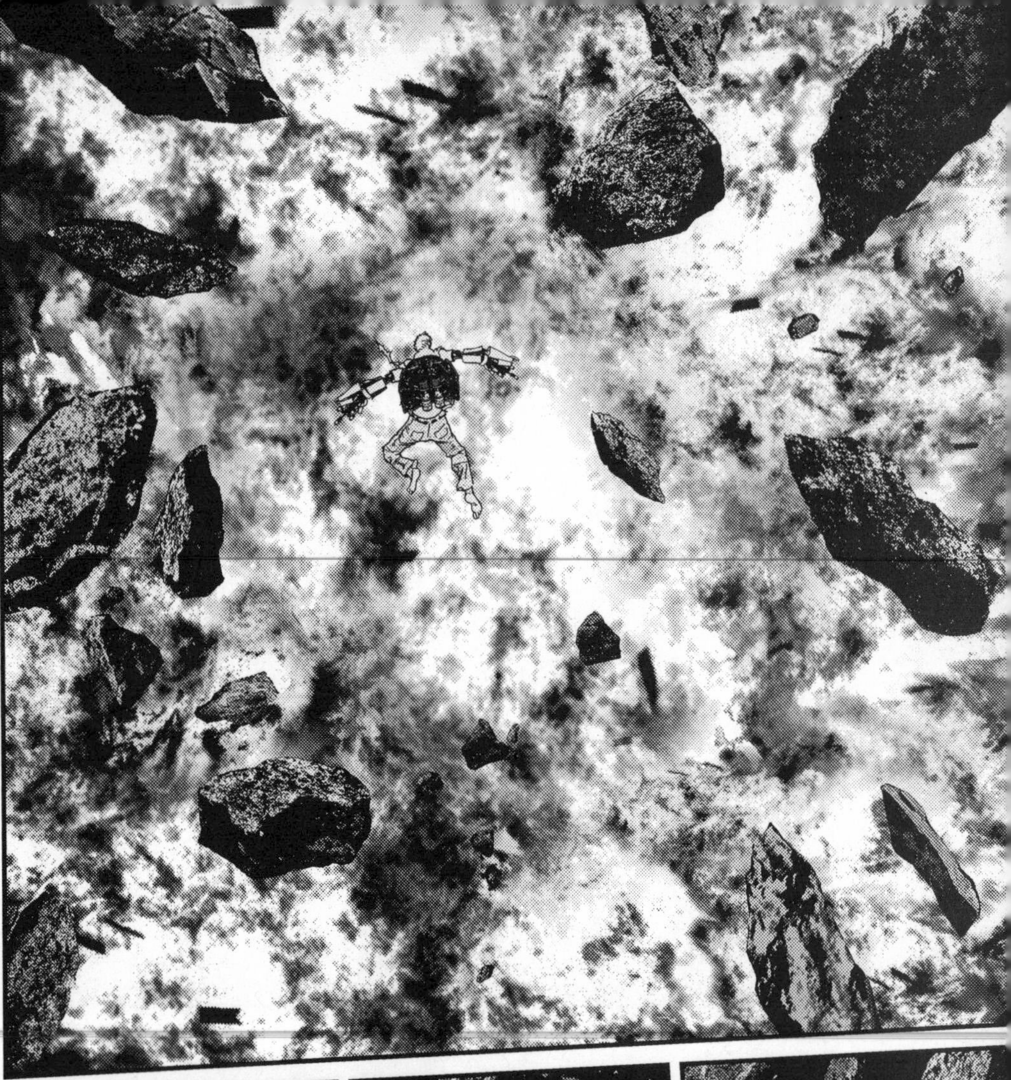
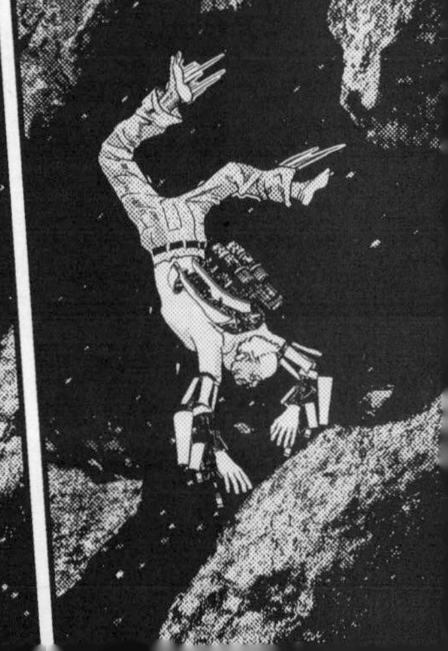
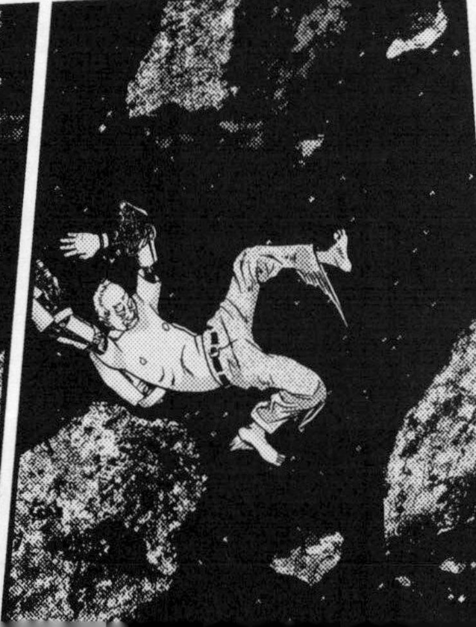
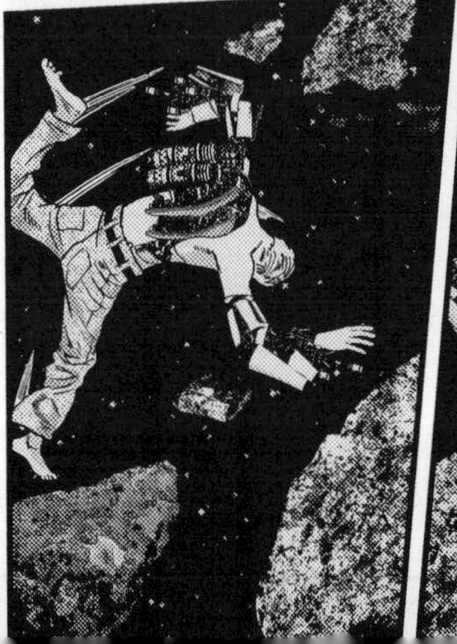

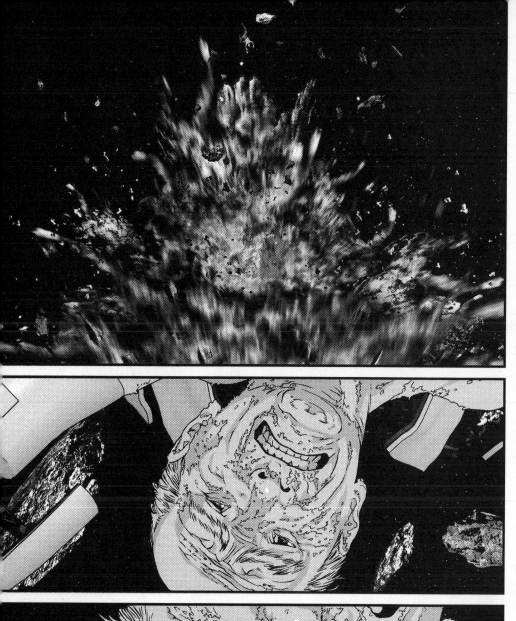
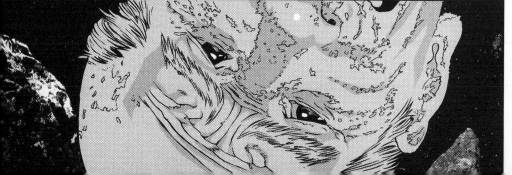

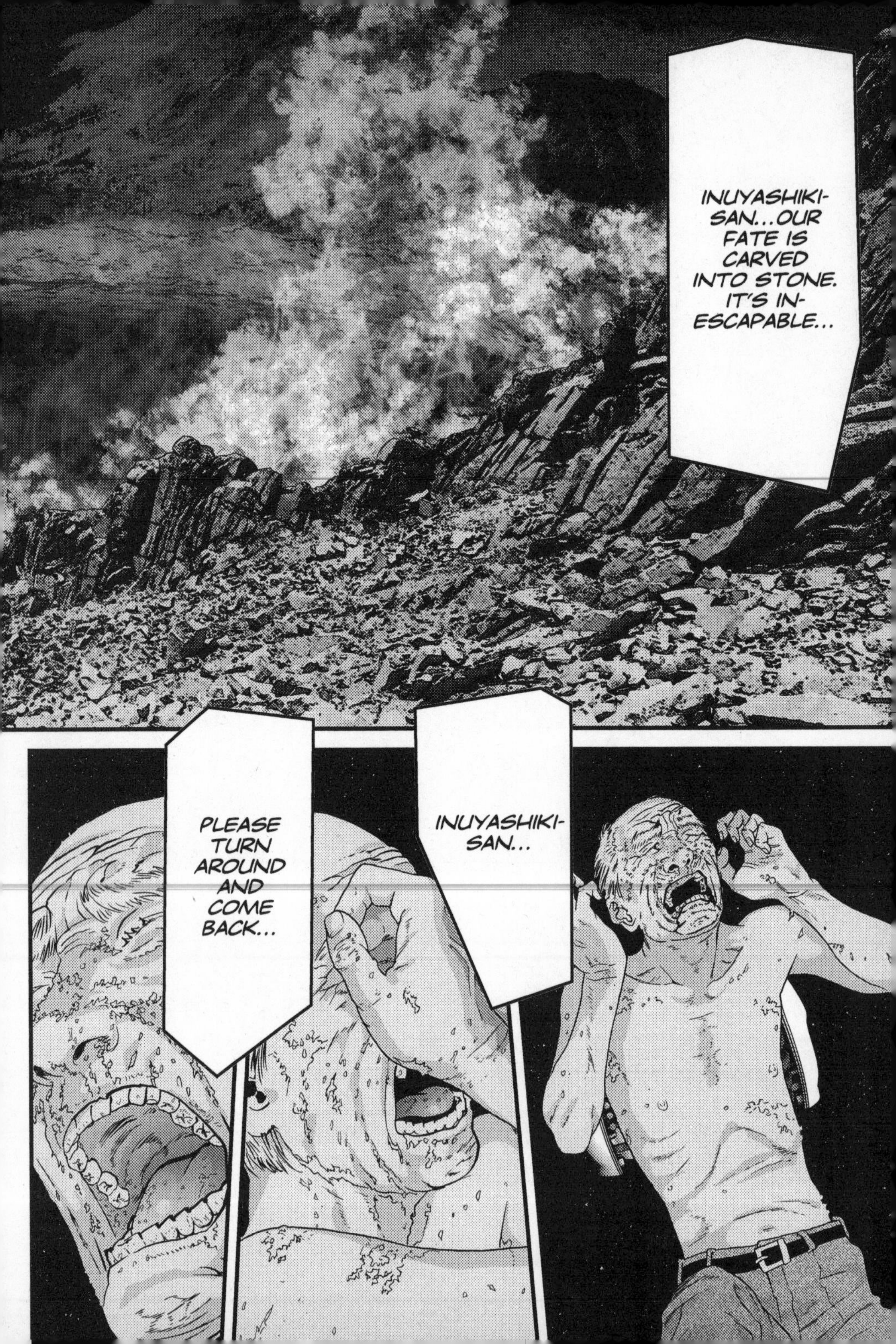
INUYASHIKI-SAN...OUR FATE IS CARVED INTO STONE. IT'S IN-ESCAPABLE...
INUYASHIKI-SAN...
PLEASE TURN AROUND AND COME BACK...

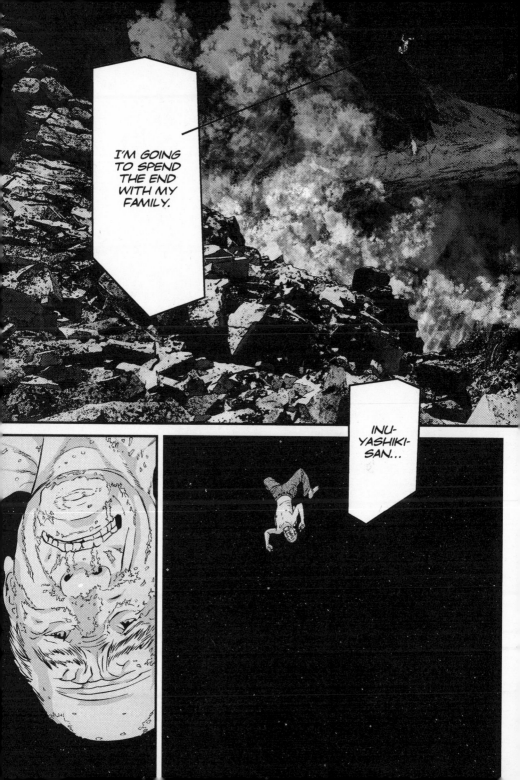

I'M GOING
TO SPEND
THE END
WITH MY
FAMILY.

INU-
YASHIKI-
SAN...

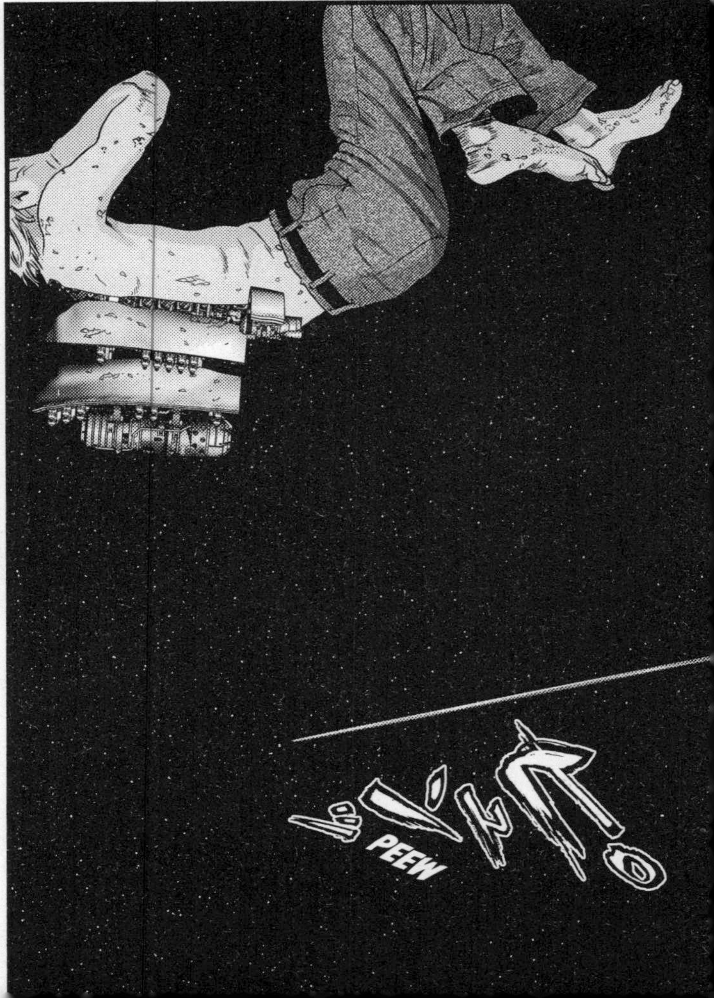
PEEW
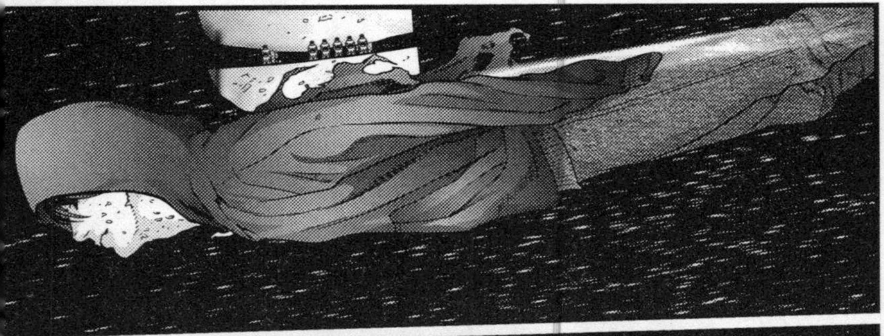
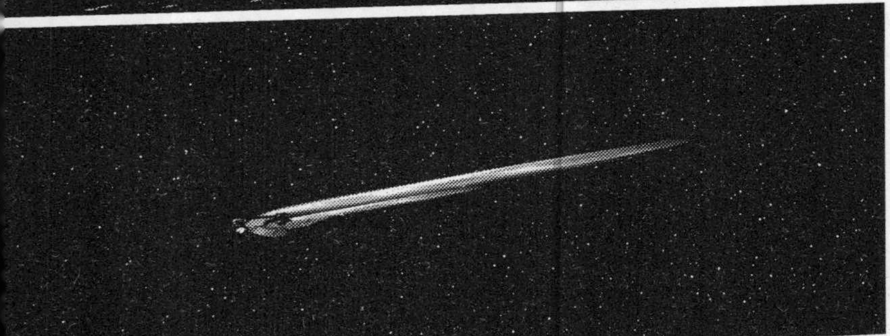
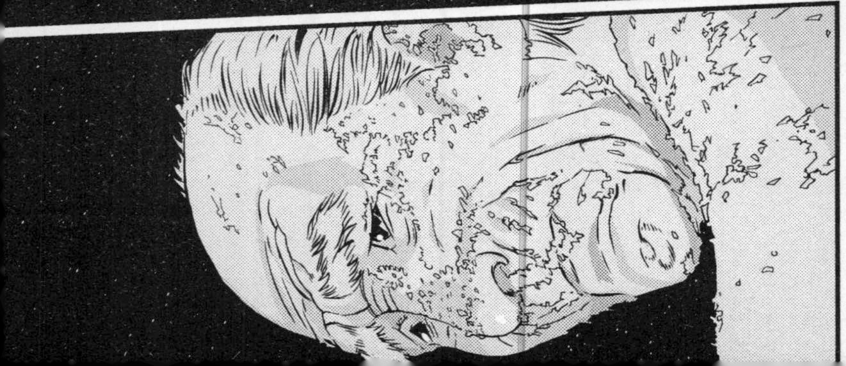

CHAPTER 81 - END

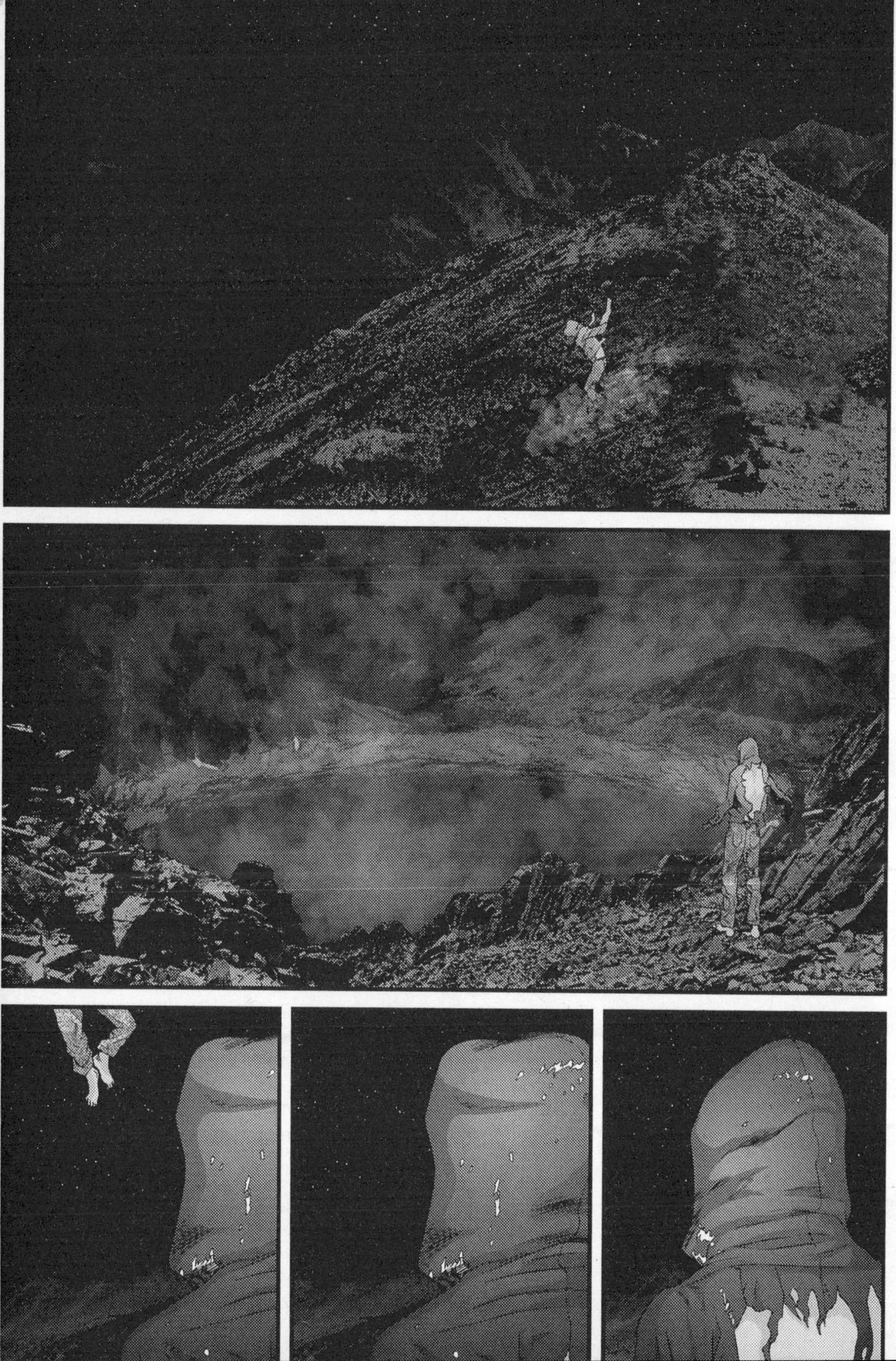

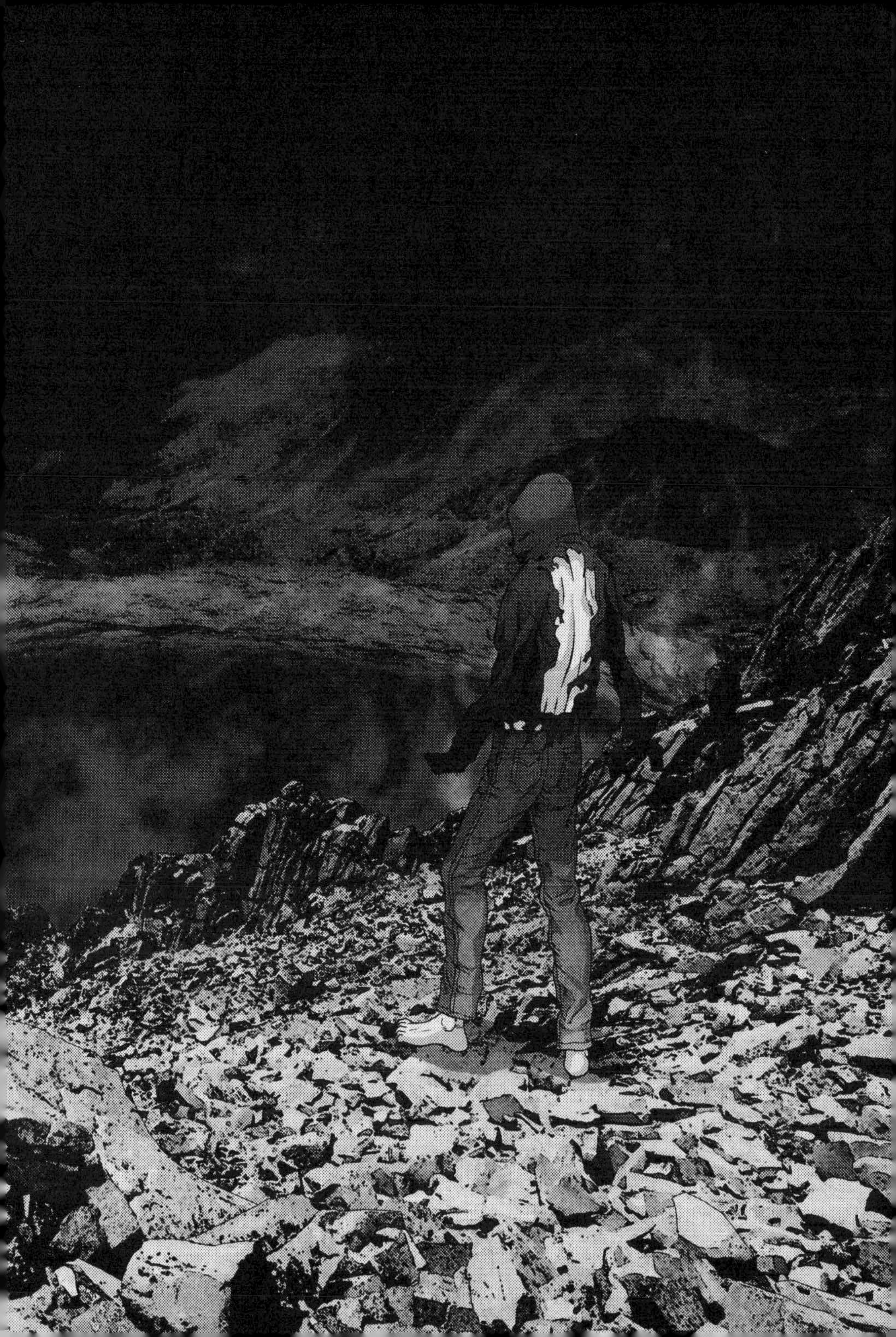

CHAPTER 82: WHY ARE YOU HERE...?

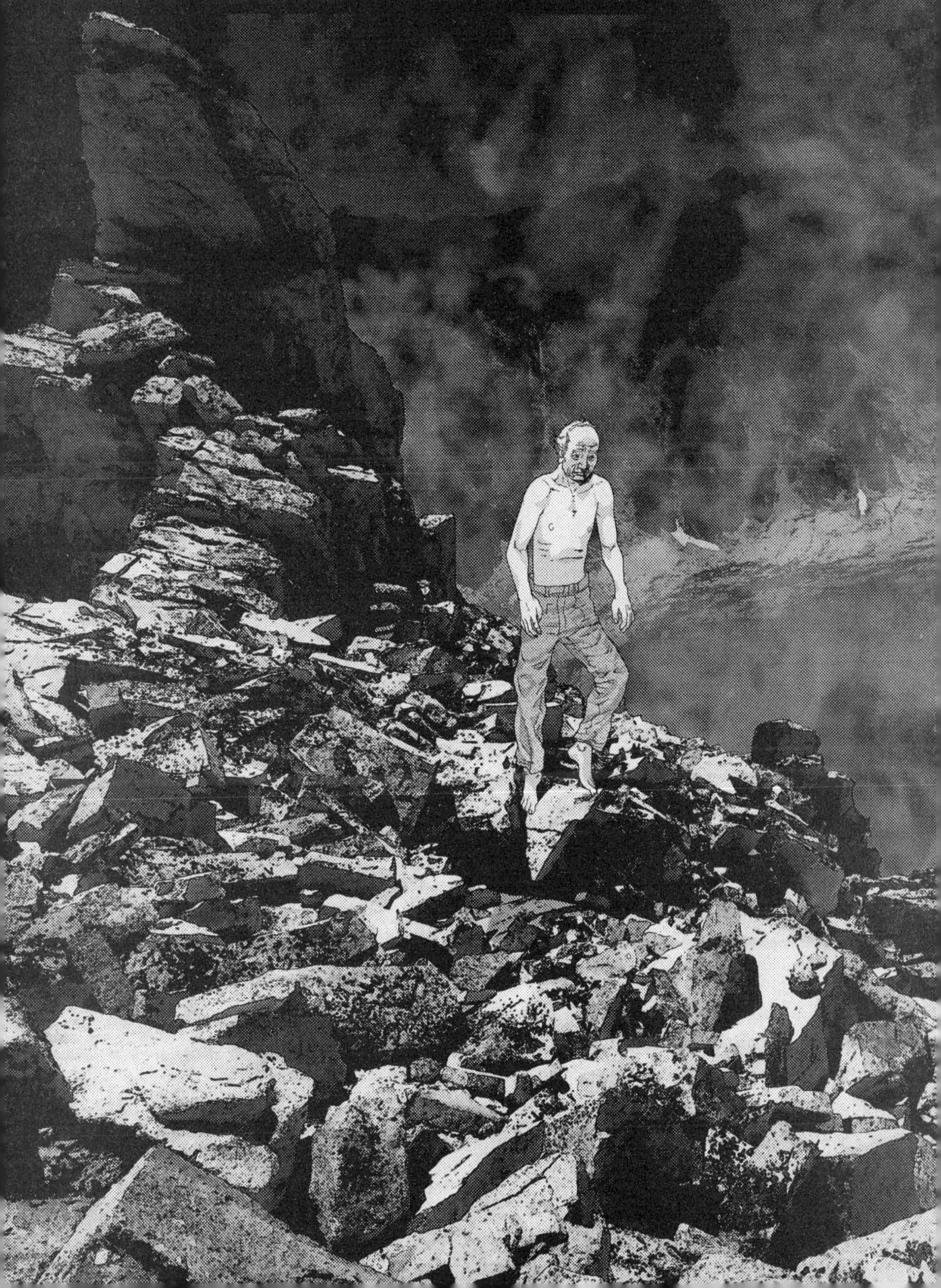

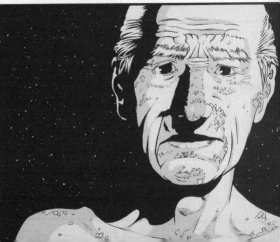

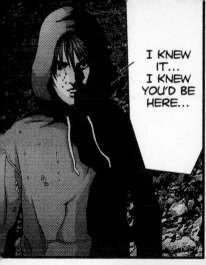

プルルルル
RRRR
Hiro Shishigami
ピッ
BEEP
I KNEW IT... I KNEW YOU'D BE HERE...
WHY... ARE YOU HERE?
...I THOUGHT ...
...I'D TRY... TO SHIFT ITS TRAJECTORY...
YOU DID...? BUT WHY...?
...
...

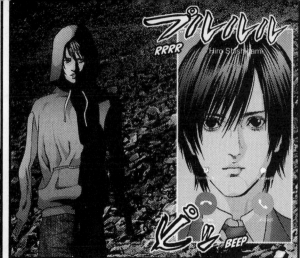

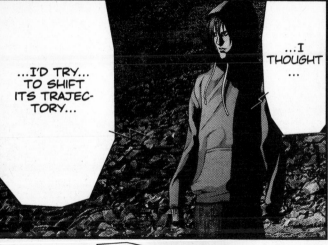

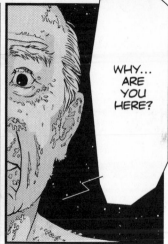

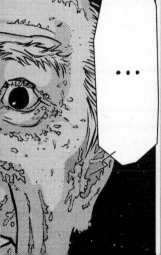

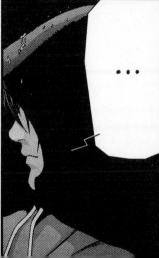

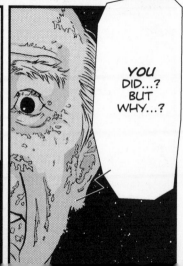

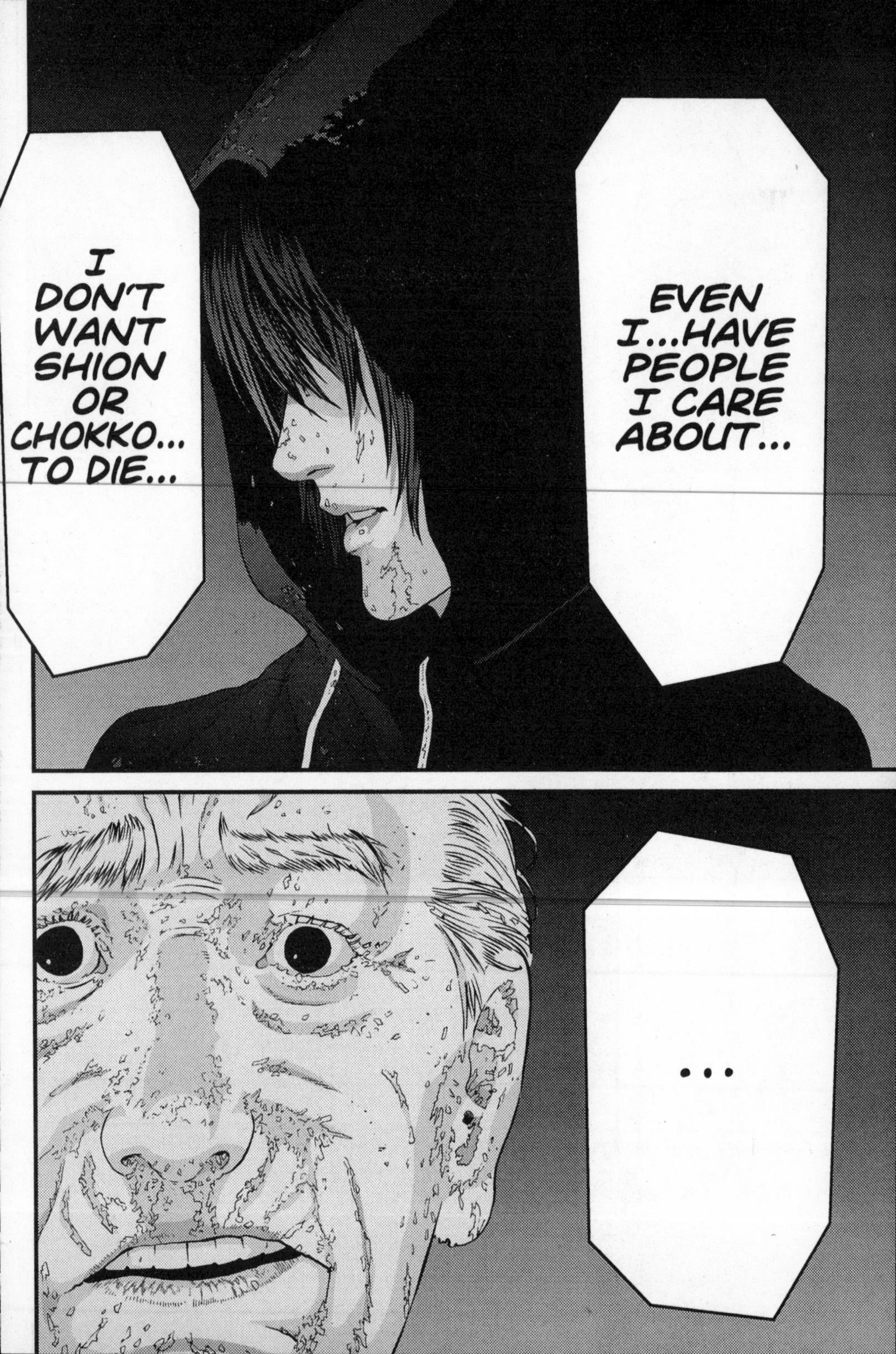
EVEN I...HAVE PEOPLE I CARE ABOUT...
I DON'T WANT SHION OR CHOKKO... TO DIE...
...

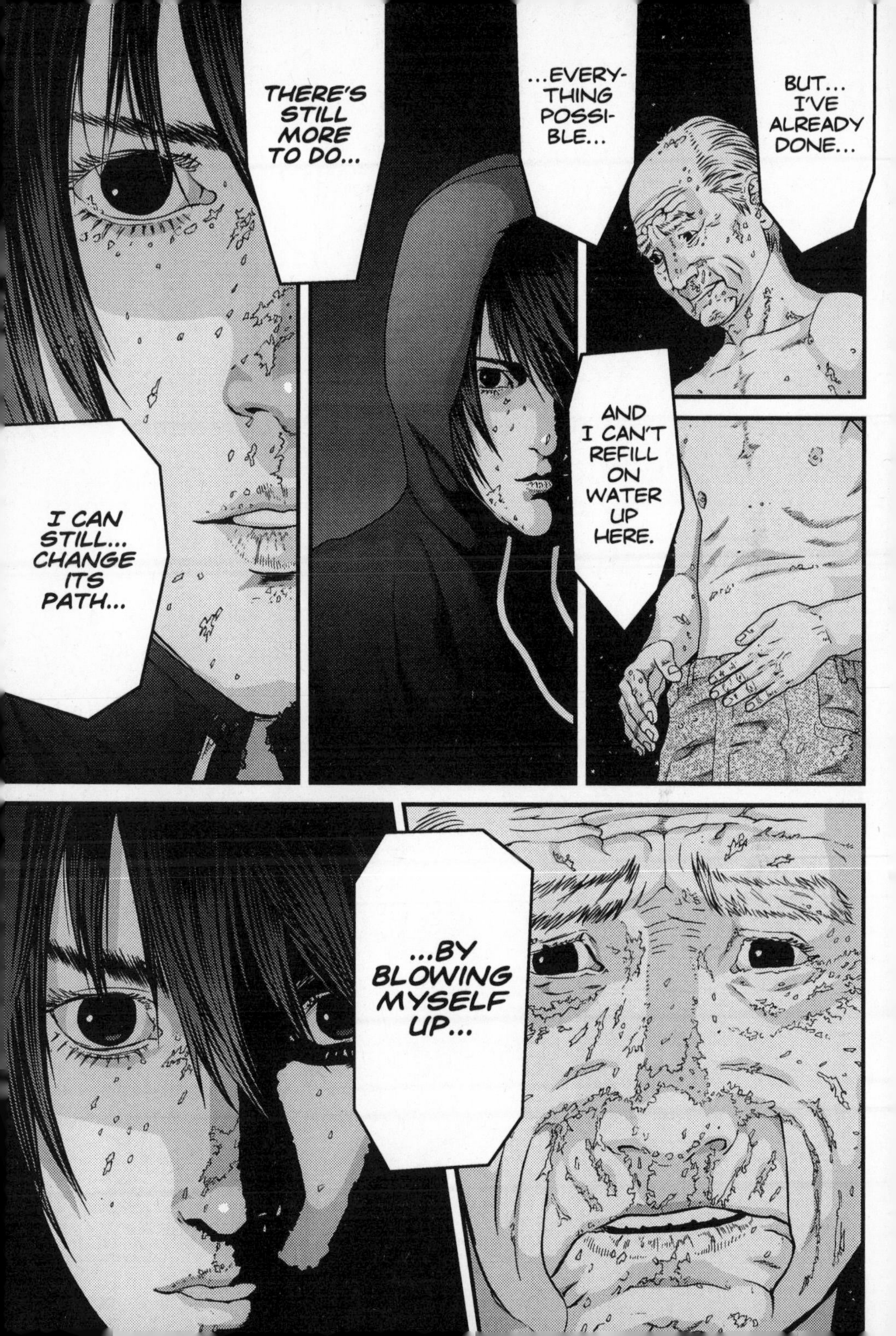
BUT... I'VE ALREADY DONE...
...EVERY-THING POSSI-BLE...
AND I CAN'T REFILL ON WATER UP HERE.
THERE'S STILL MORE TO DO...
I CAN STILL... CHANGE ITS PATH...
...BY BLOWING MYSELF UP...

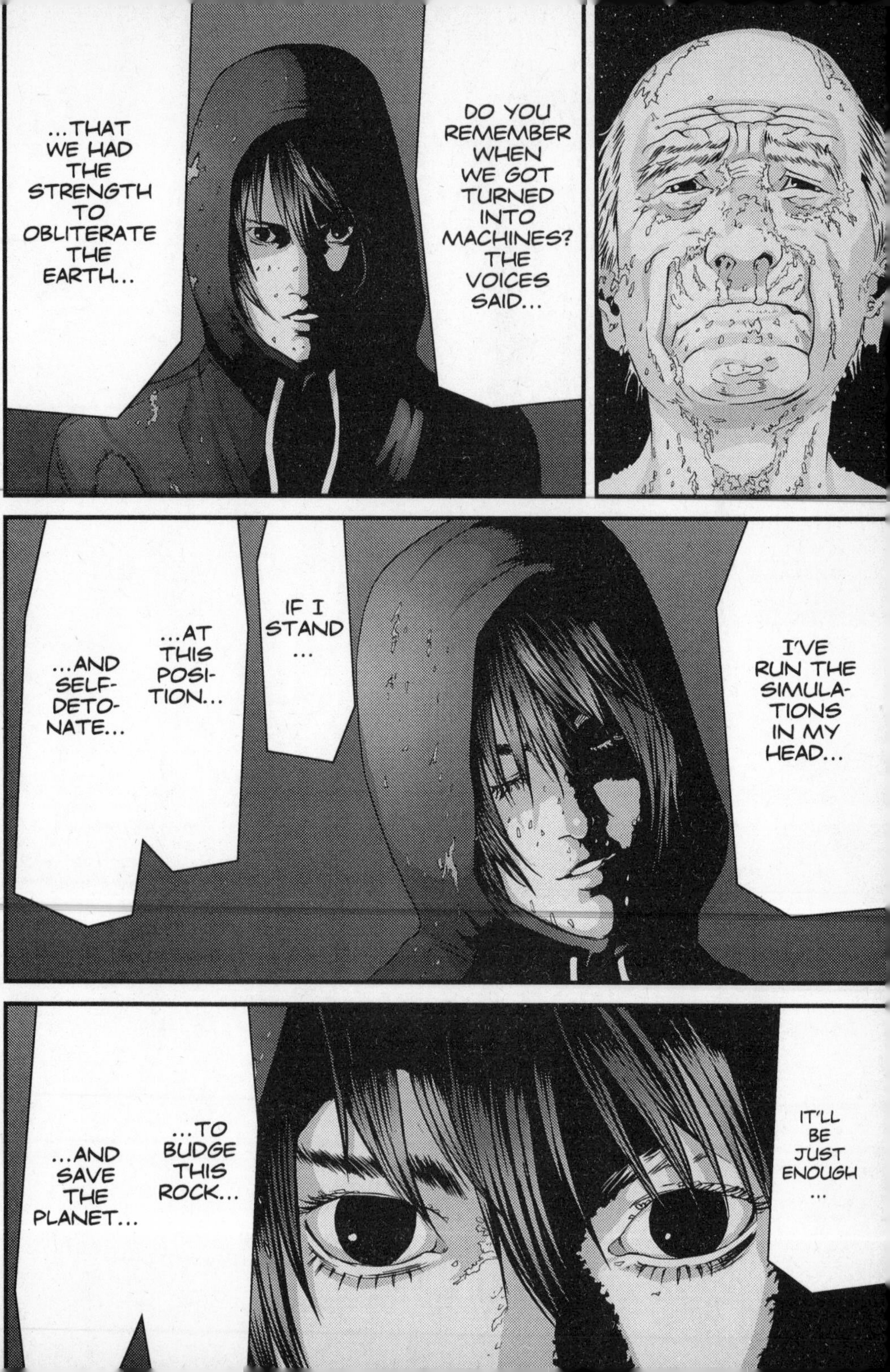
DO YOU REMEMBER WHEN WE GOT TURNED INTO MACHINES? THE VOICES SAID...
...THAT WE HAD THE STRENGTH TO OBLITERATE THE EARTH...
I'VE RUN THE SIMULATIONS IN MY HEAD...
IF I STAND ...
...AT THIS POSITION...
...AND SELF-DETONATE...
IT'LL BE JUST ENOUGH ...
...TO BUDGE THIS ROCK...
...AND SAVE THE PLANET...

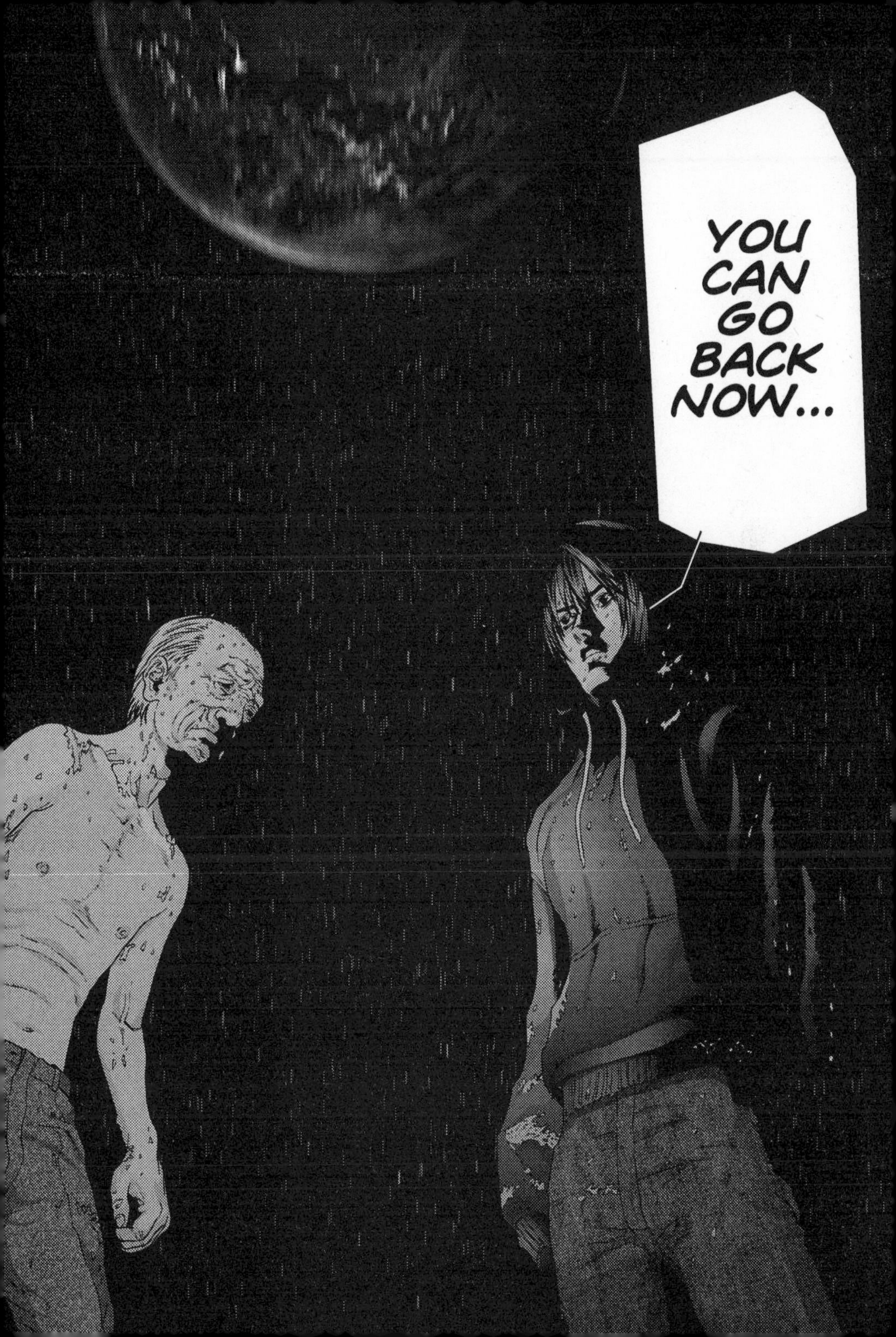
YOU CAN GO BACK NOW...

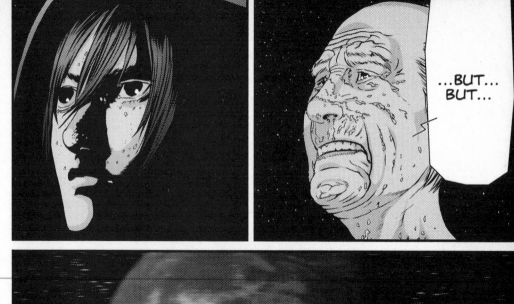

...BUT...
BUT...

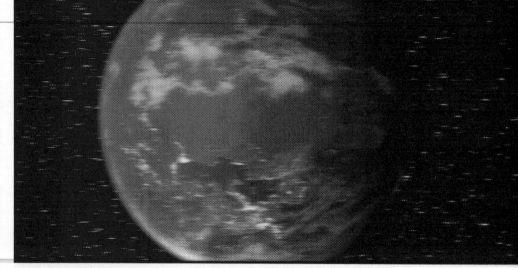

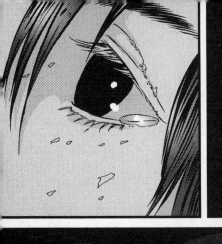

WHERE ARE YOU?

SHISHI-GAMI-KUN...

HNNGH...

SHISHI-GAMI-KUN...

SHISHI-GAMI-KUN...

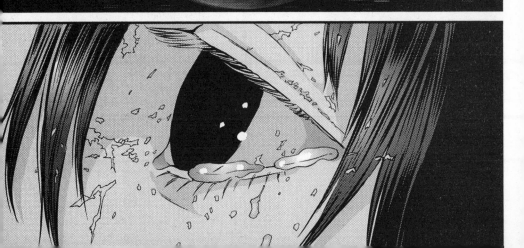

I HAVE A FAVOR TO ASK YOU...
HUH? WHAT?
MY HANDS... ARE GONE NOW.
I WANT YOU TO USE YOUR FINGERS...
...TO PUSH MY EYES INWARD...
THAT'S...THE ACTIVATION SWITCH...
...FOR DETONATION...

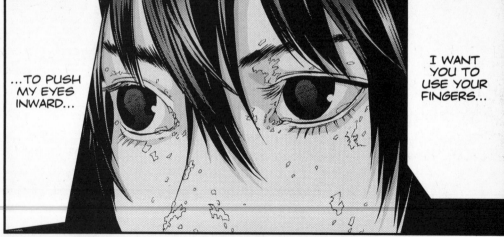

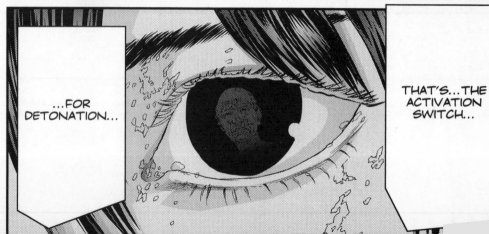

...

ONCE YOU ACTIVATE THE SWITCH, YOU SHOULD LEAVE AT ONCE...

...

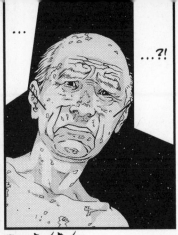

...?!

TRRRR

Ando-kun

WHERE ARE YOU NOW, INUYA-SHIKI-SAN?

BEEP

SHISHI-GAMI IS... RIGHT HERE... WITH ME...

INUYA-SHIKI-SAN?

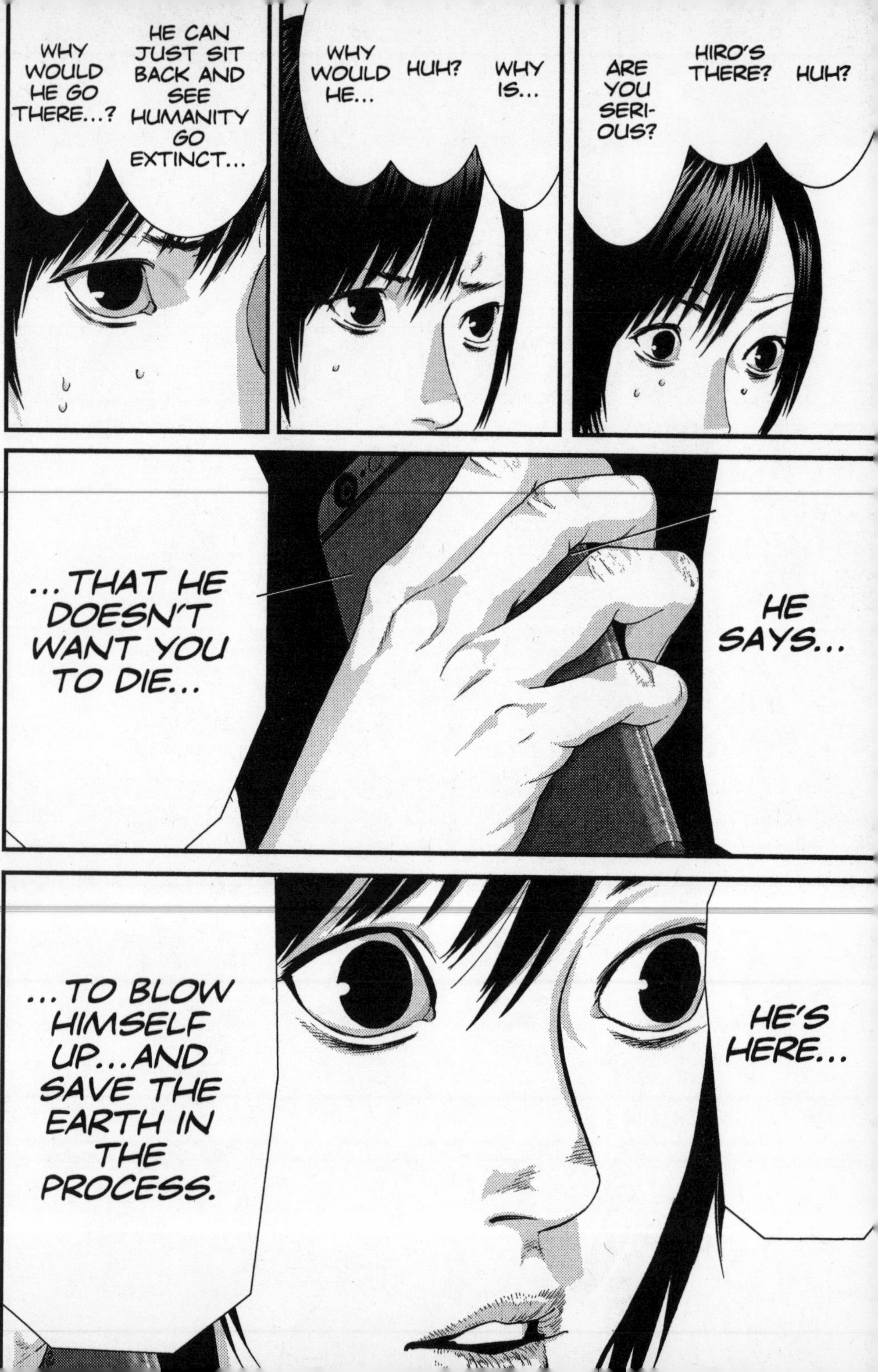
HUH?
HIRO'S THERE?
ARE YOU SERIOUS?
WHY IS...
HUH?
WHY WOULD HE...
HE CAN JUST SIT BACK AND SEE HUMANITY GO EXTINCT...
WHY WOULD HE GO THERE...?
HE SAYS...
...THAT HE DOESN'T WANT YOU TO DIE...
HE'S HERE...
...TO BLOW HIMSELF UP...AND SAVE THE EARTH IN THE PROCESS.

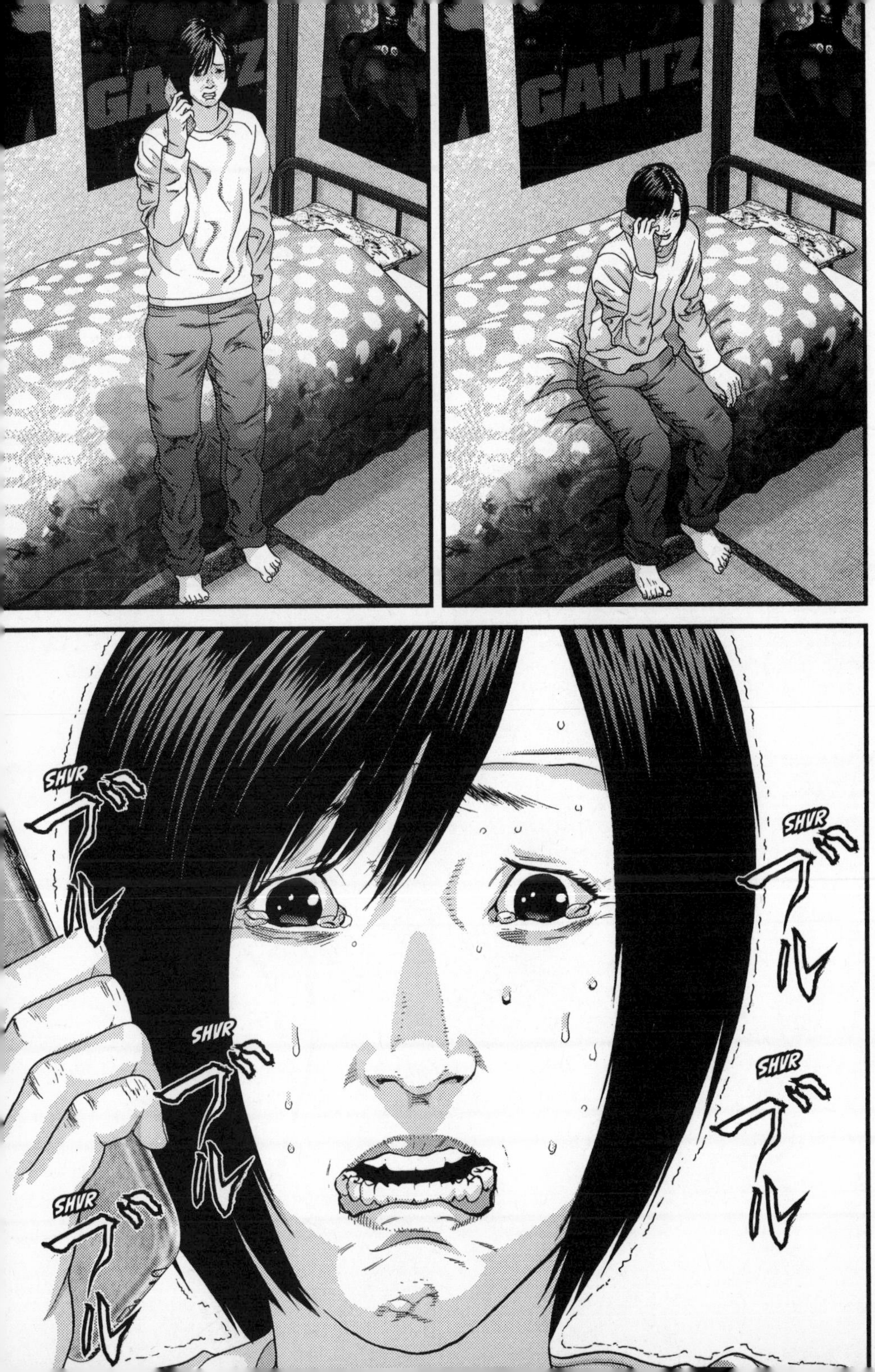
GANTZ
GANTZ
SHVR
ブル
SHVR
ブル
SHVR
ブル
SHVR
ブル

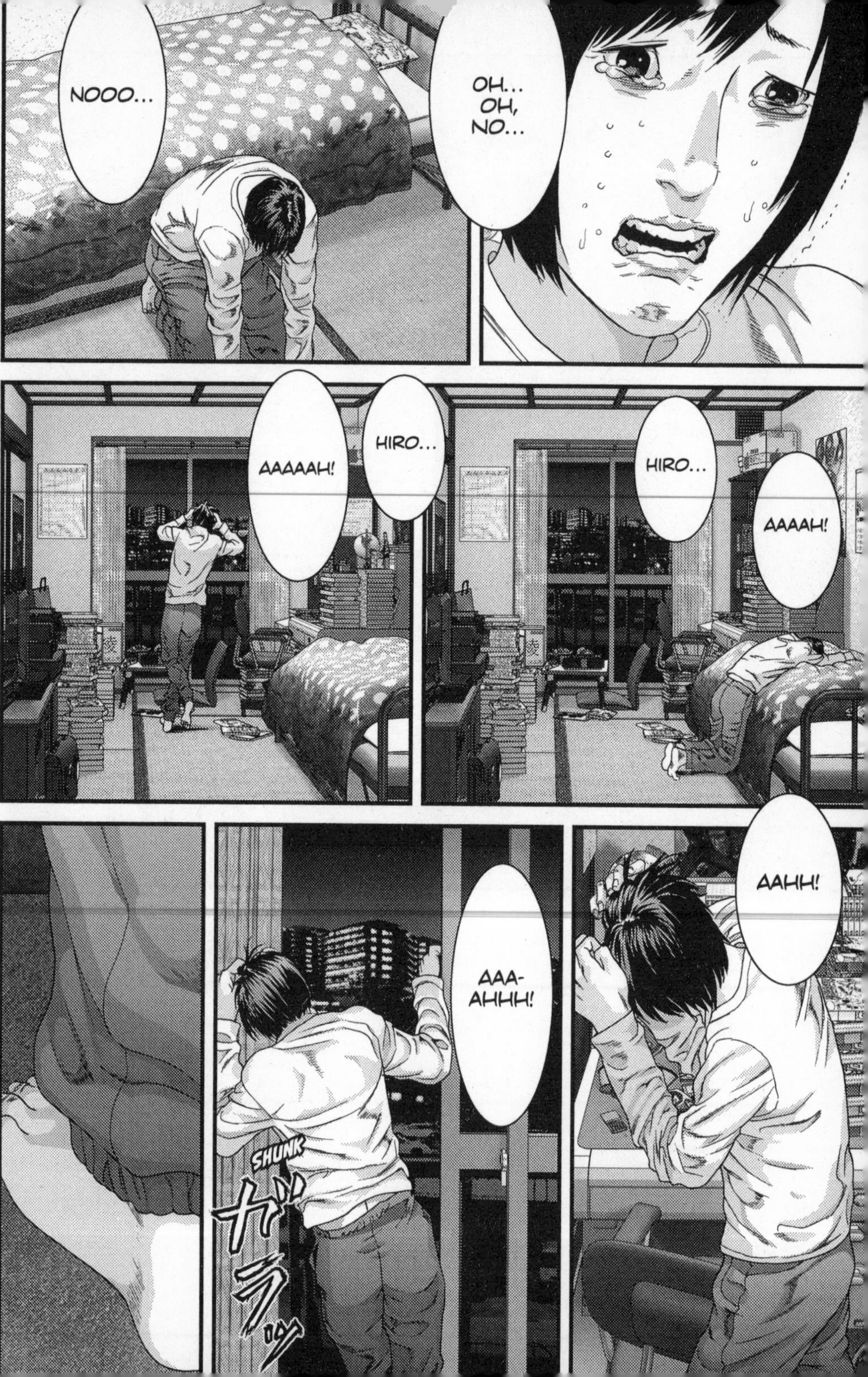
OH... OH, NO...
NOOO...
HIRO...
AAAAH!
HIRO...
AAAAAH!
AAHH!
AAA-AHHH!
SHUNK

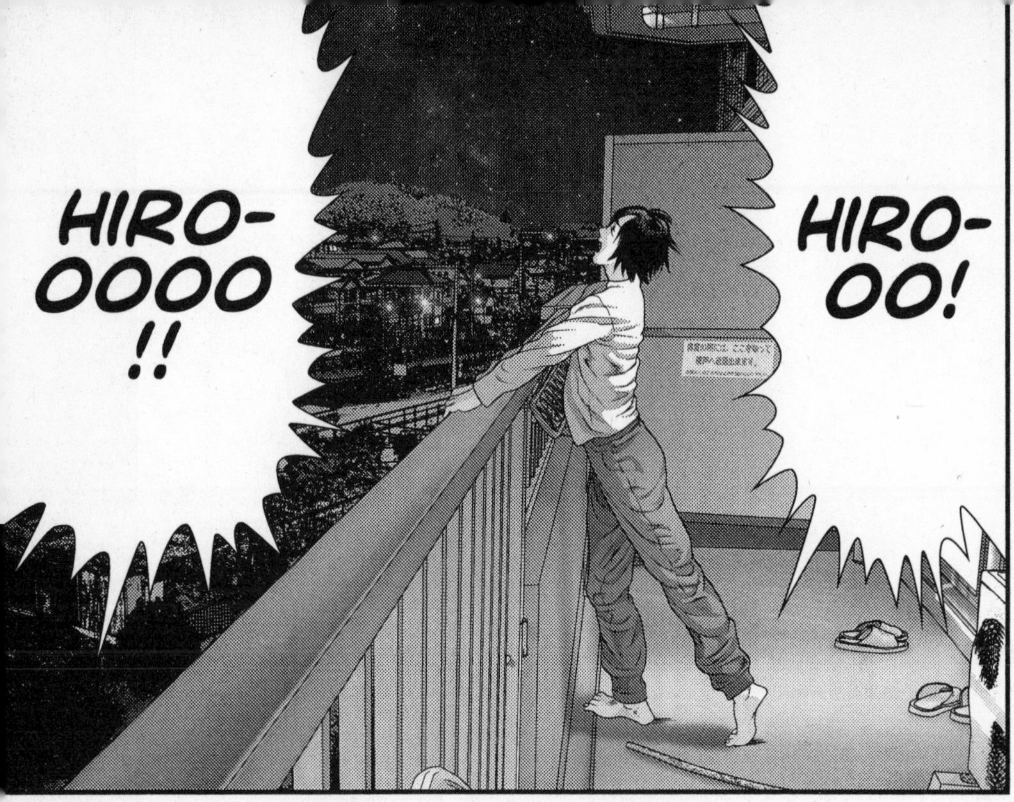
HIRO-OO!
HIRO-OOOO!!

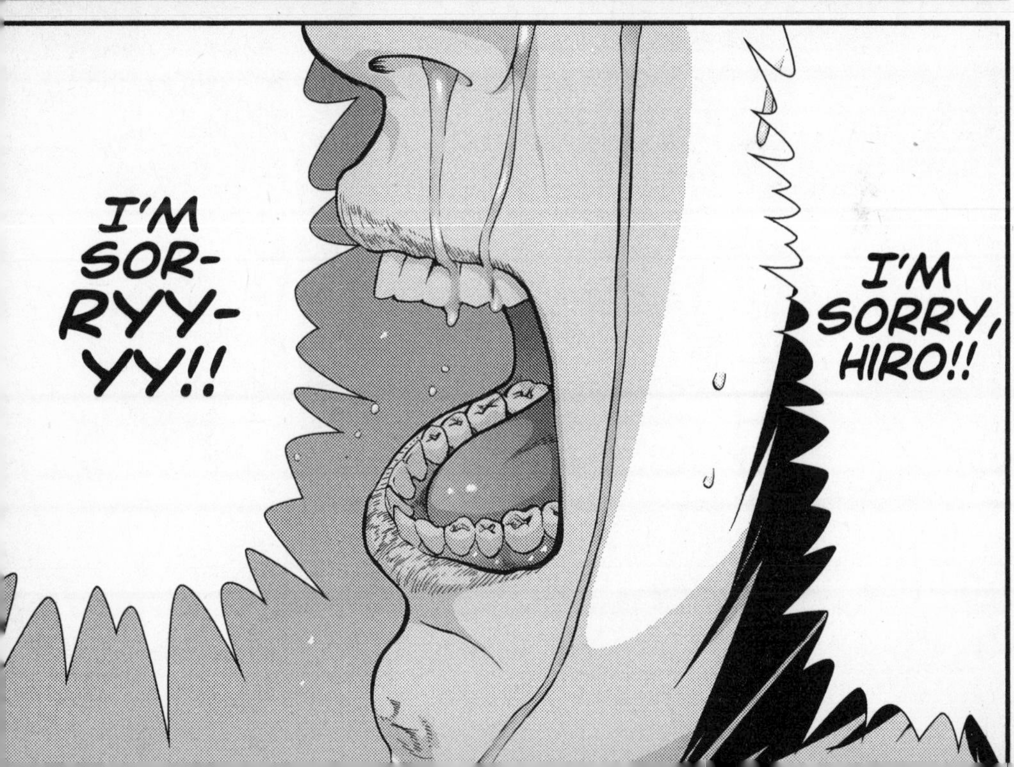
I'M SORRY, HIRO!!
I'M SOR-RYYY-YY!!

GO AHEAD...

HIROOOO!

I'M SORRY, HIRO!

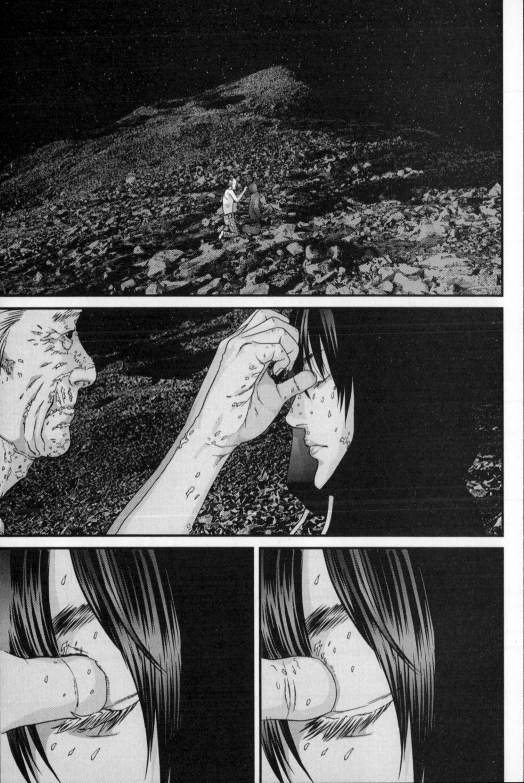

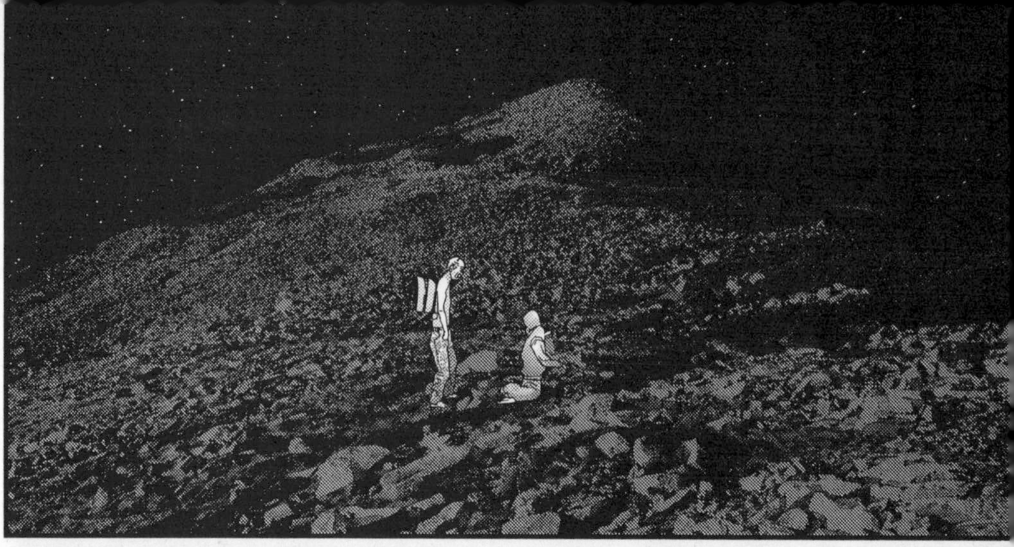
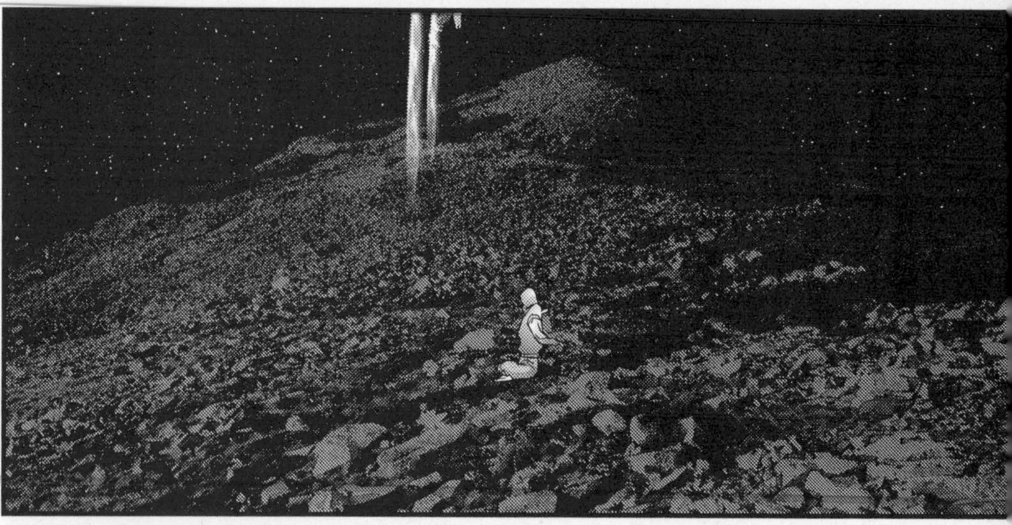
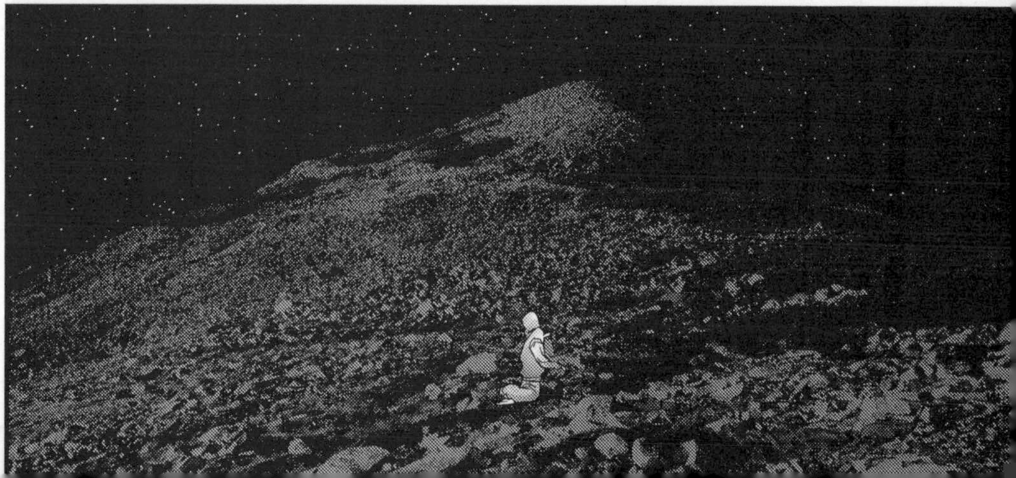

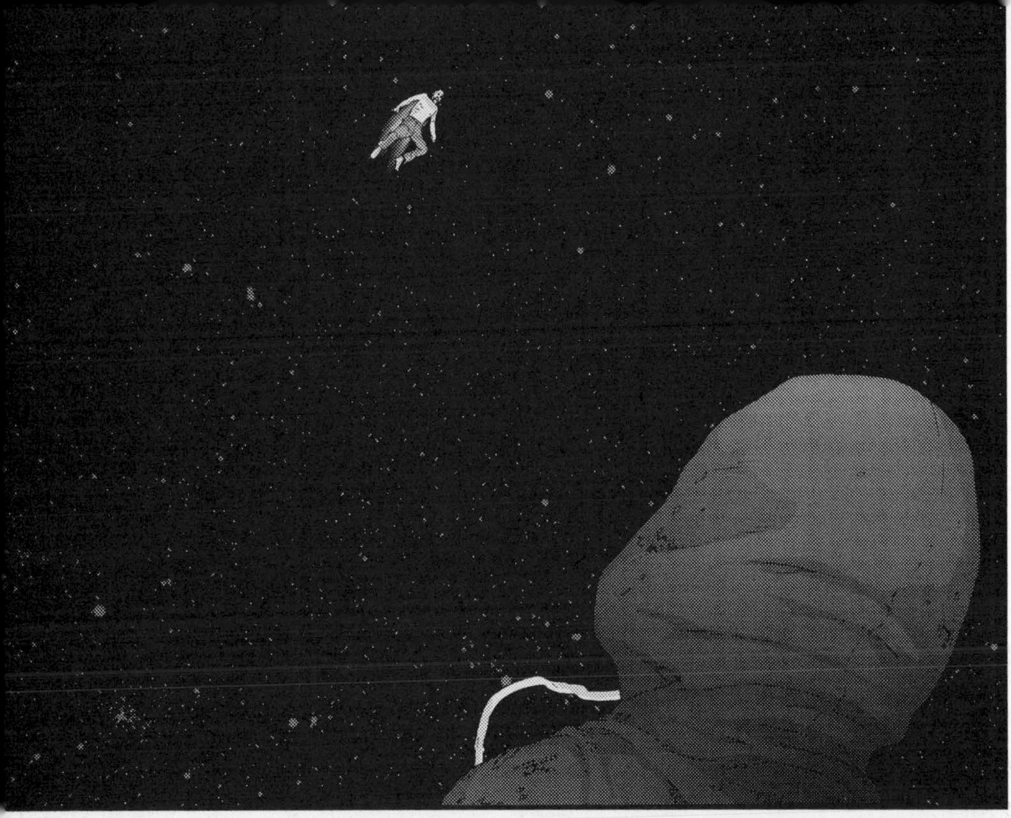

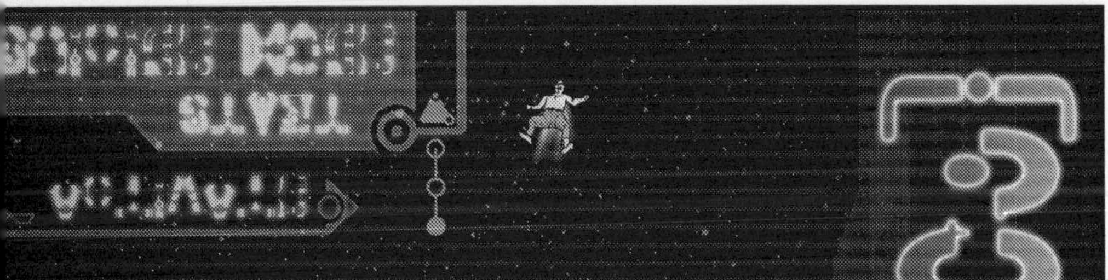
3

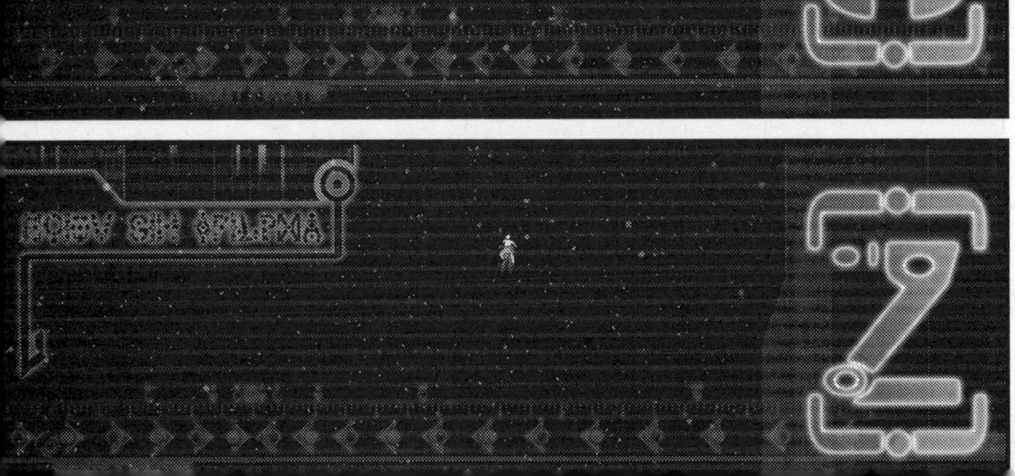
2

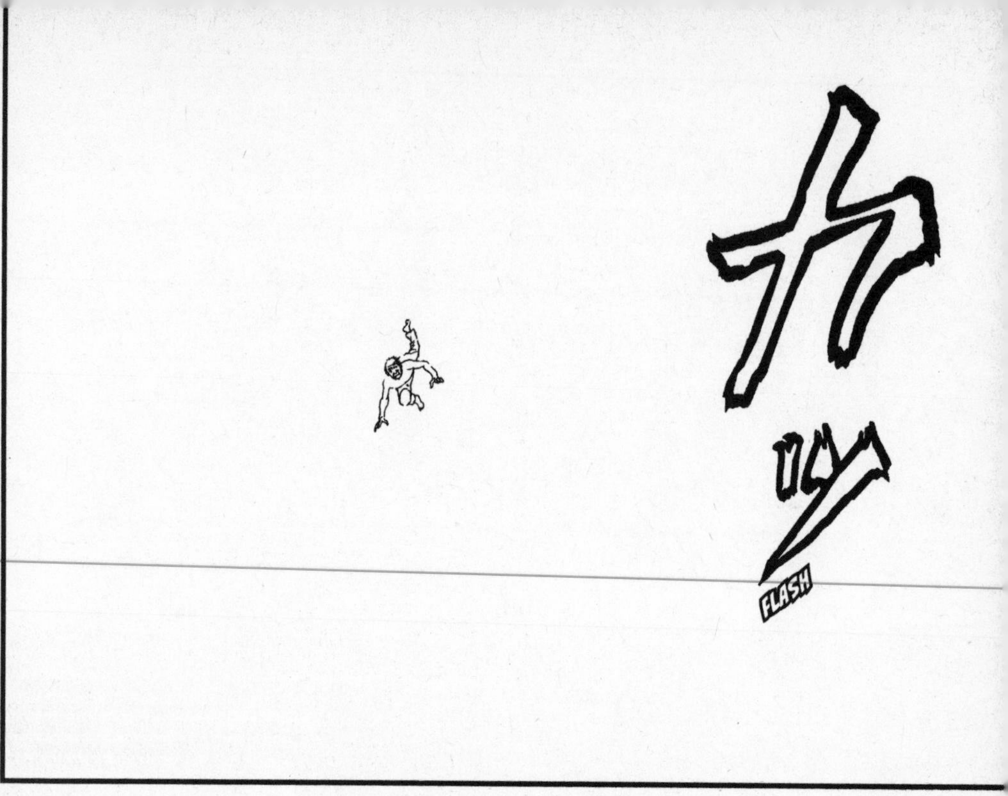
カッ
FLASH

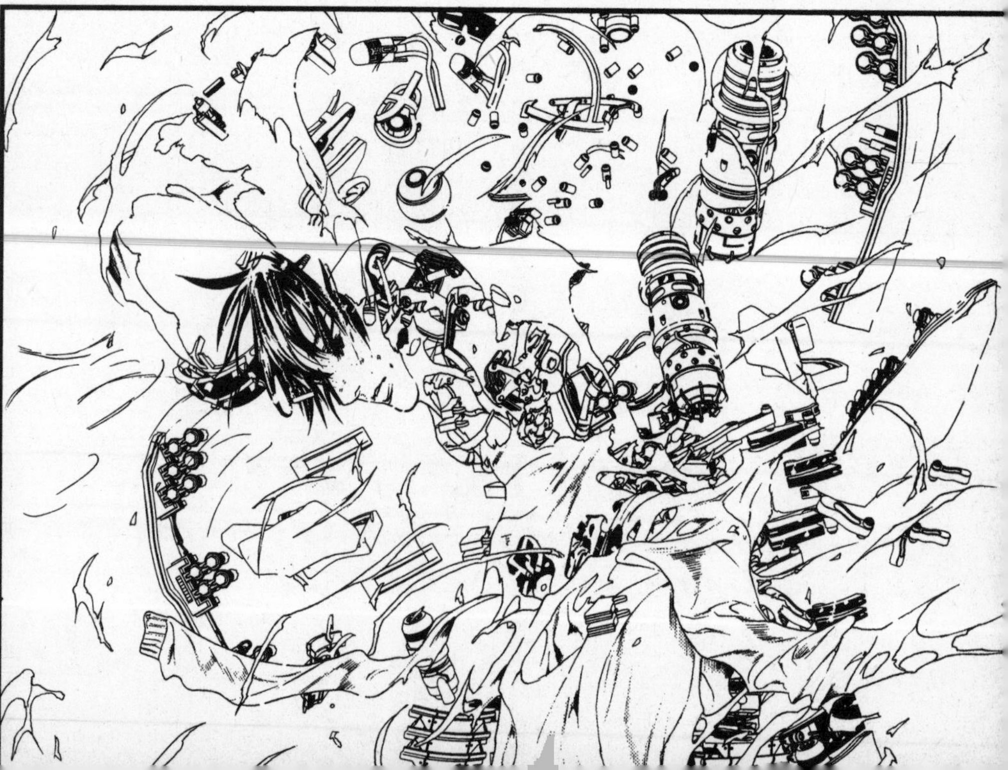

CHAPTER 82 - END

I N U Y A S H I K I

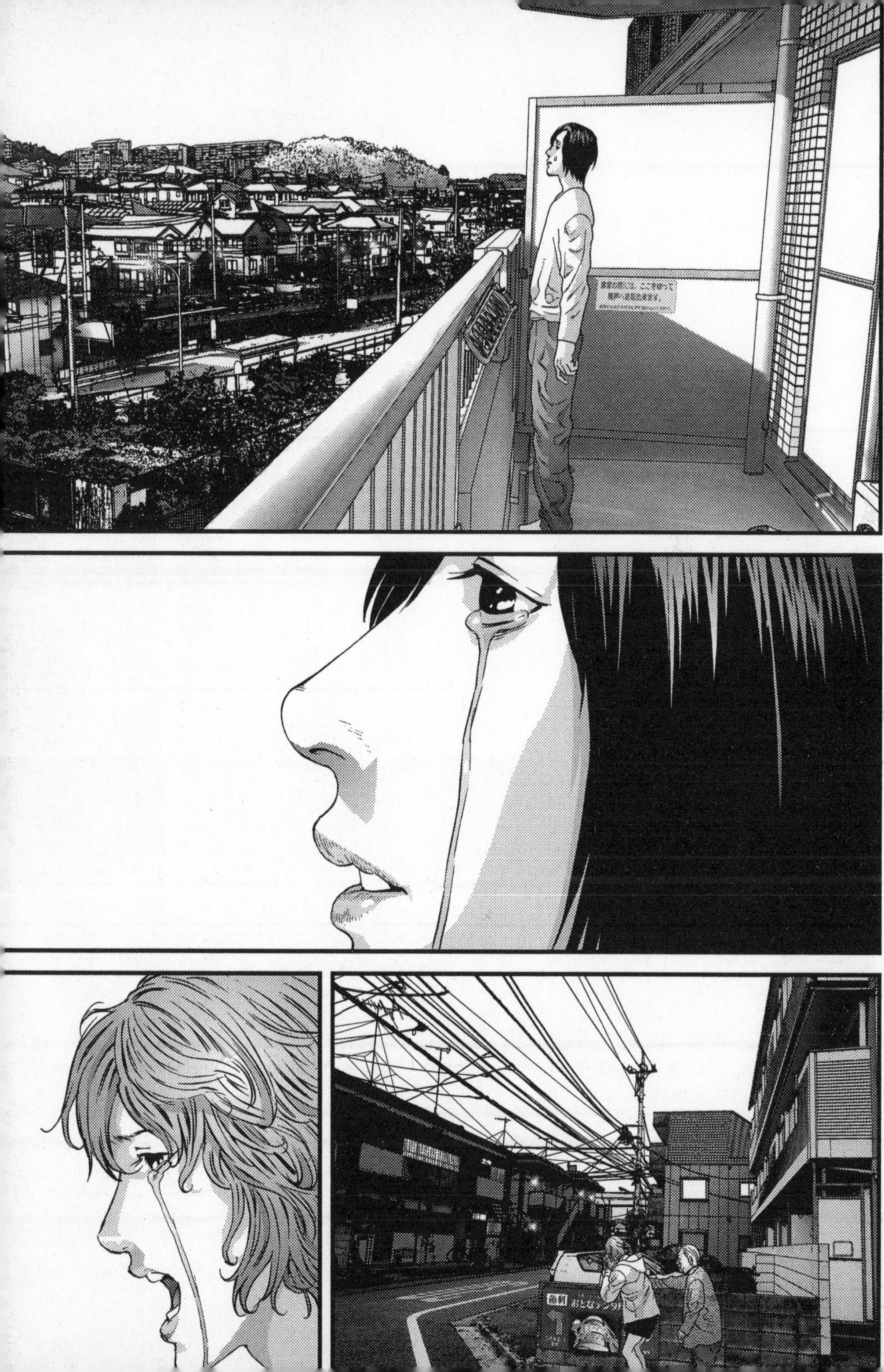

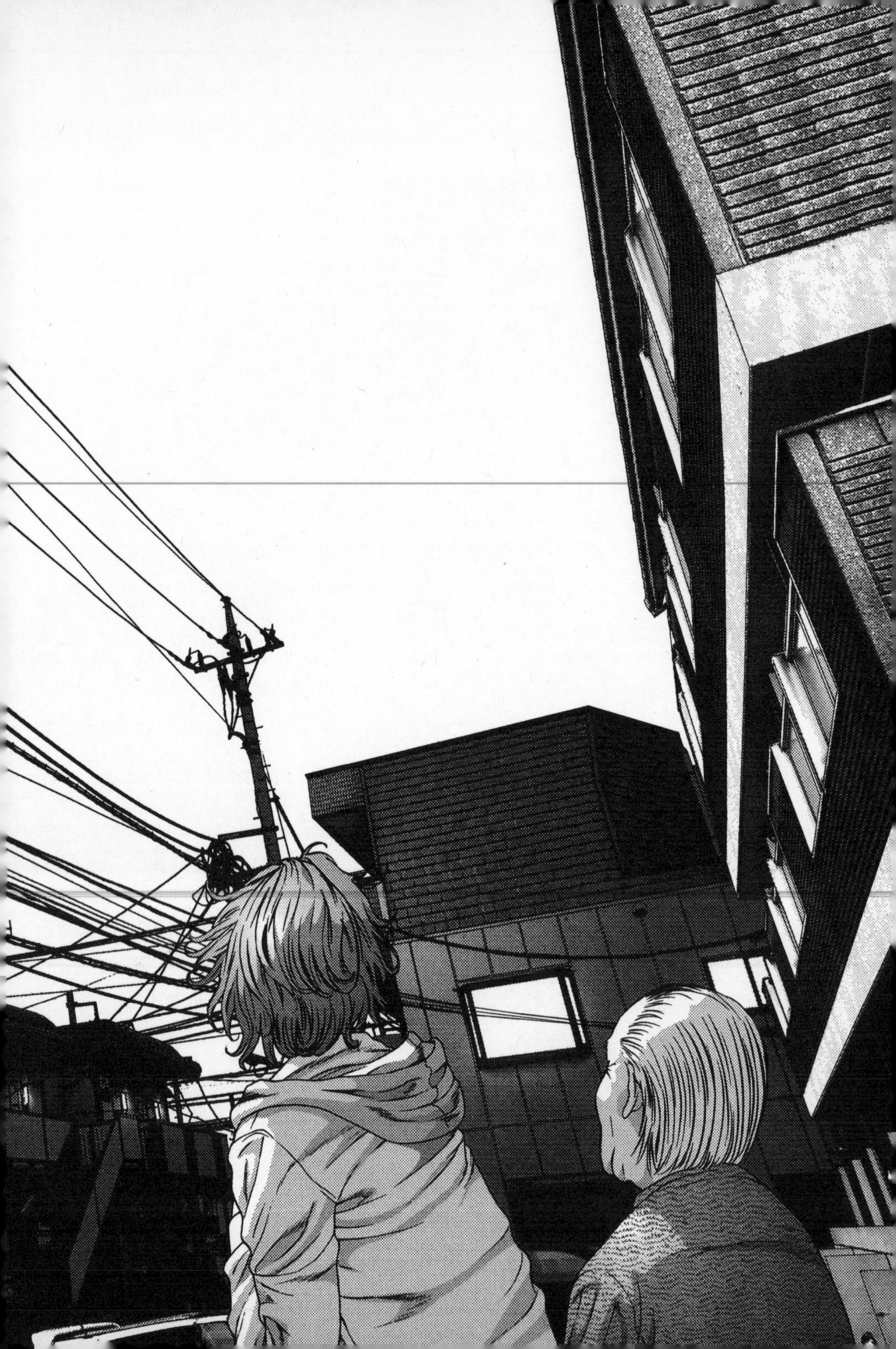

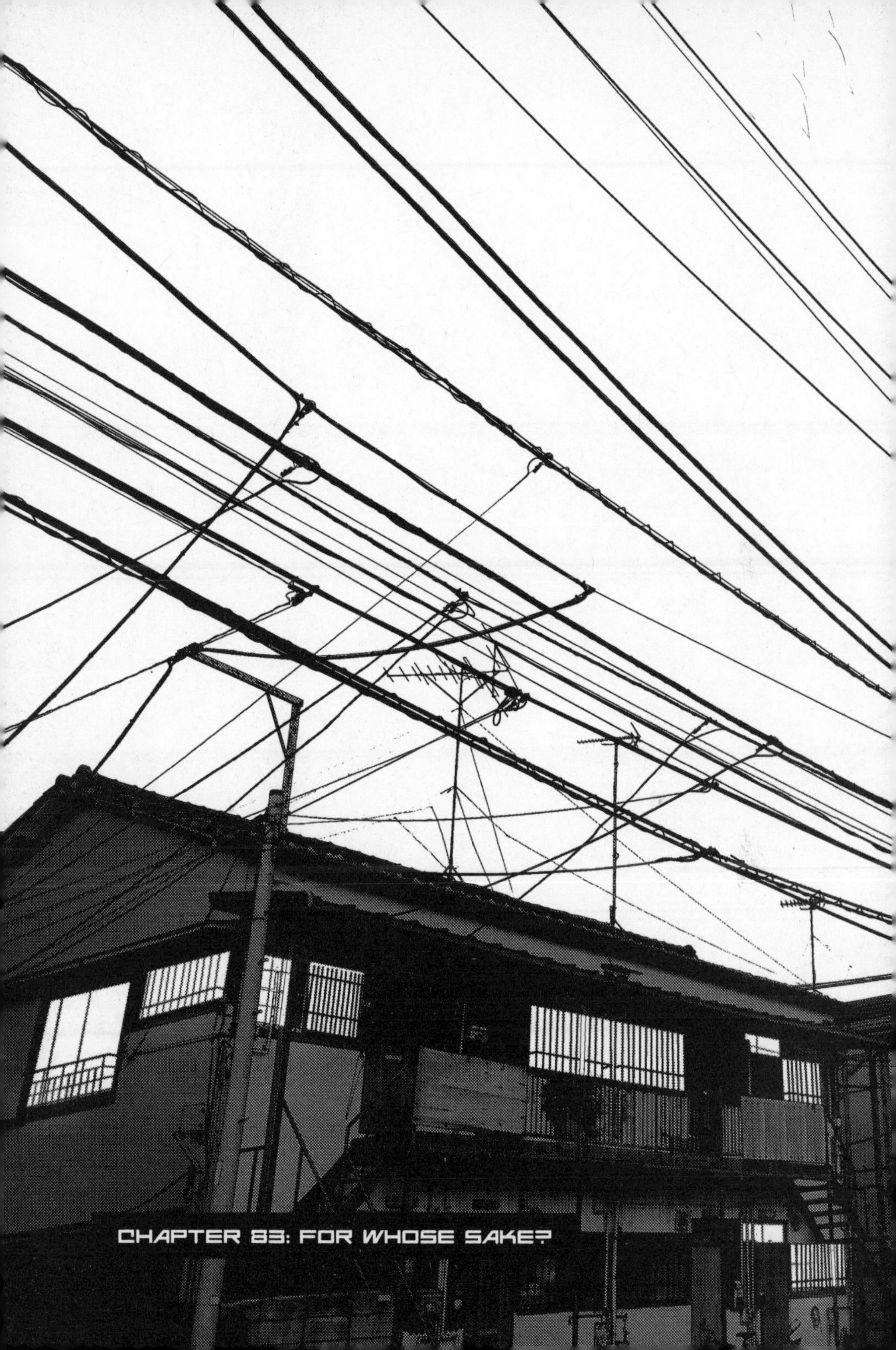
CHAPTER 83: FOR WHOSE SAKE?

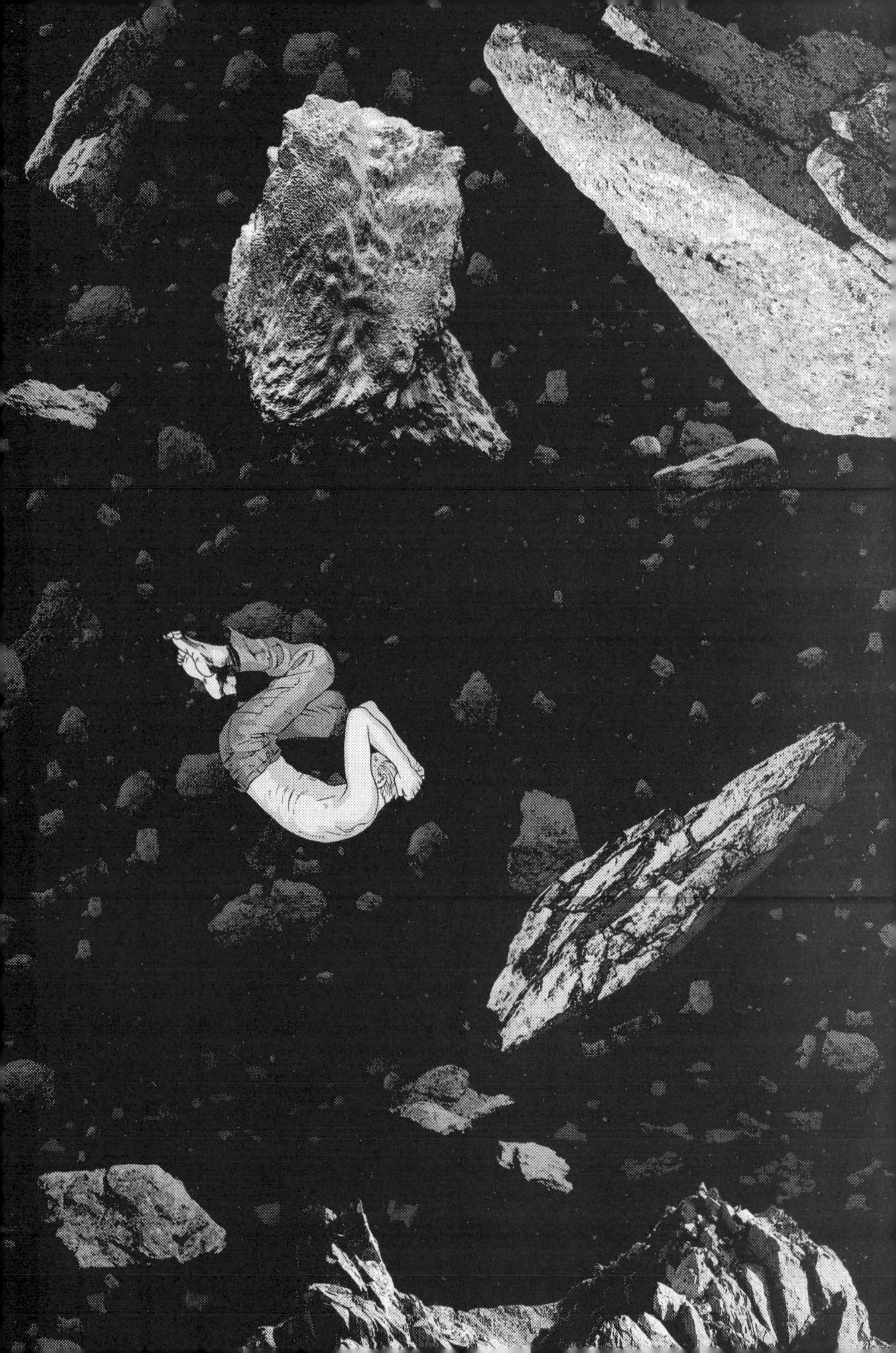

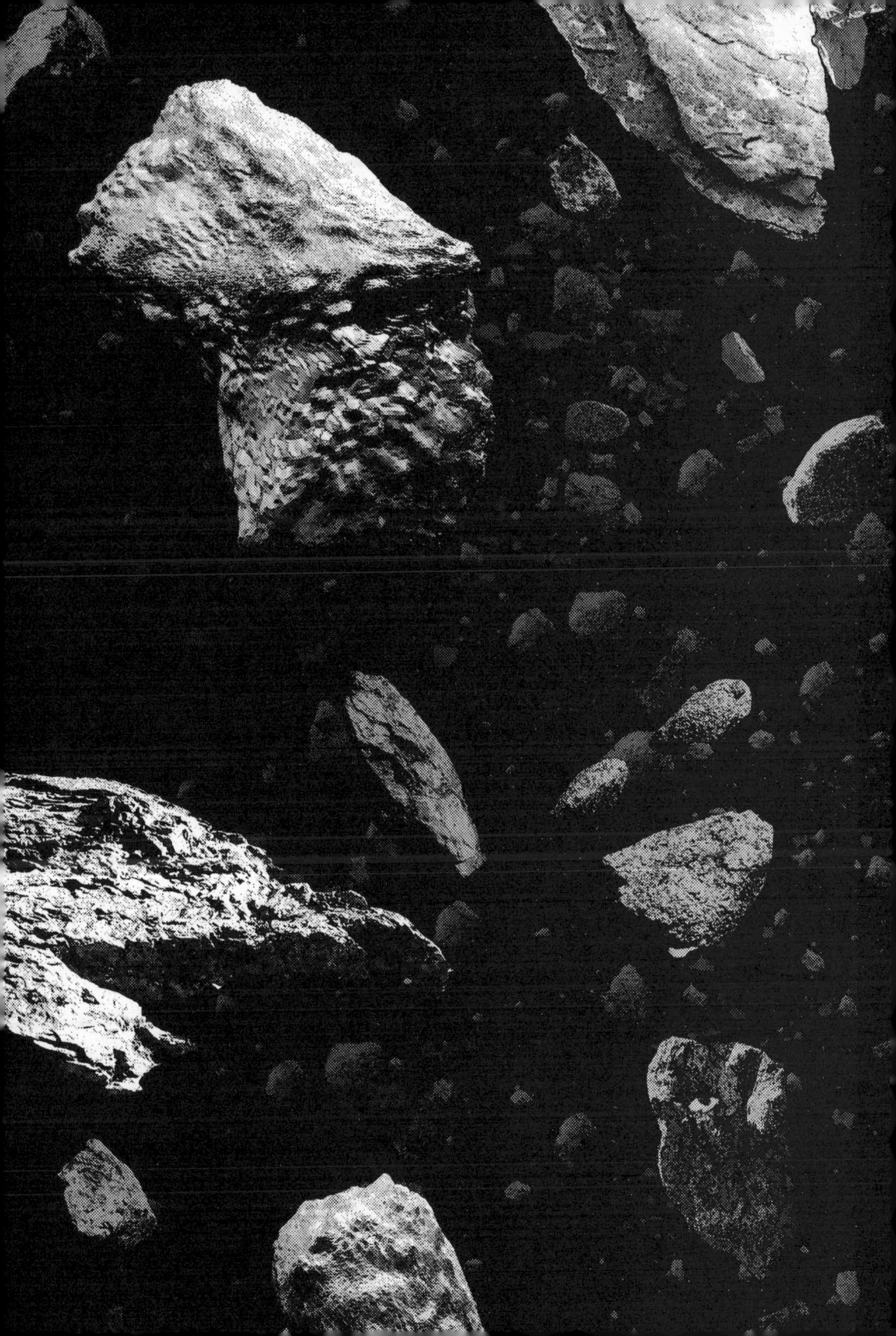

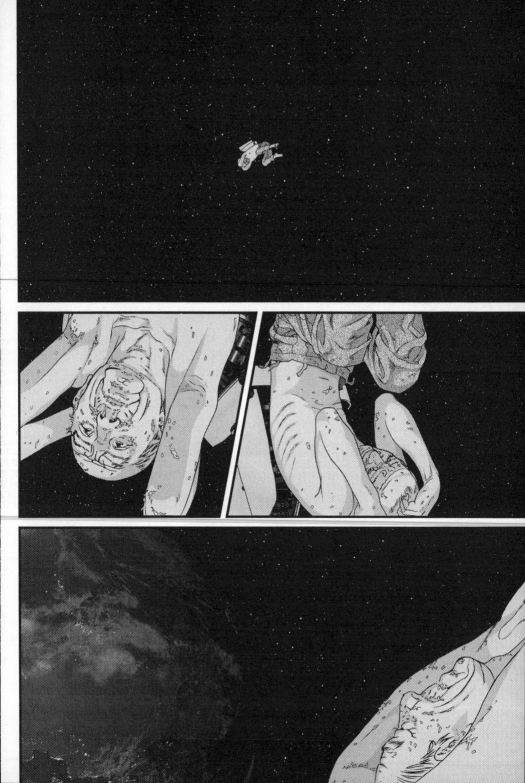

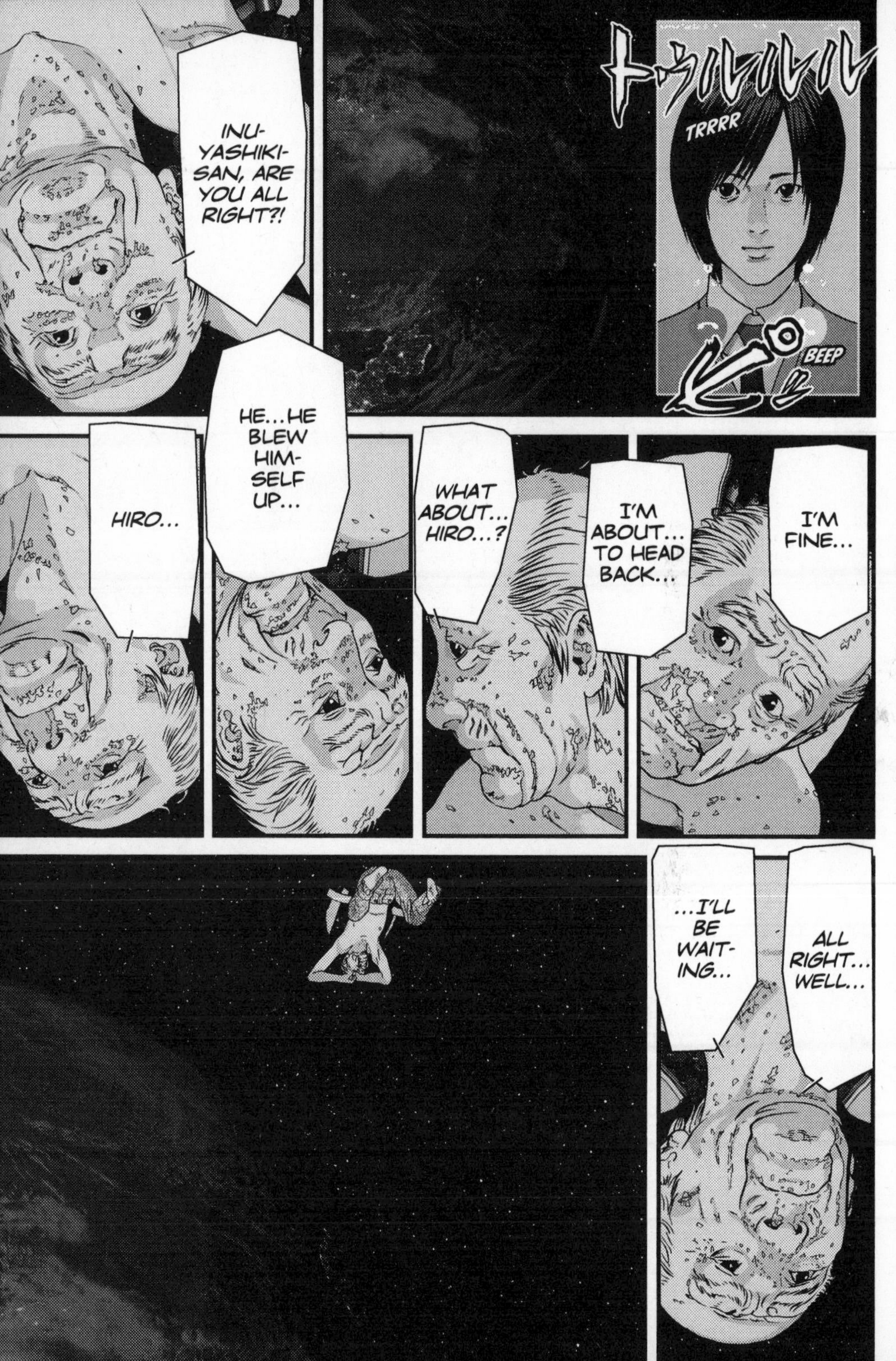

トゥルルルル
TRRRR
ピッ
BEEP
INU-YASHIKI-SAN, ARE YOU ALL RIGHT?!
I'M FINE...
I'M ABOUT... TO HEAD BACK...
WHAT ABOUT... HIRO...?
HE...HE BLEW HIMSELF UP...
HIRO...
ALL RIGHT... WELL...
...I'LL BE WAITING...

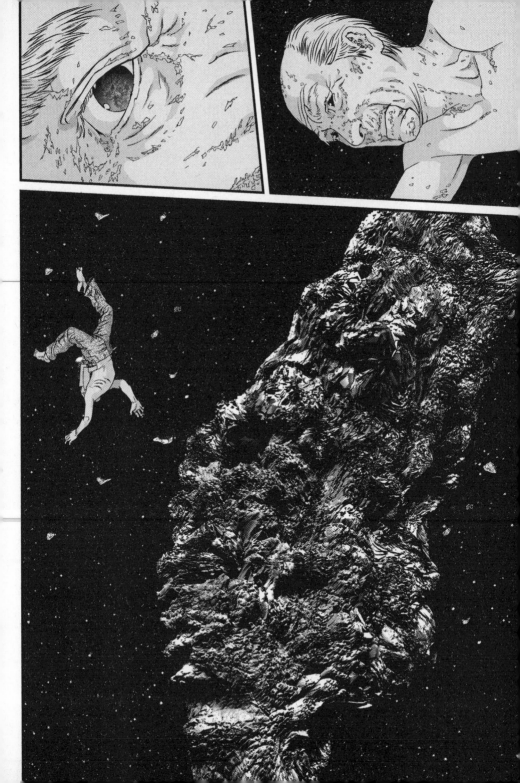

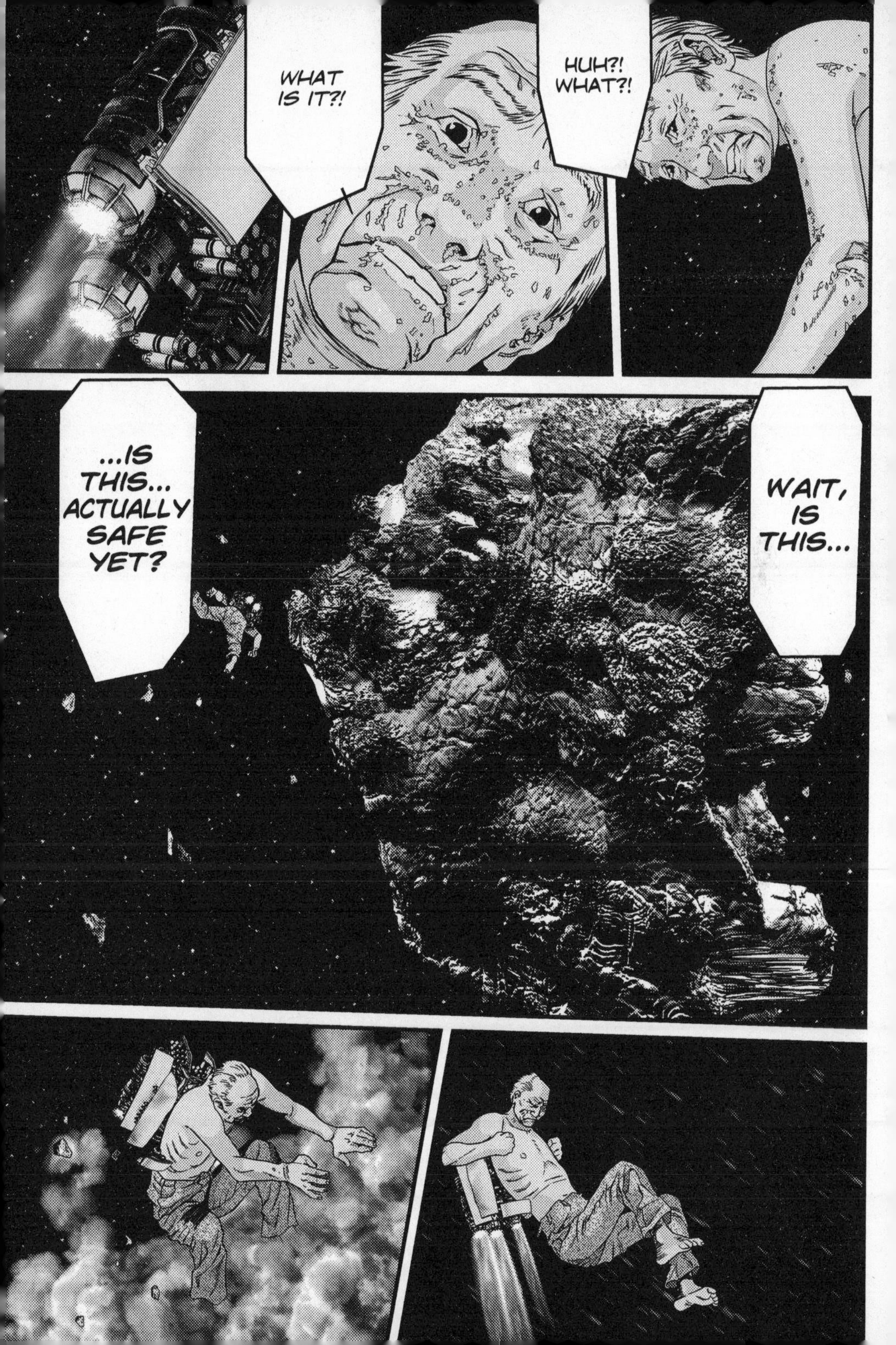
HUH?! WHAT?!
WHAT IS IT?!
WAIT, IS THIS...
...IS THIS... ACTUALLY SAFE YET?

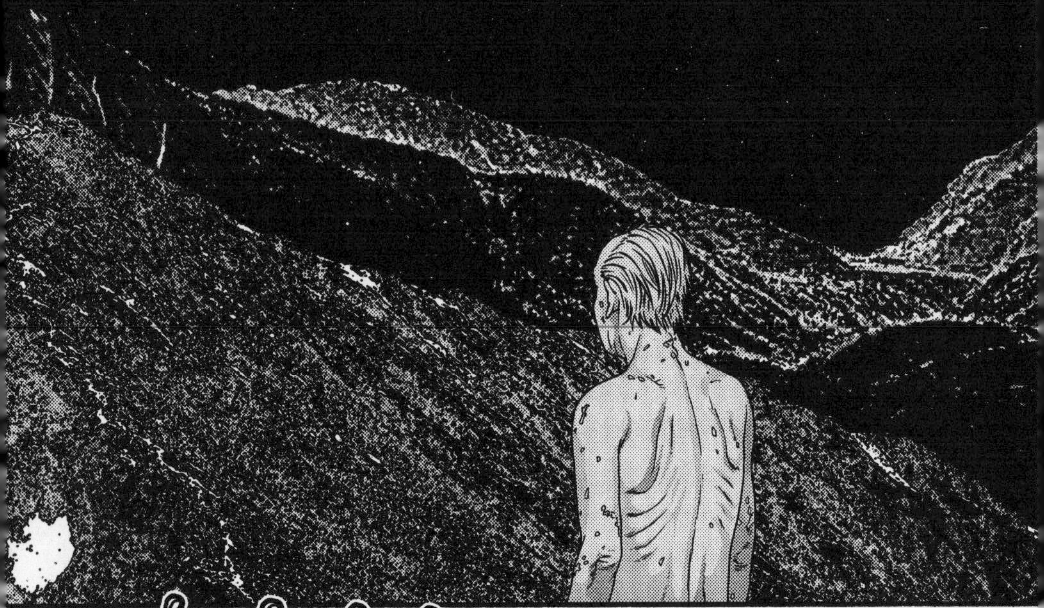

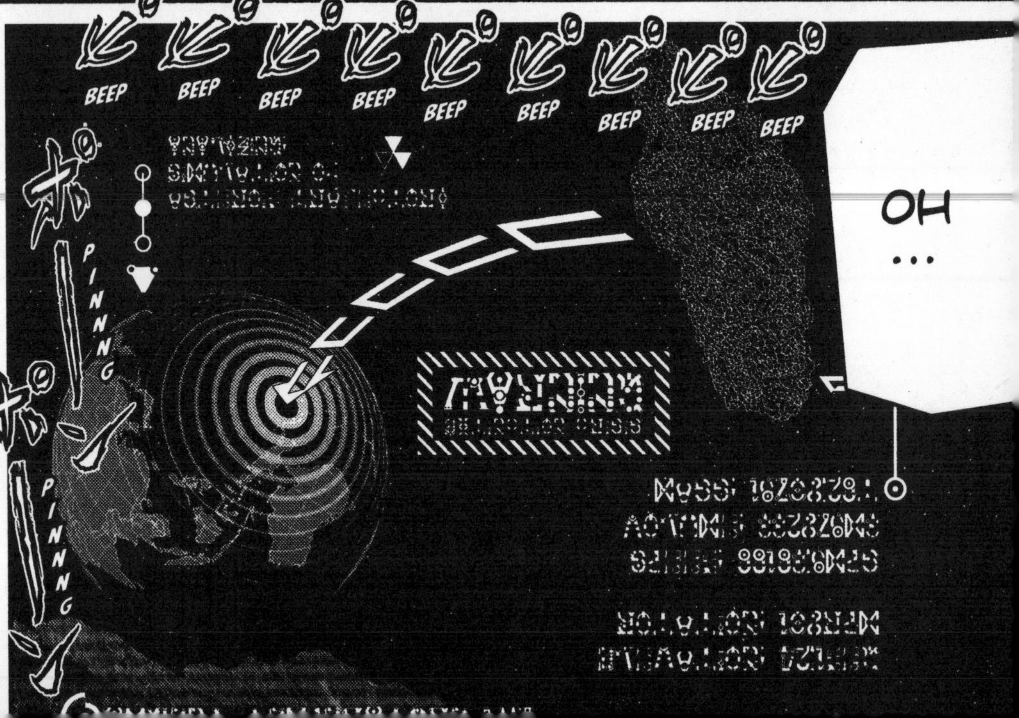
OH ...
ピ ピ ピ ピ ピ ピ ピ ピ ピ
BEEP BEEP BEEP BEEP BEEP BEEP BEEP BEEP BEEP
ポーン
PINNNG
ポーン
PINNNG

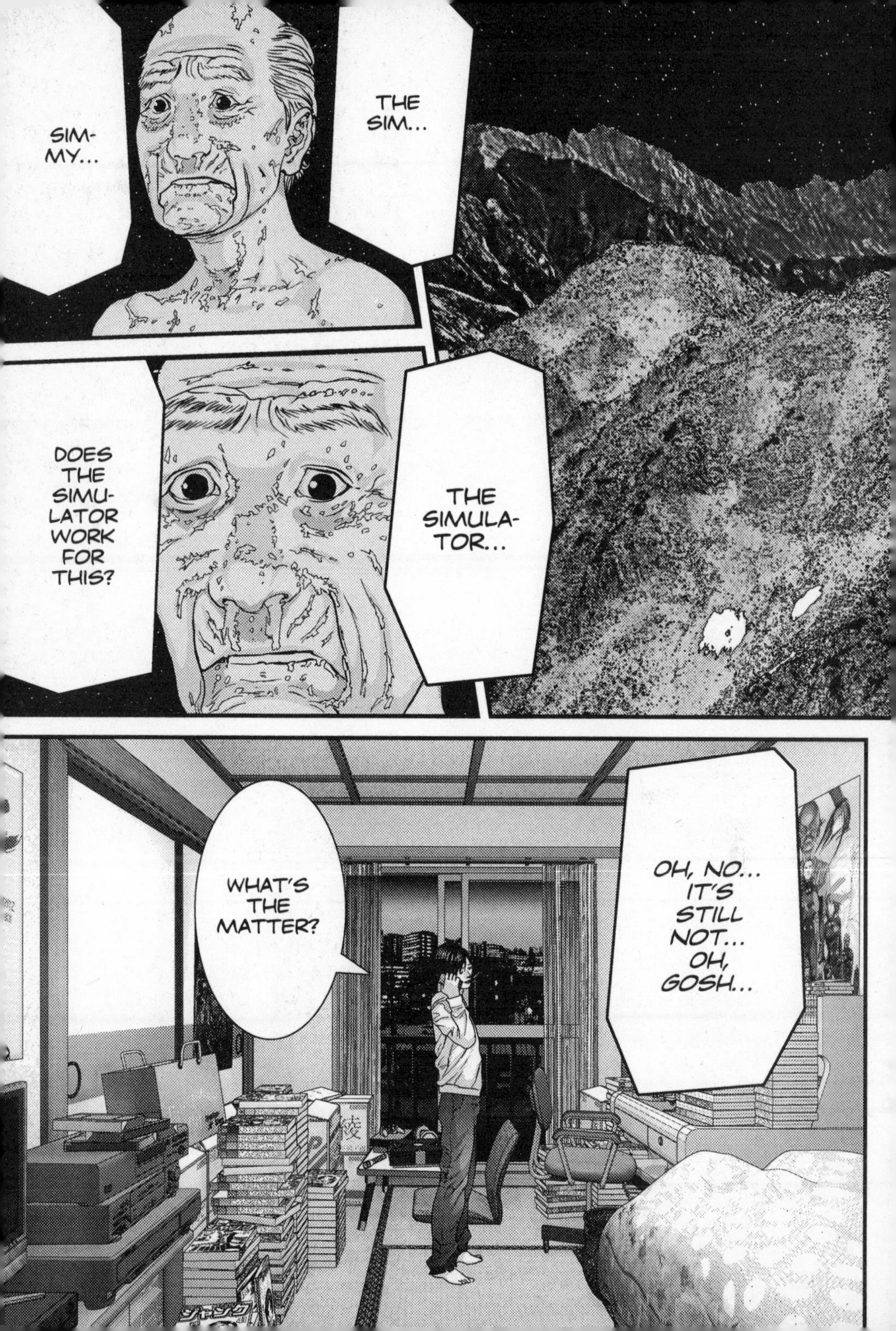
THE SIM...
SIM-MY...
THE SIMULATOR...
DOES THE SIMULATOR WORK FOR THIS?
OH, NO... IT'S STILL NOT... OH, GOSH...
WHAT'S THE MATTER?

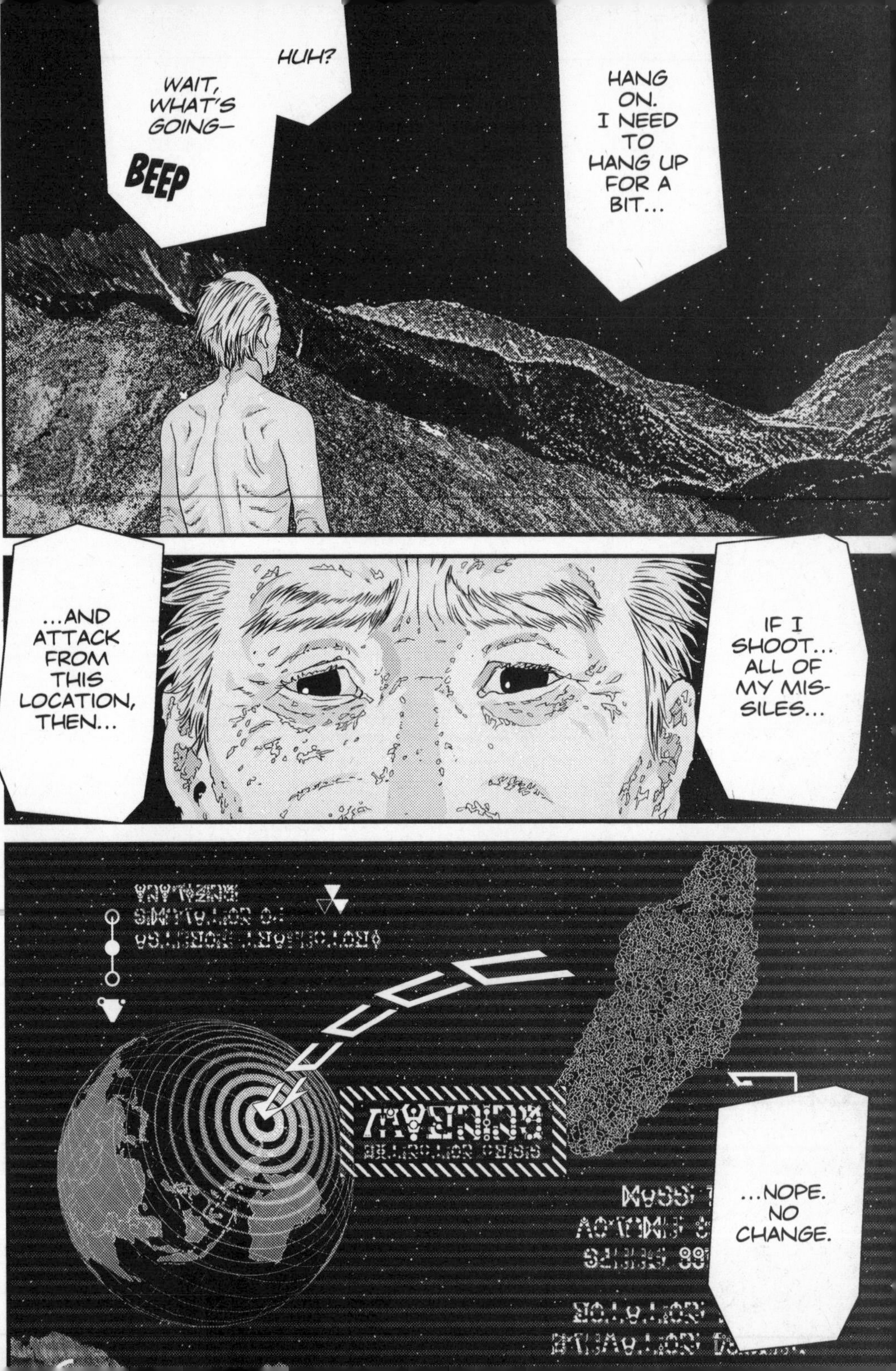
HANG ON. I NEED TO HANG UP FOR A BIT...
HUH?
WAIT, WHAT'S GOING—
BEEP
IF I SHOOT... ALL OF MY MIS-SILES...
...AND ATTACK FROM THIS LOCATION, THEN...
...NOPE. NO CHANGE.

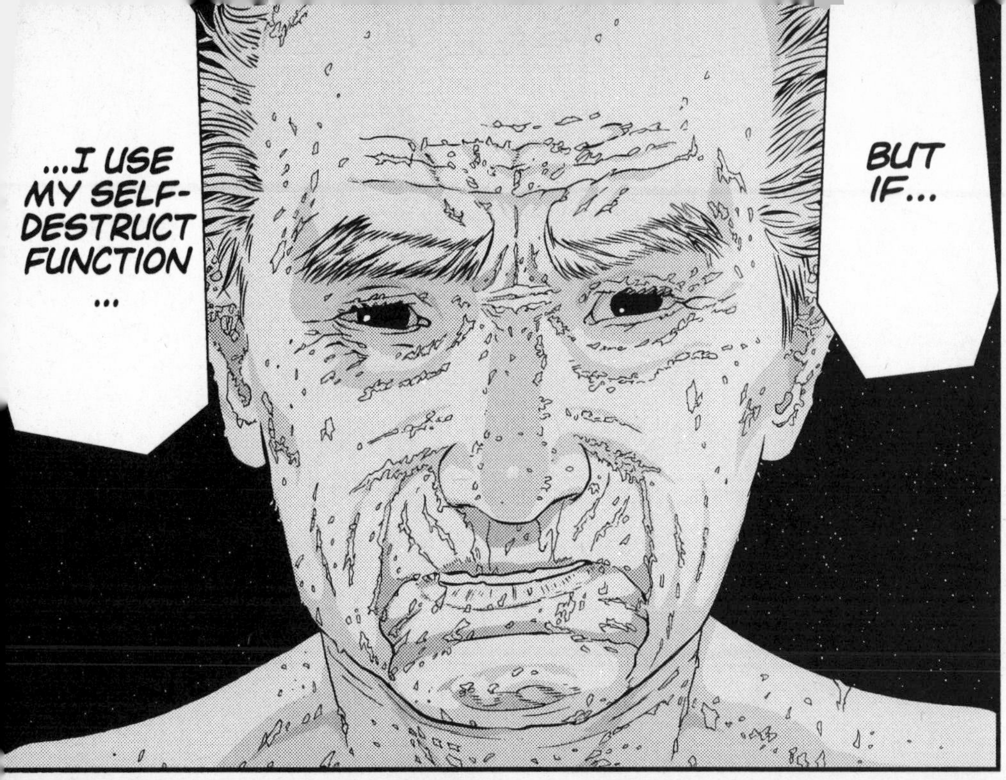
BUT IF...
...I USE MY SELF-DESTRUCT FUNCTION ...

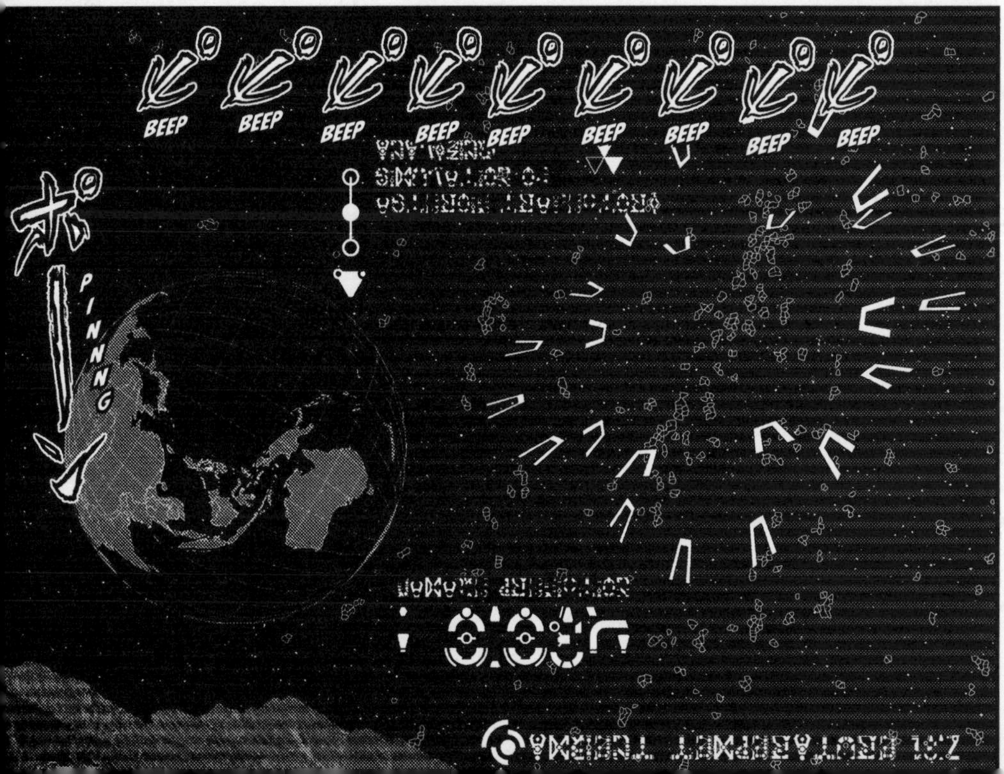
BEEP BEEP BEEP BEEP BEEP BEEP BEEP BEEP BEEP
PINNNG

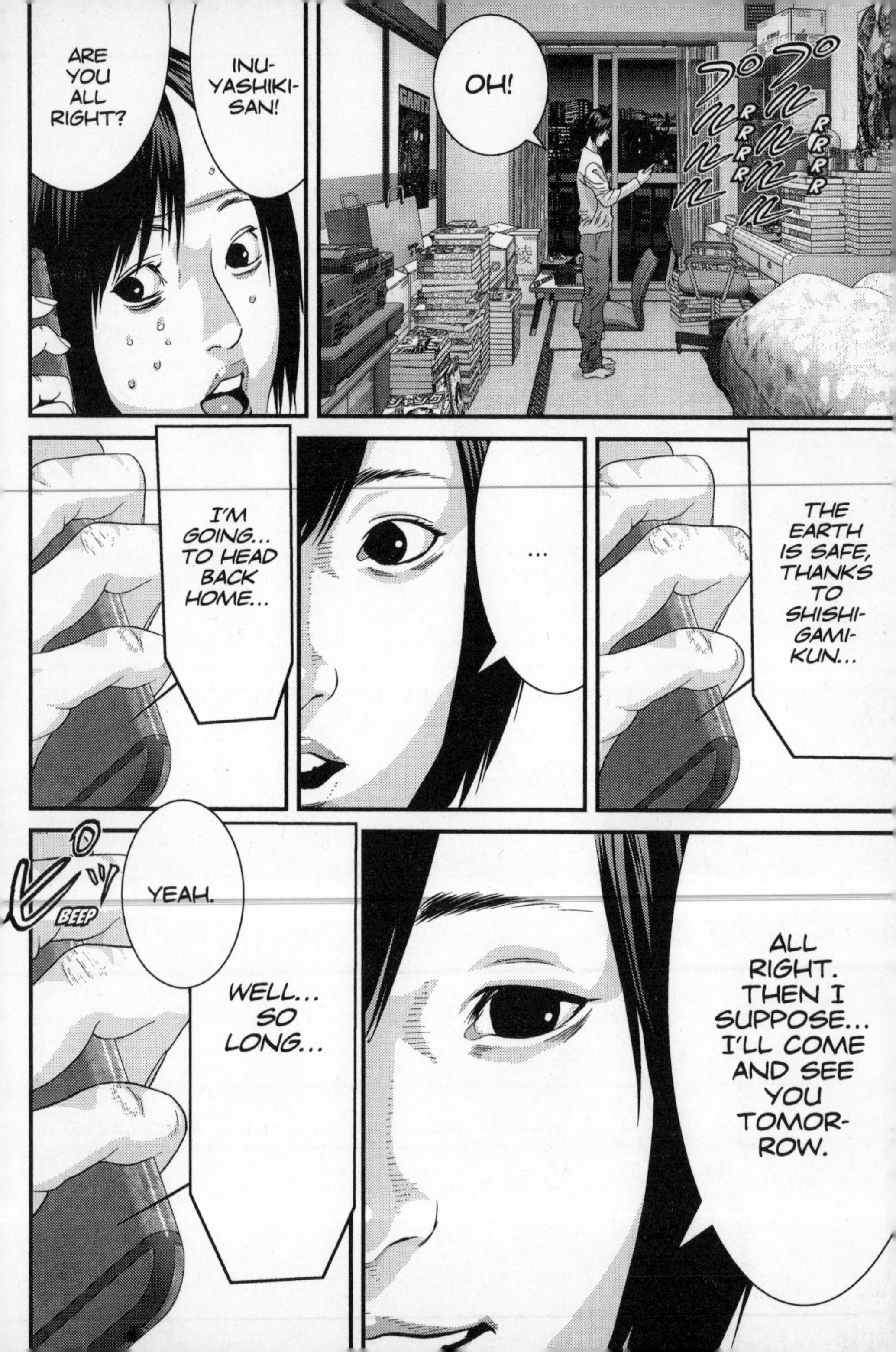
OH!
RRRR
RRRR
INU-YASHIKI-SAN!
ARE YOU ALL RIGHT?
THE EARTH IS SAFE, THANKS TO SHISHI-GAMI-KUN...
...
I'M GOING... TO HEAD BACK HOME...
ALL RIGHT. THEN I SUPPOSE... I'LL COME AND SEE YOU TOMOR-ROW.
YEAH.
WELL... SO LONG...
BEEP

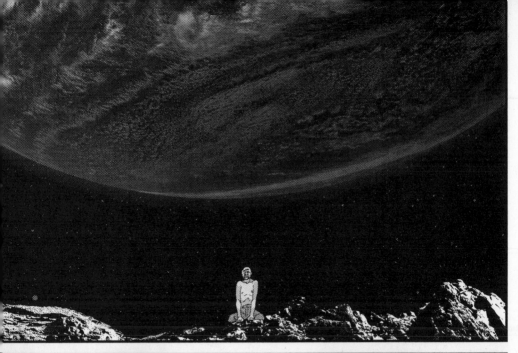

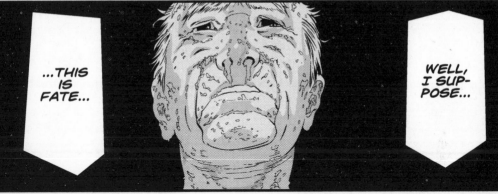

WELL, I SUP-POSE...
...THIS IS FATE...
I'M SORRY, EVERY-ONE...
I'M SORRY I COULDN'T KEEP... MY PRO-MISE...

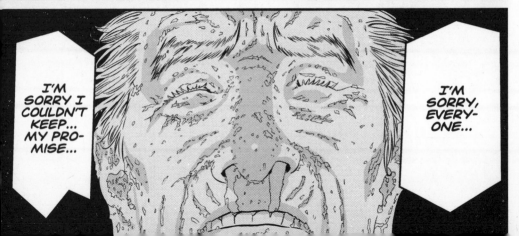

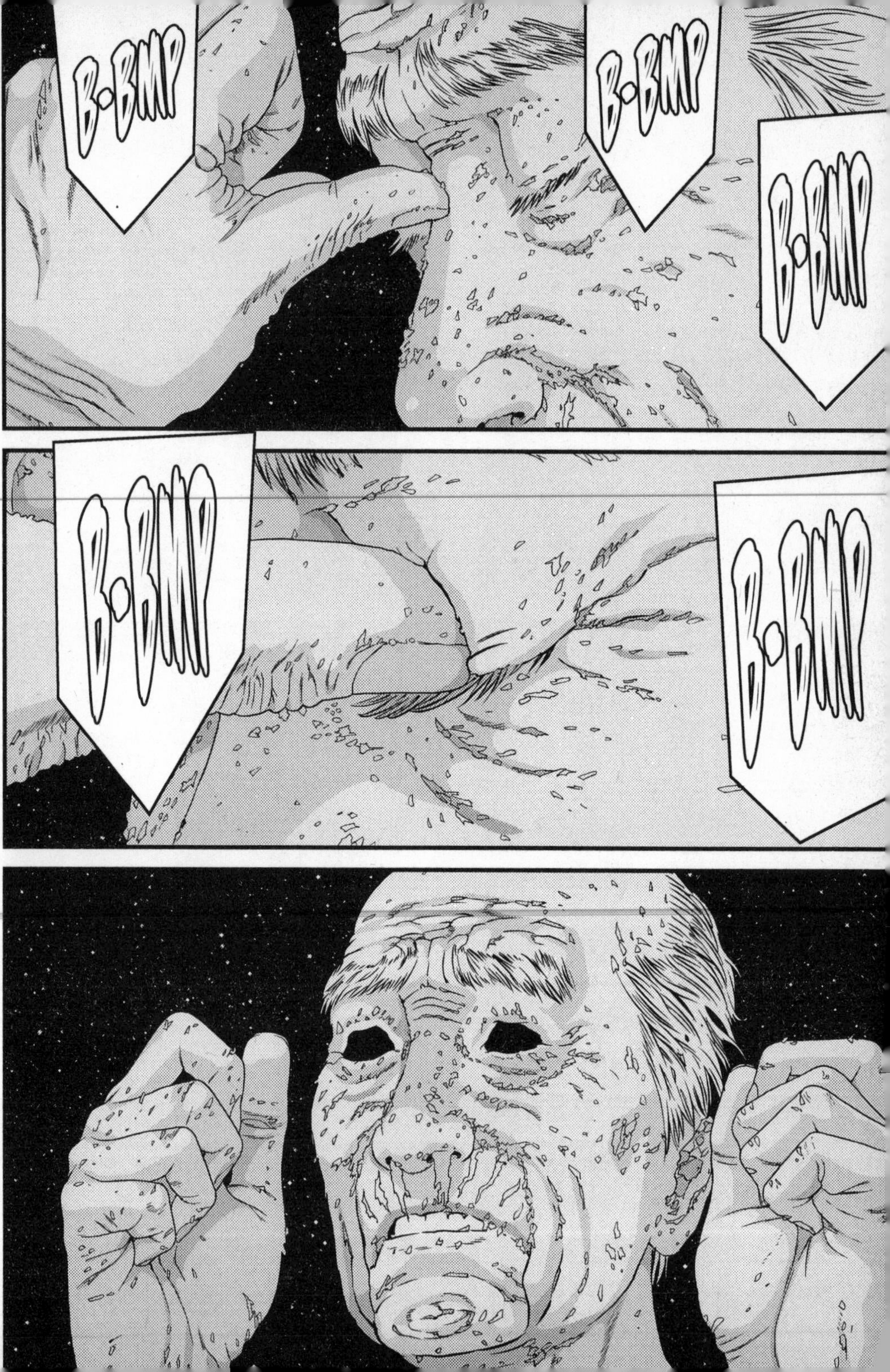
B-BMP
B-BMP
B-BMP
B-BMP
B-BMP

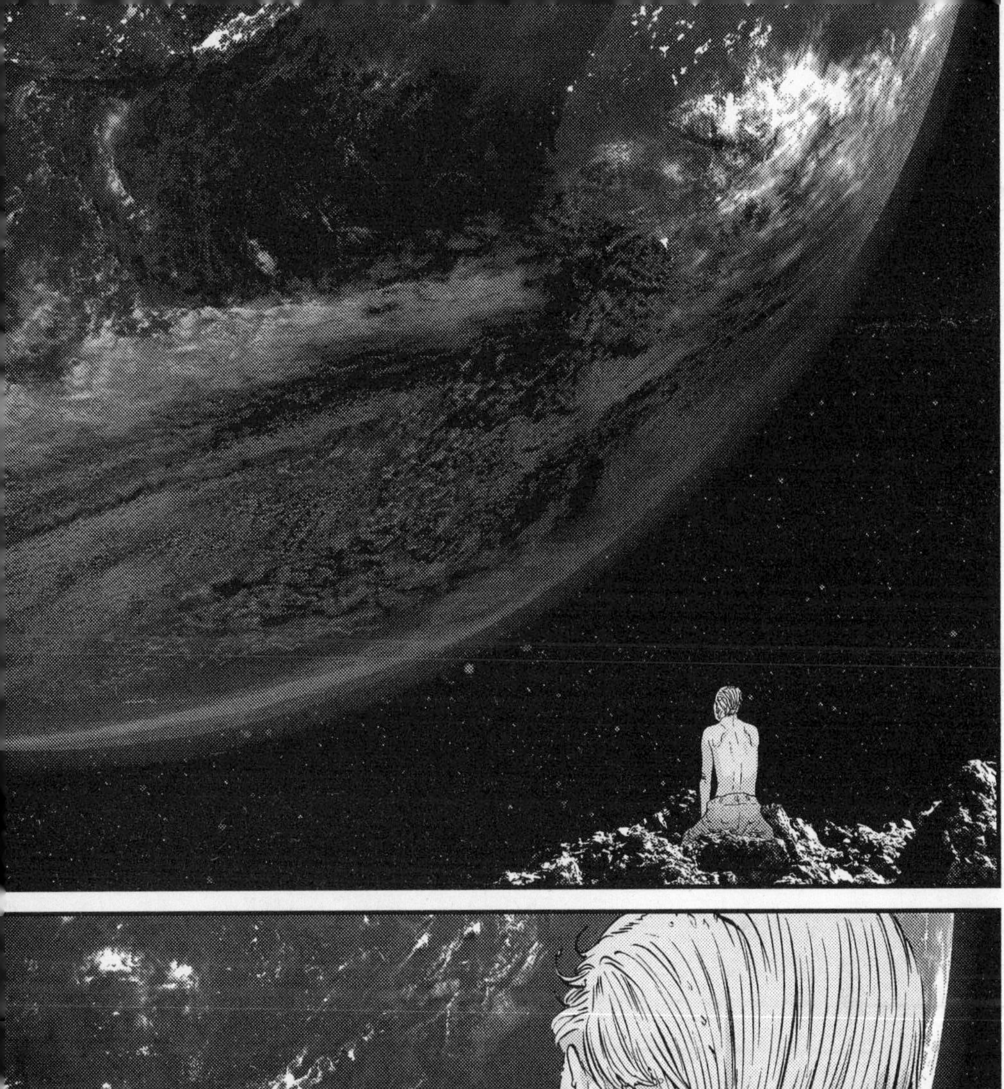
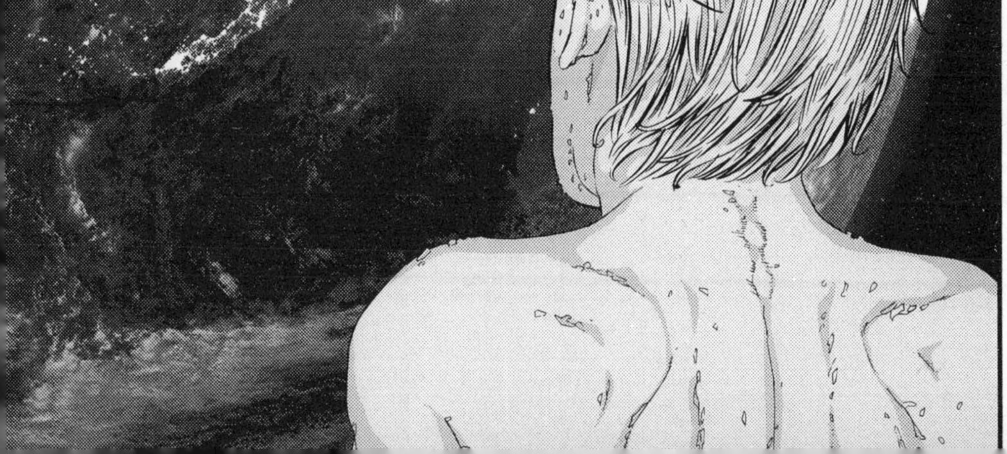

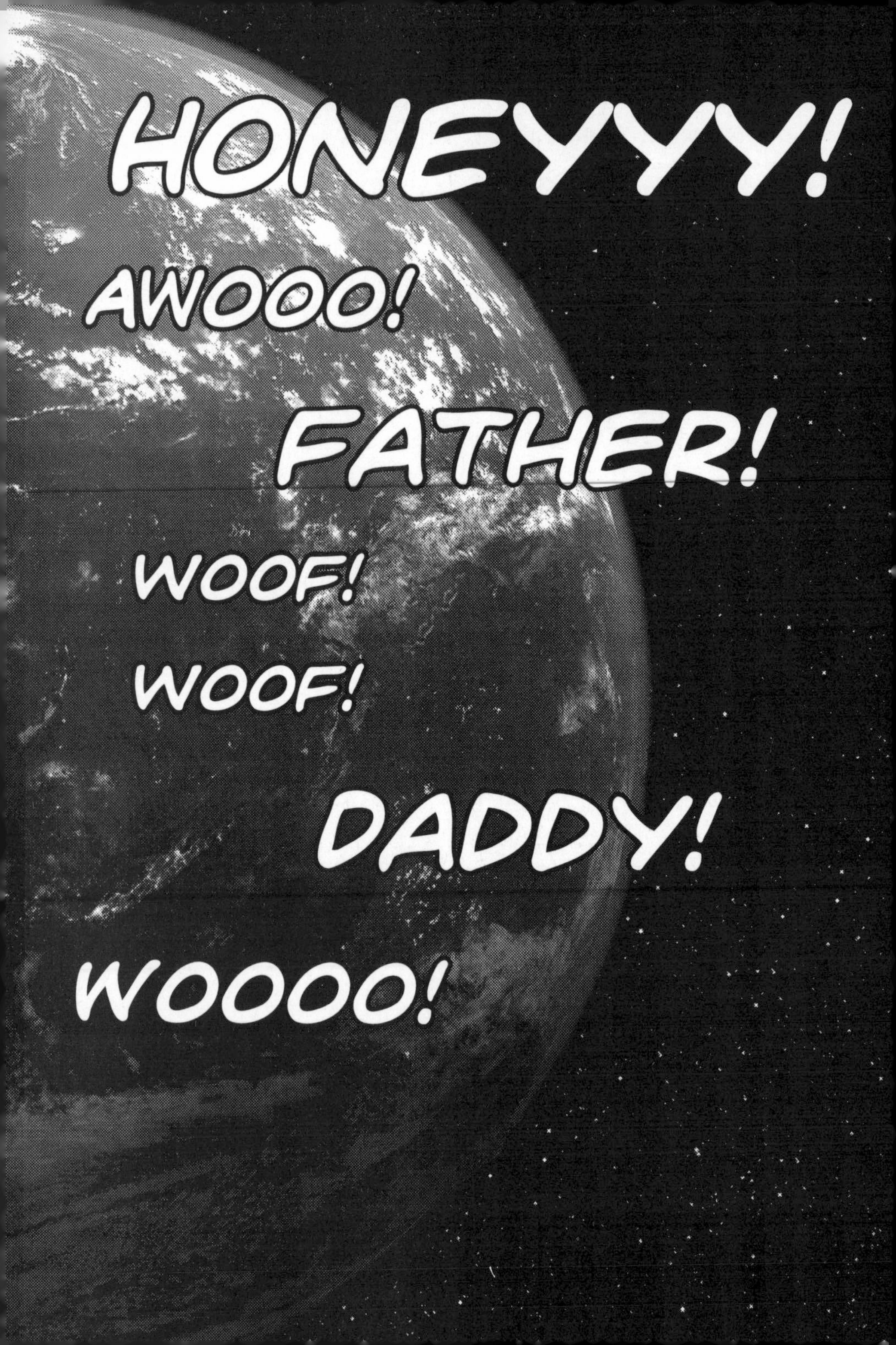
HONEYYY!
AWOOO!
FATHER!
WOOF!
WOOF!
DADDY!
WOOOO!

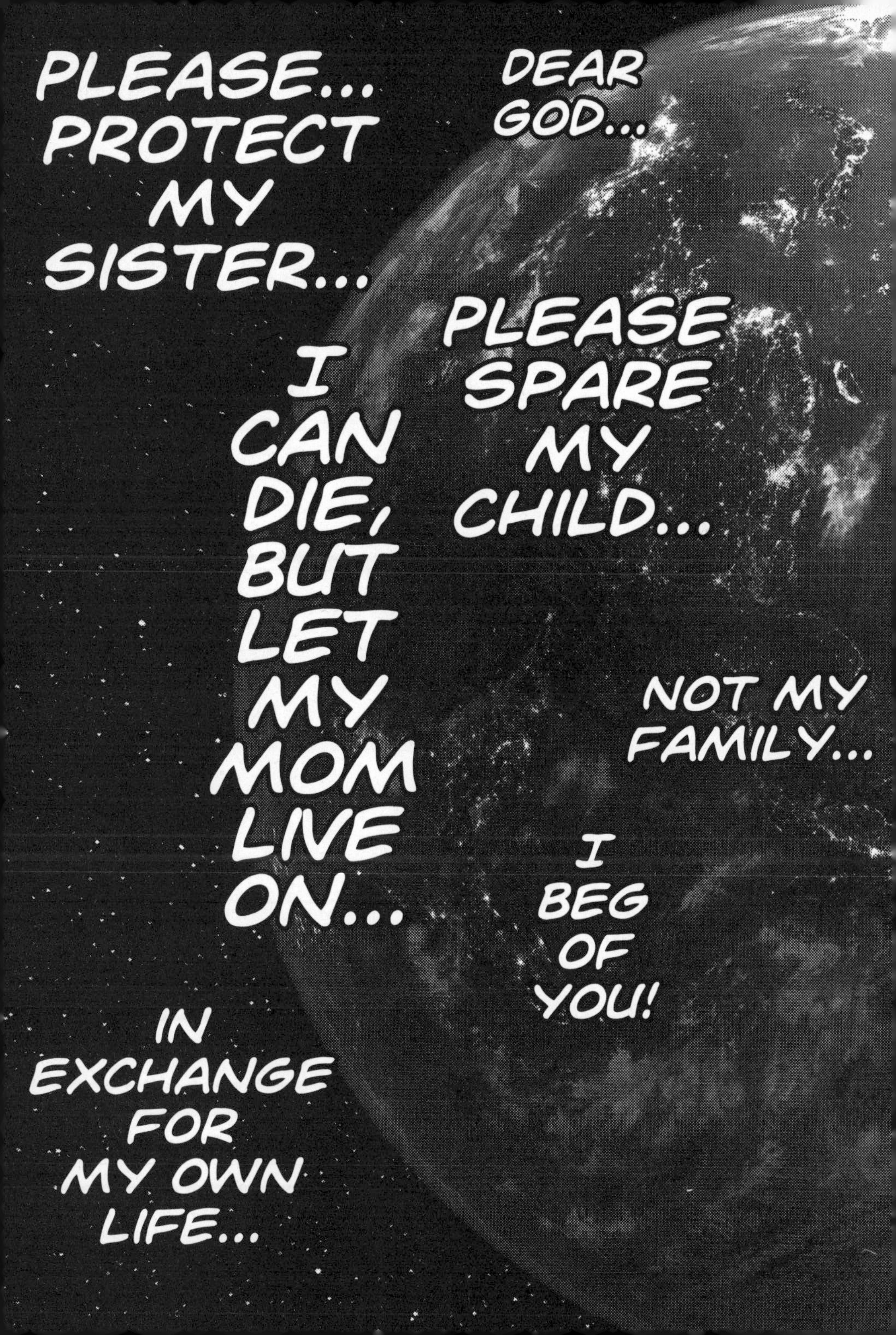
DEAR GOD...
PLEASE SPARE MY CHILD...
PLEASE... PROTECT MY SISTER...
I CAN DIE, BUT LET MY MOM LIVE ON...
NOT MY FAMILY...
I BEG OF YOU!
IN EXCHANGE FOR MY OWN LIFE...

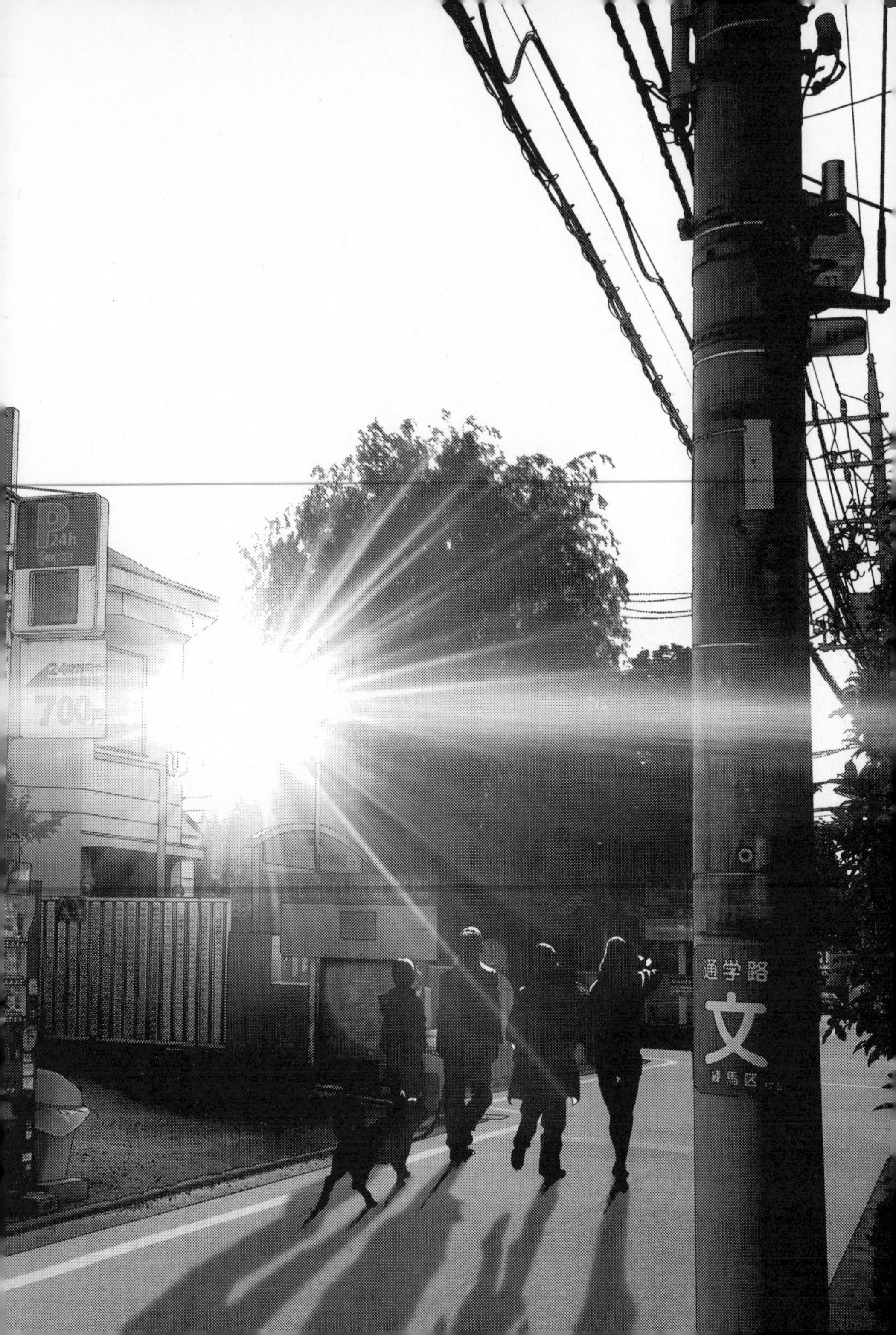
通学路
文
700

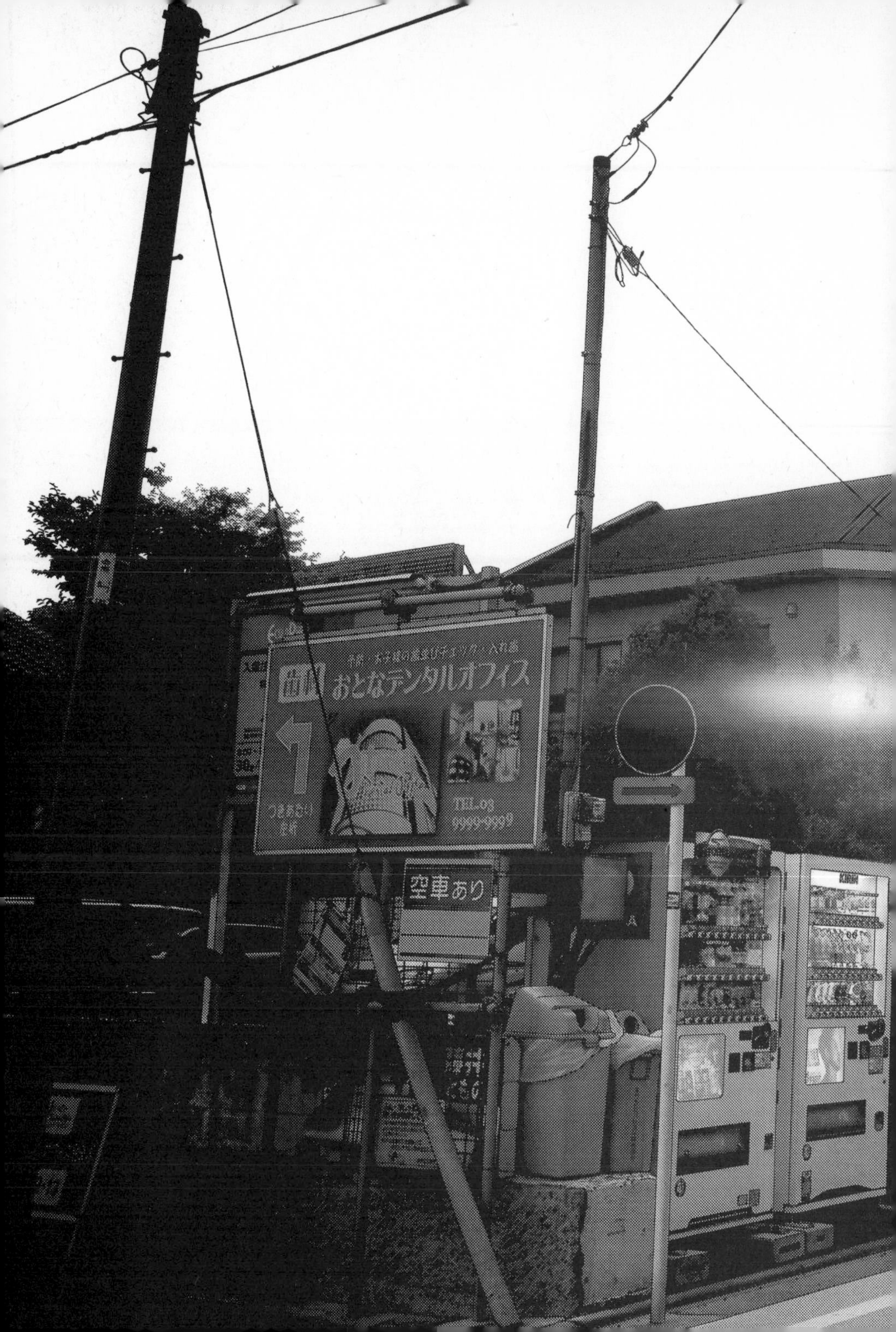
歯科
おとなデンタルオフィス
つきあたり
左折
TEL.03
9999-9999
空車あり

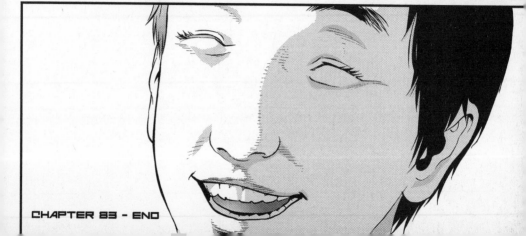

CHAPTER 83 - END

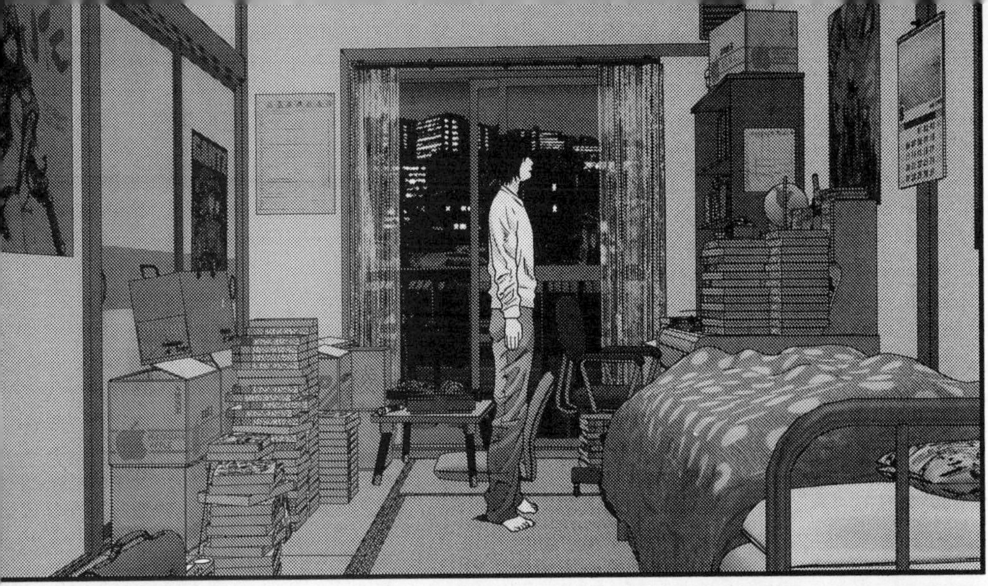
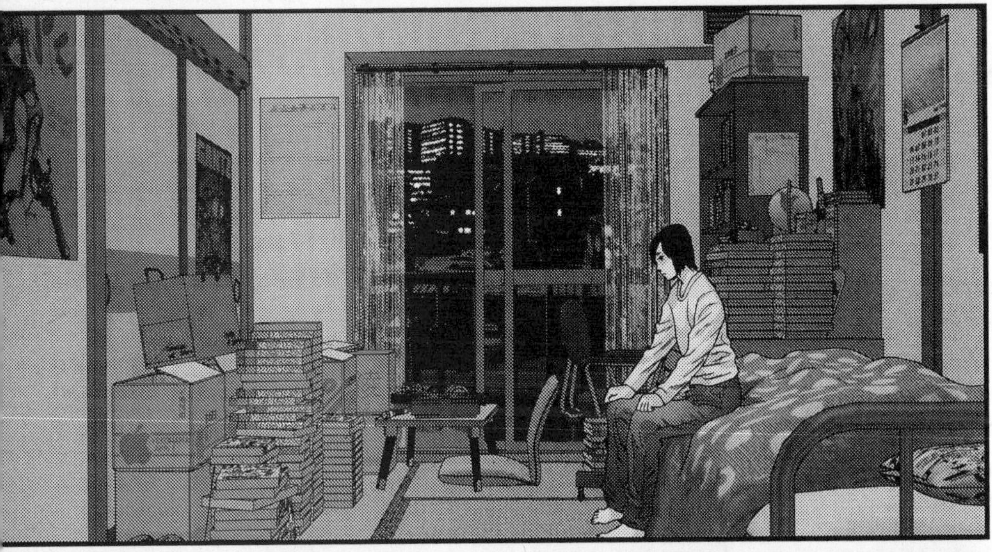
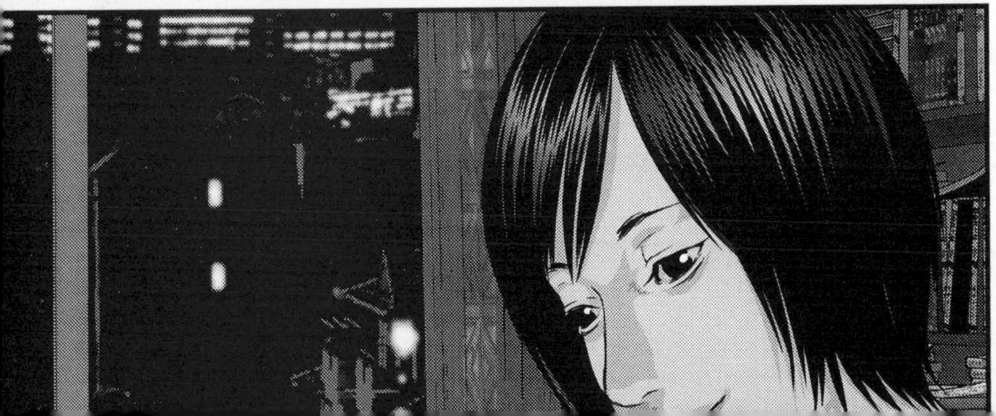

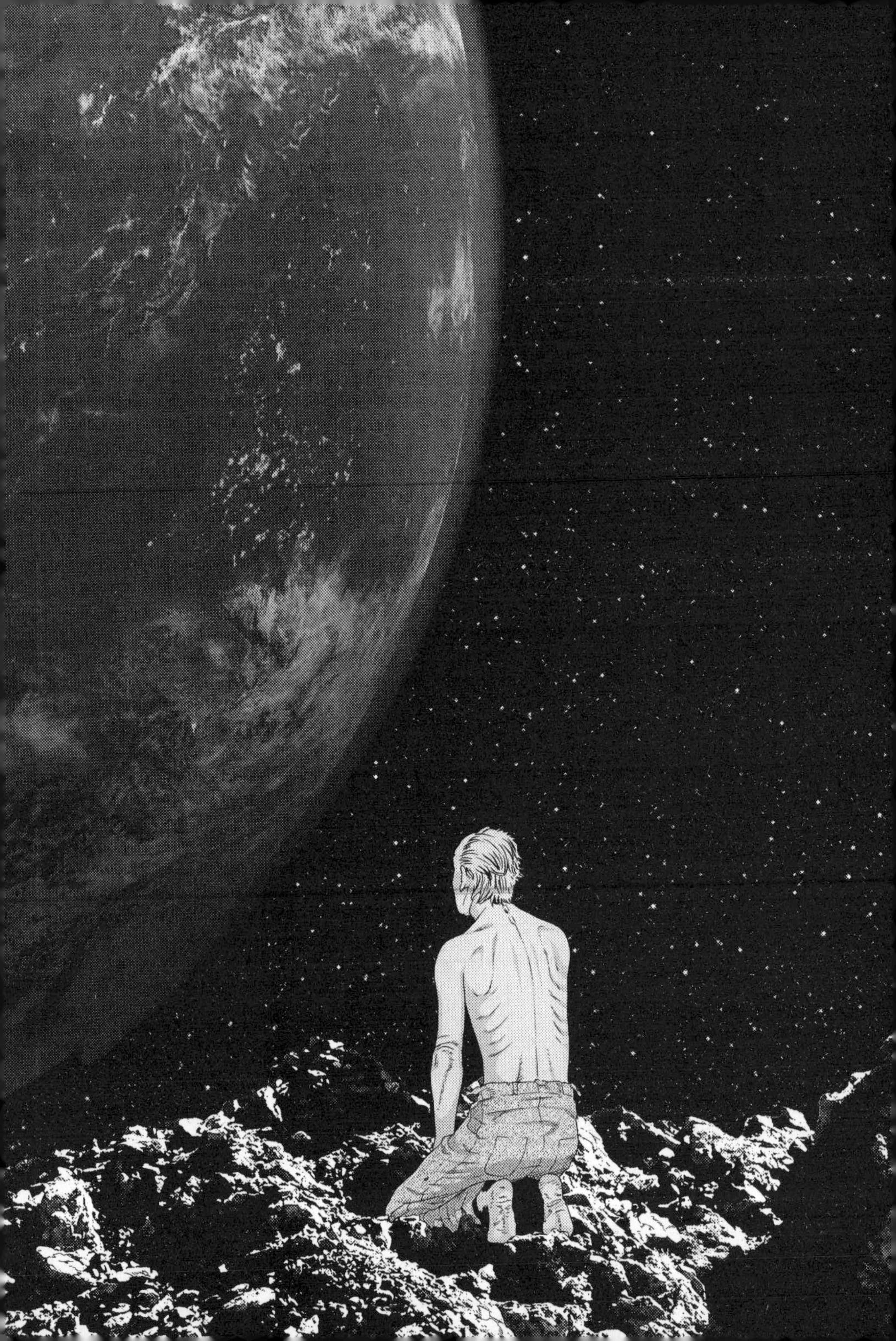

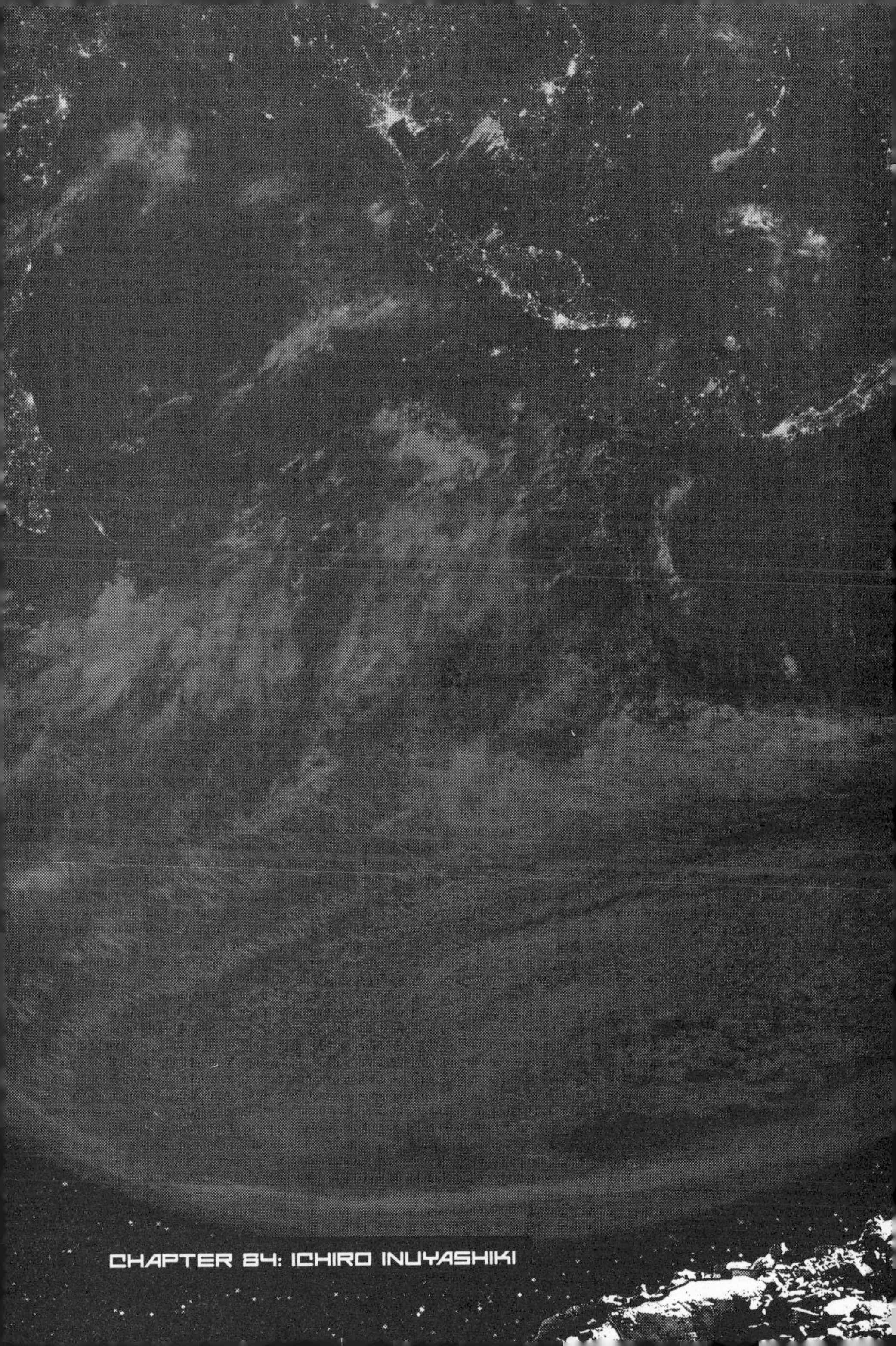
CHAPTER 84: ICHIRO INUYASHIKI

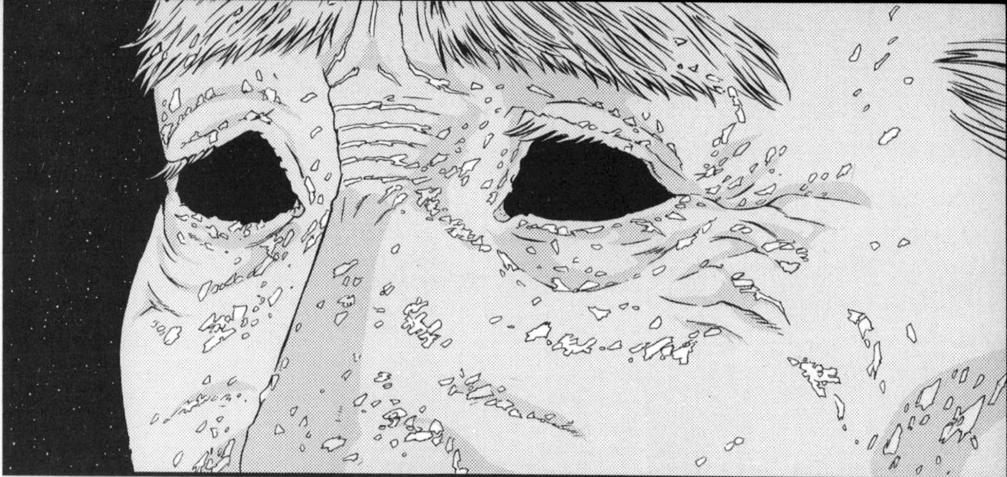
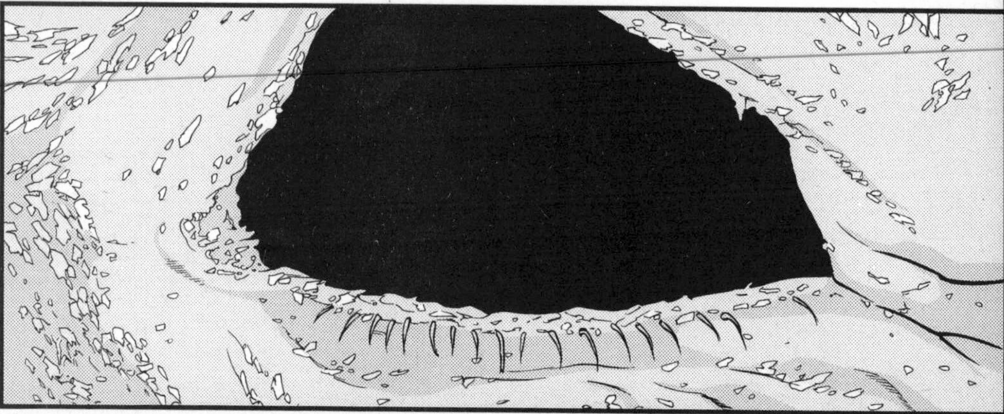
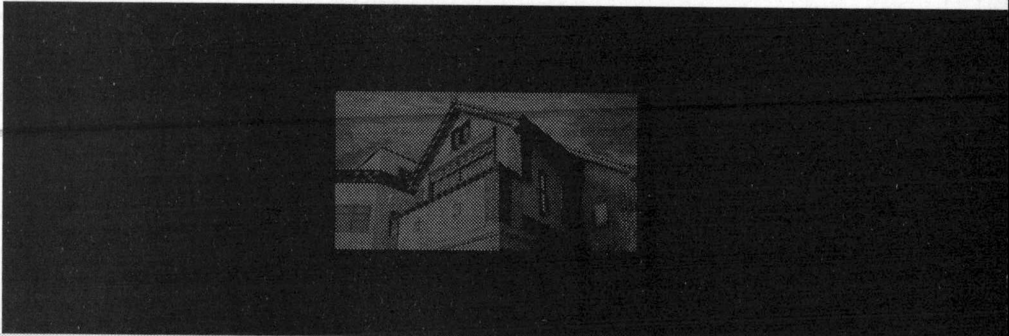
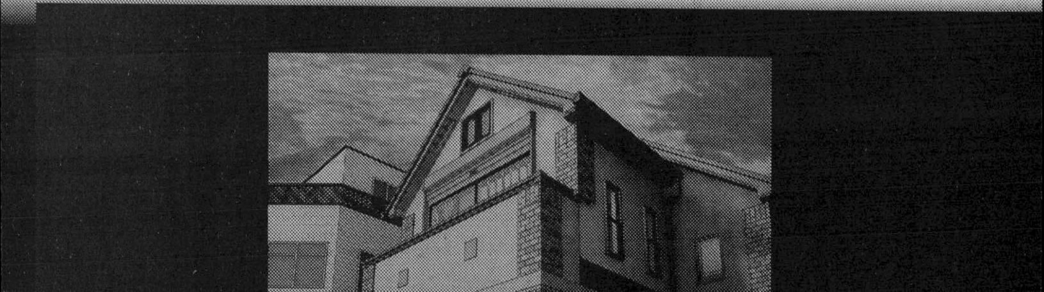

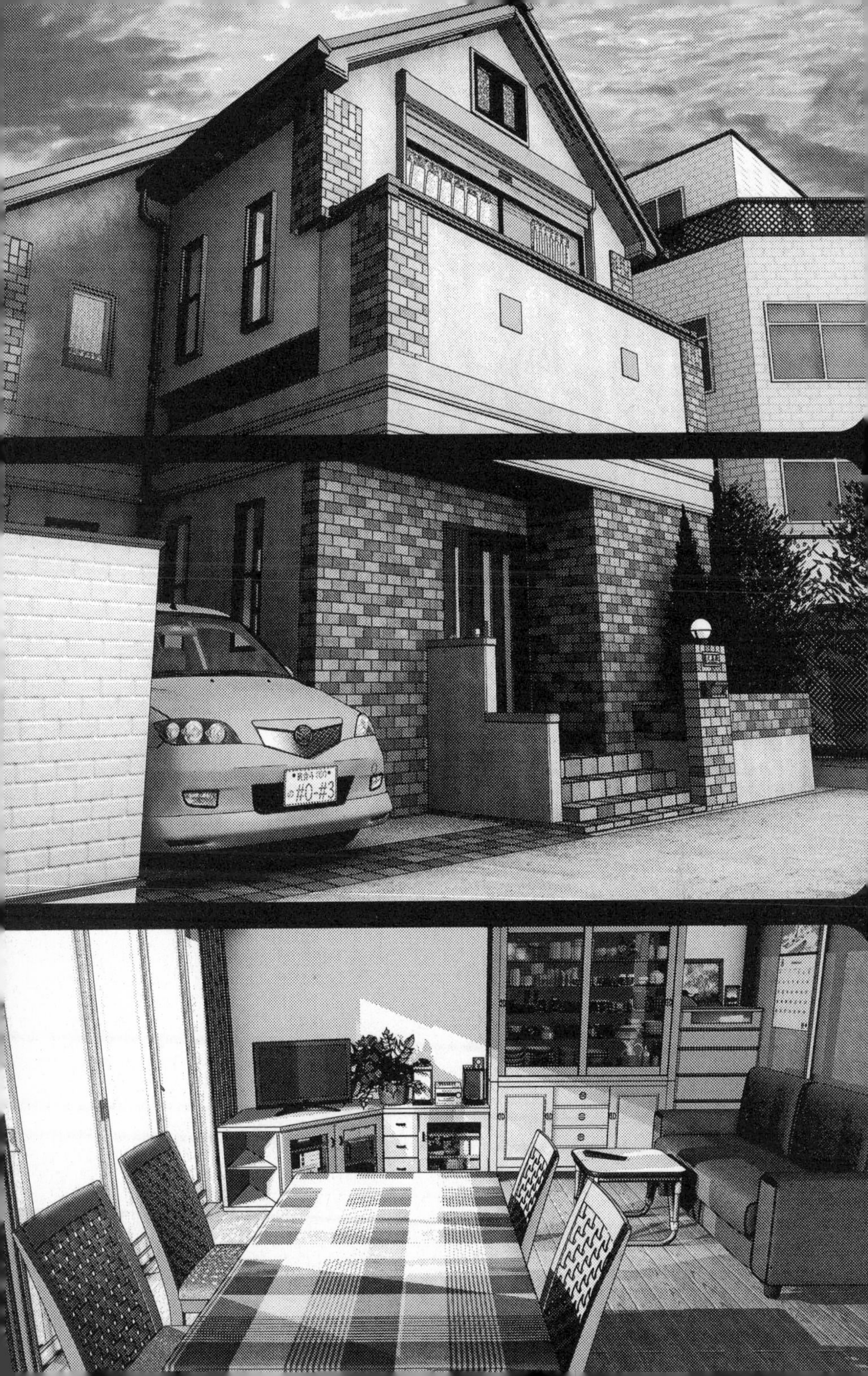
#0-#3

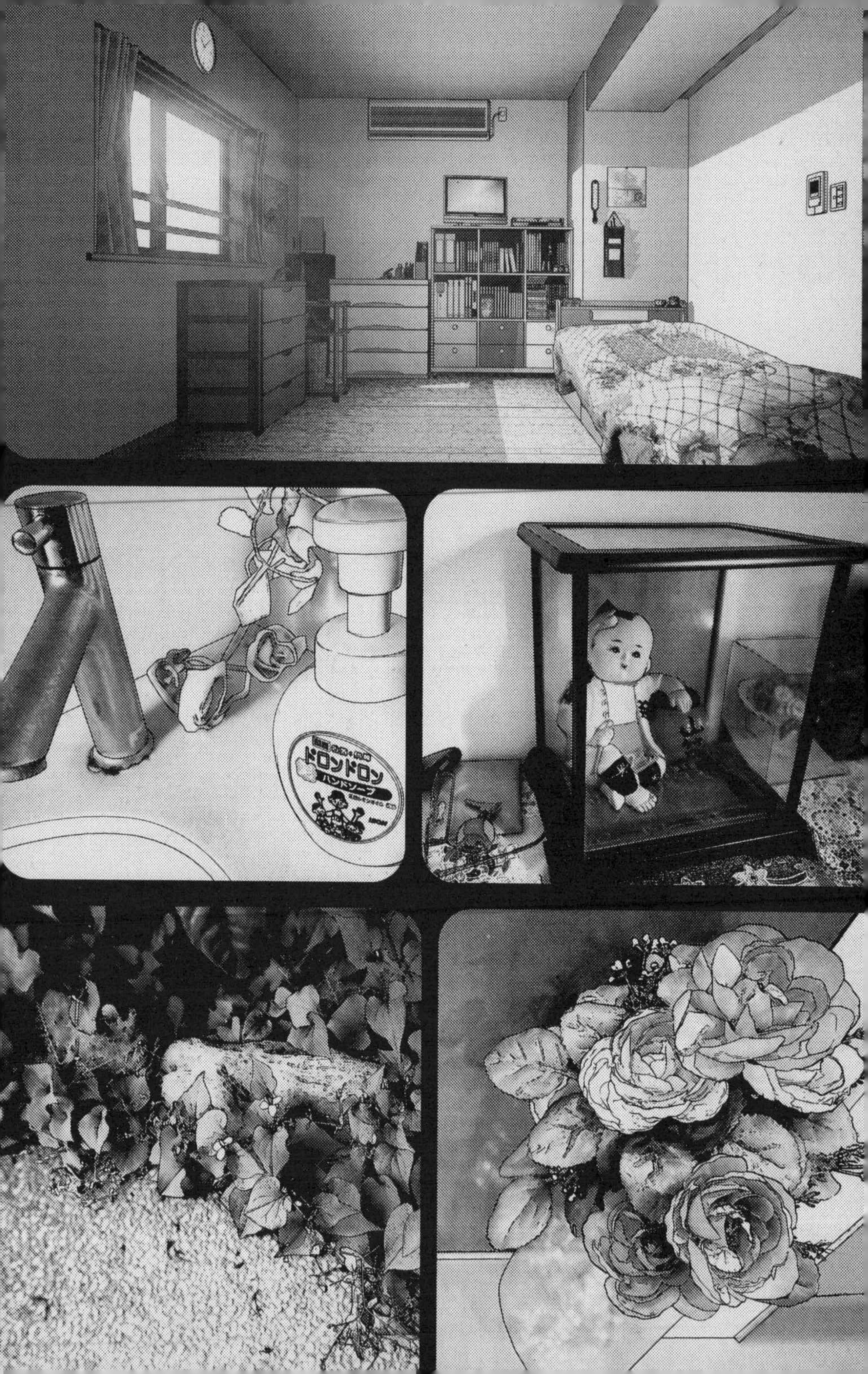
ドロンドロン
ハンドソープ

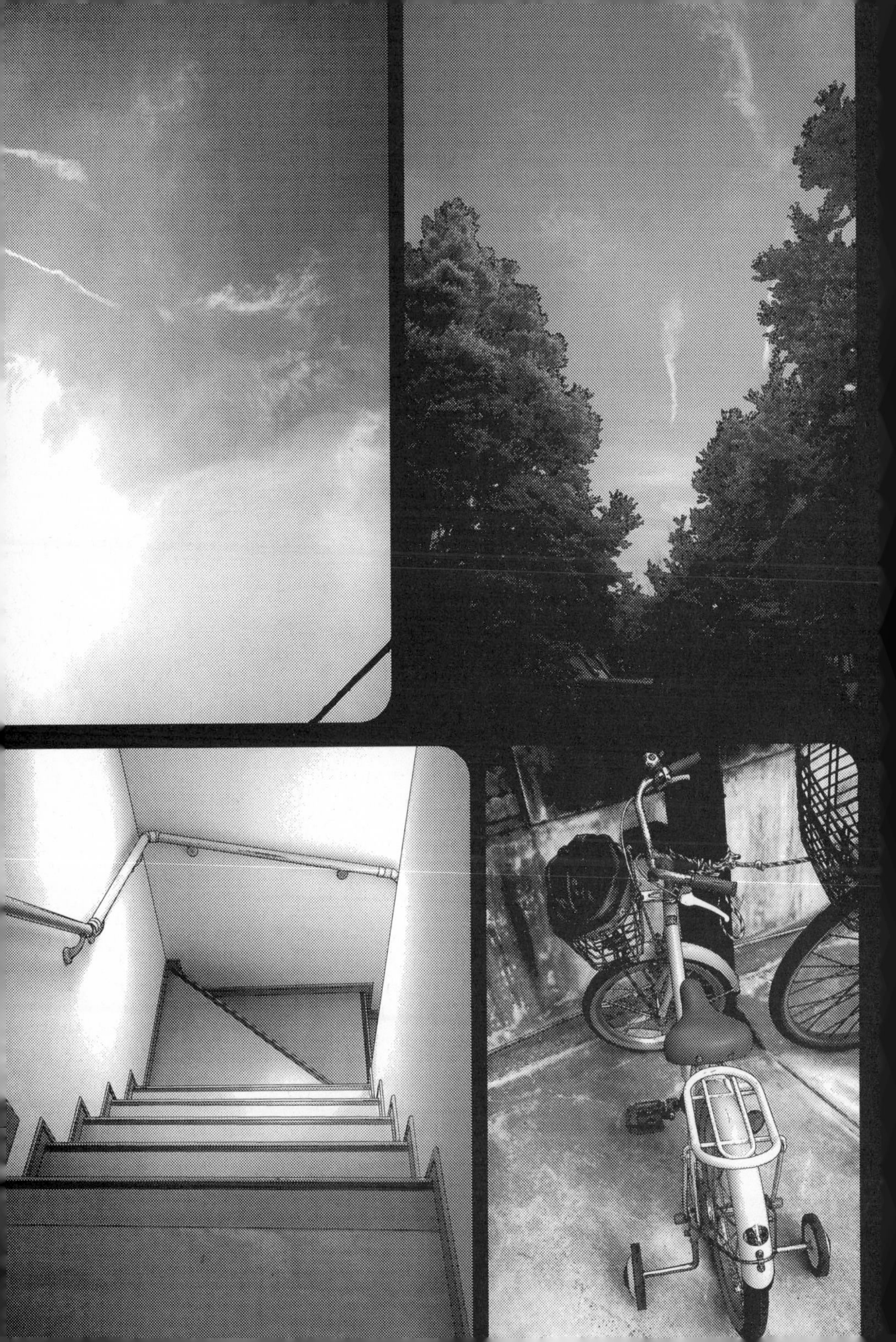

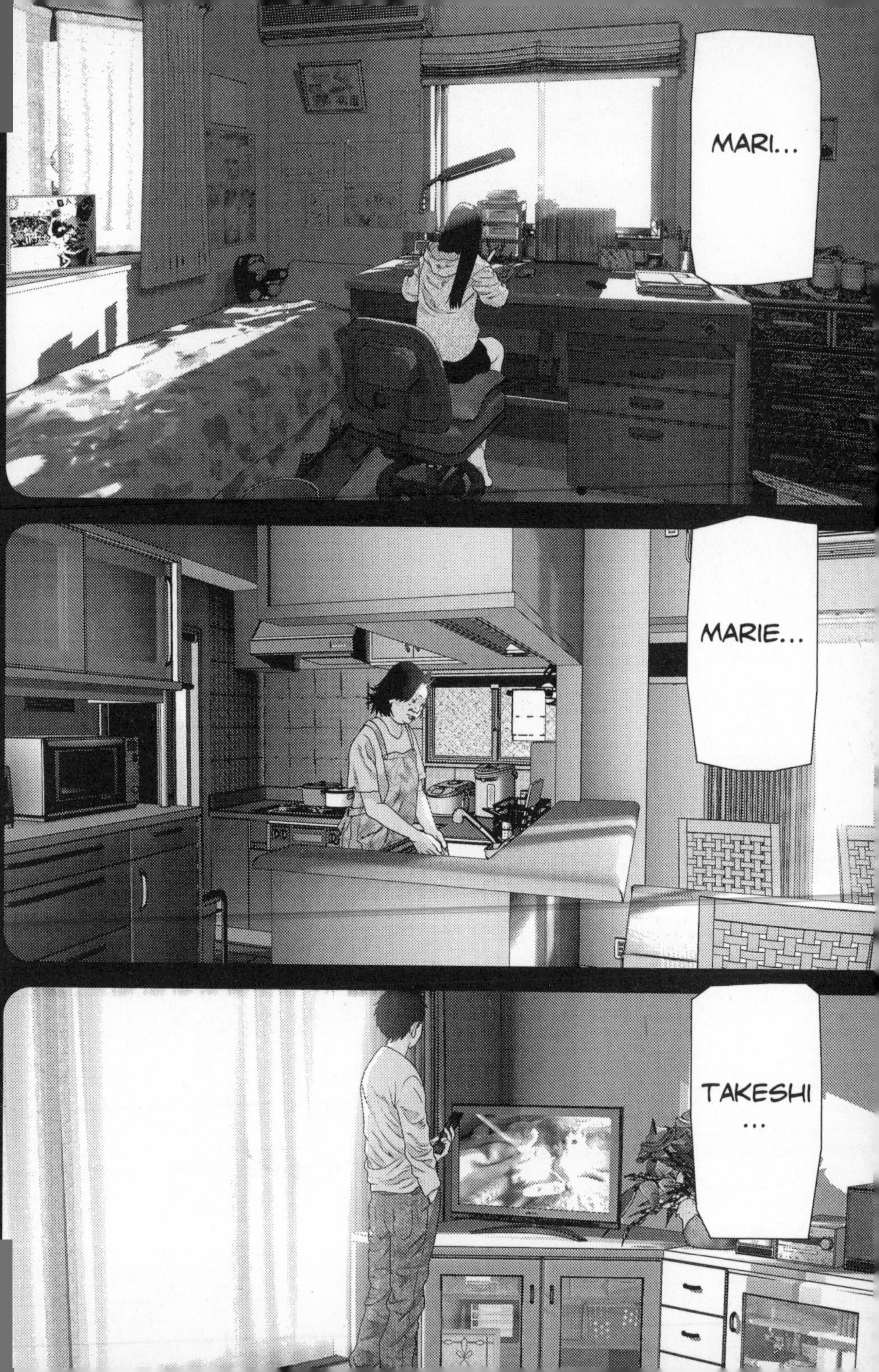
MARI...
MARIE...
TAKESHI ...

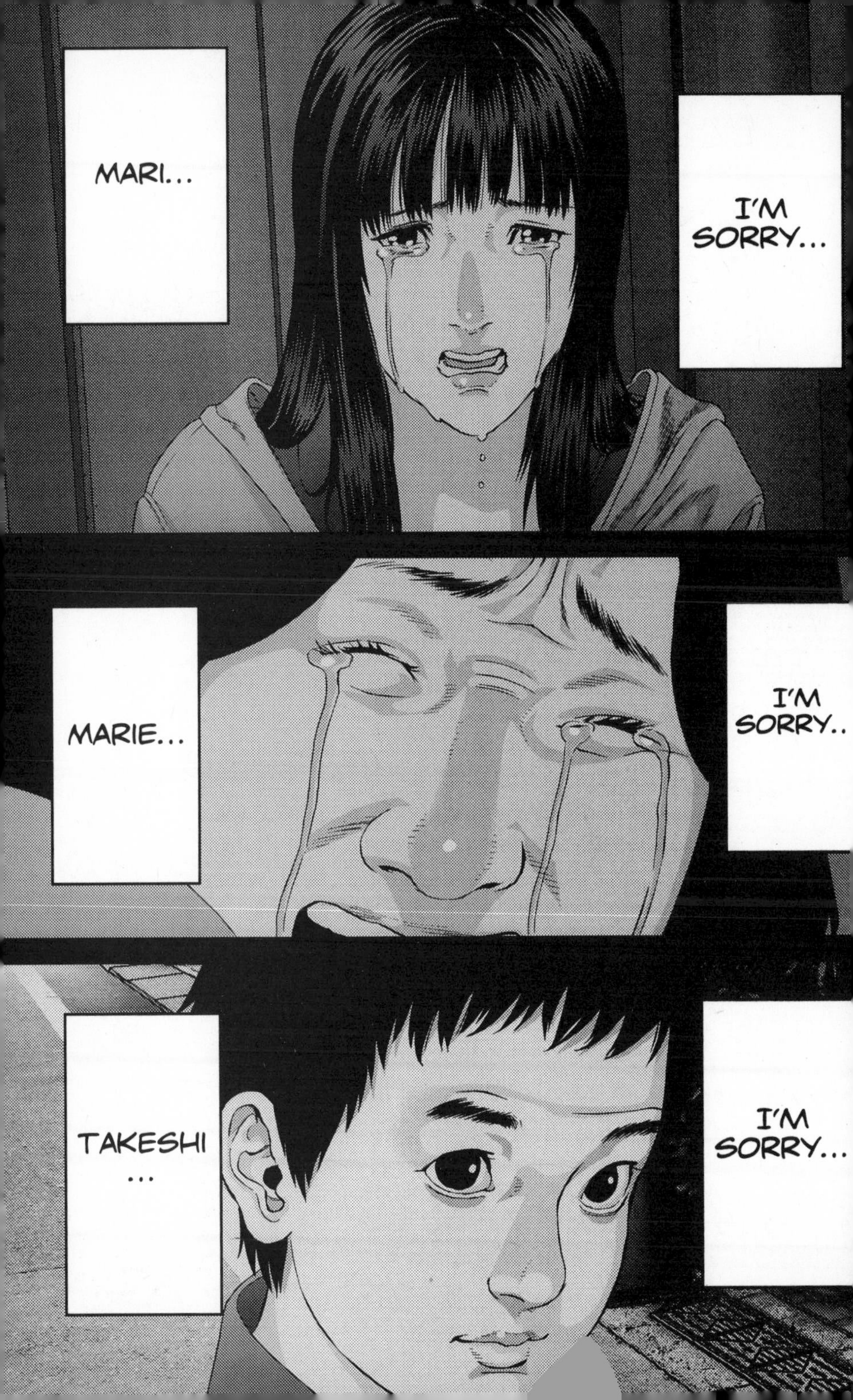
MARI...
I'M SORRY...
MARIE...
I'M SORRY..
TAKESHI ...
I'M SORRY...

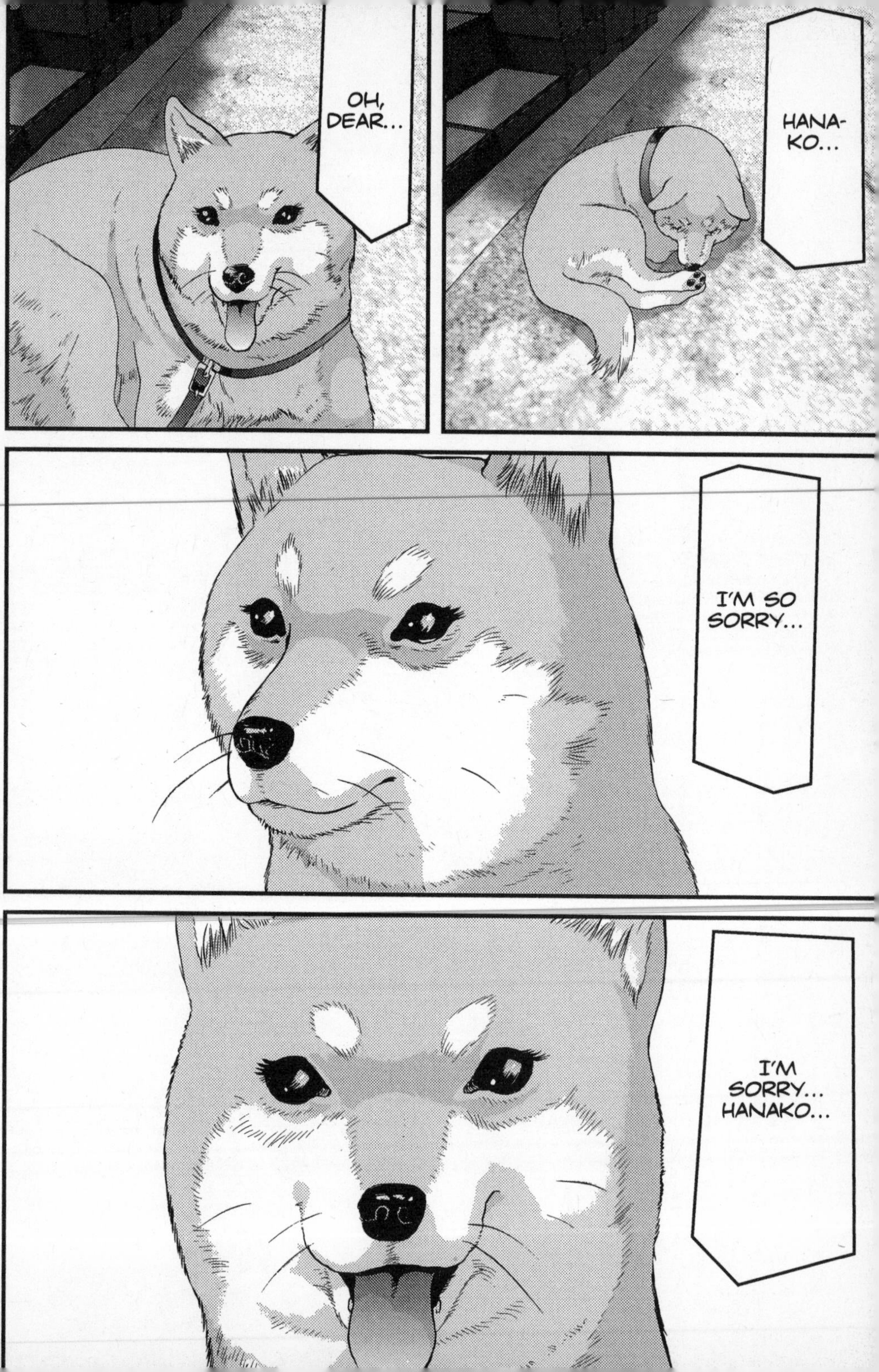
HANA-KO...
OH, DEAR...
I'M SO SORRY...
I'M SORRY... HANAKO...

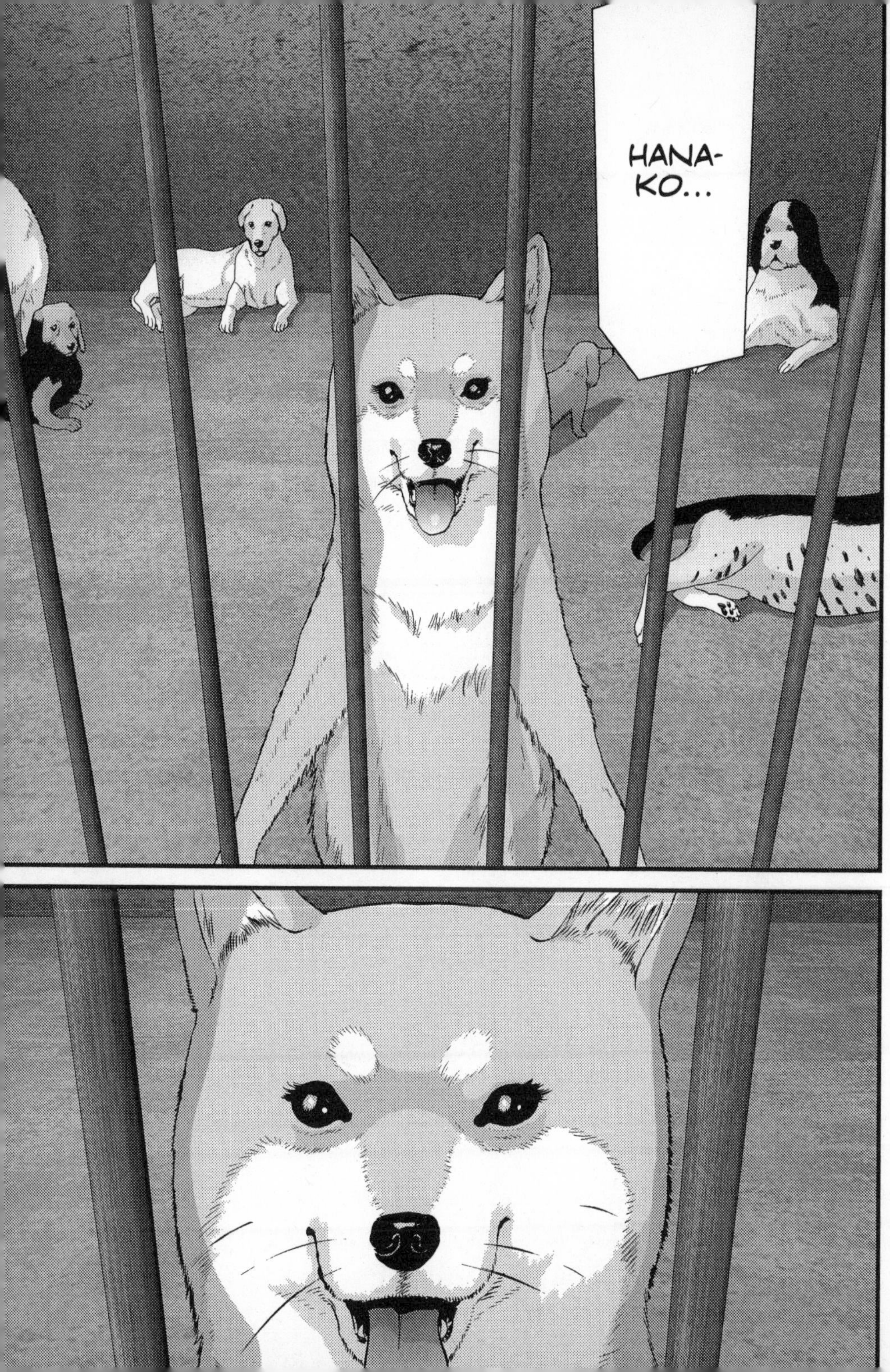
HANA-
KO...

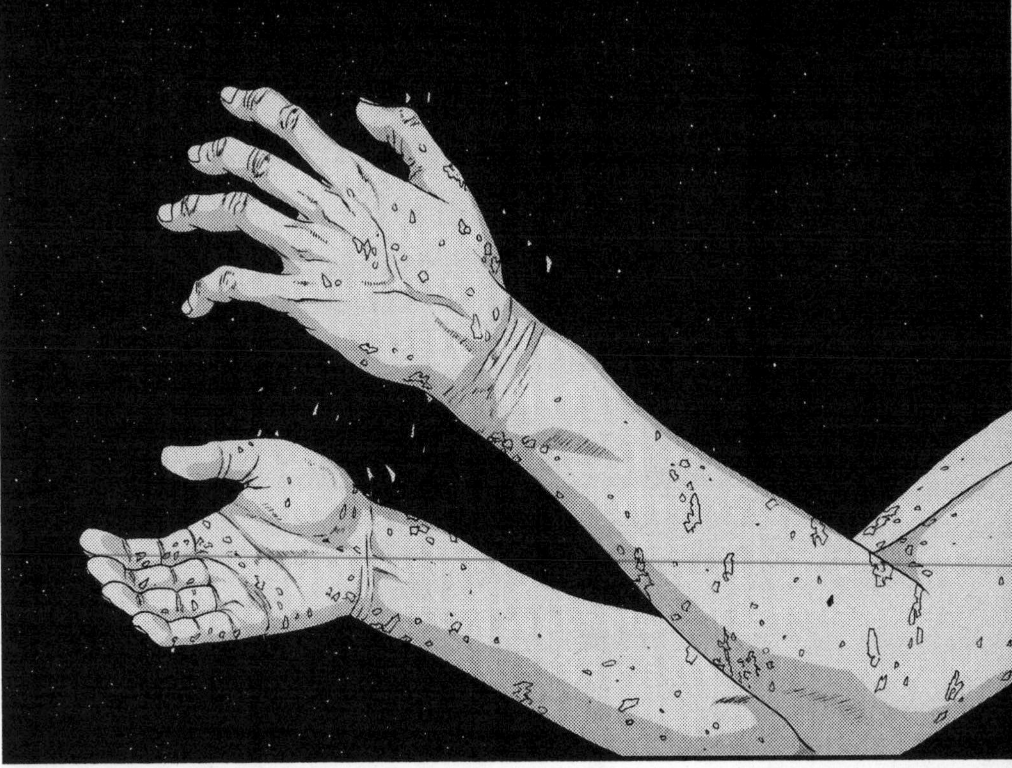
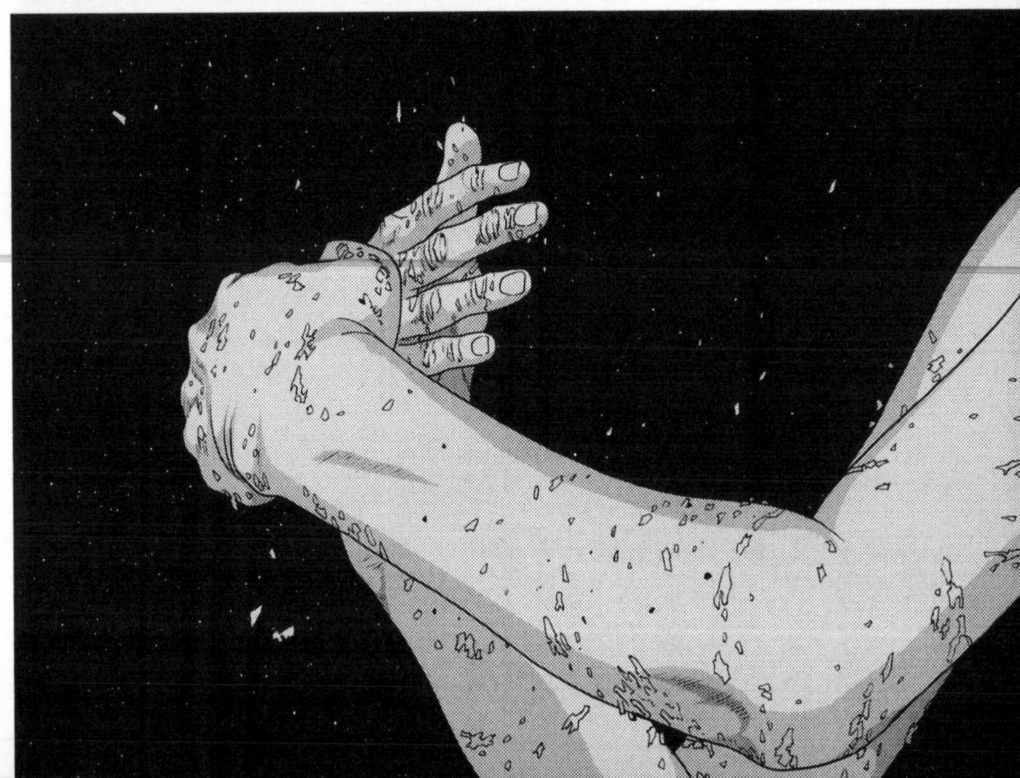

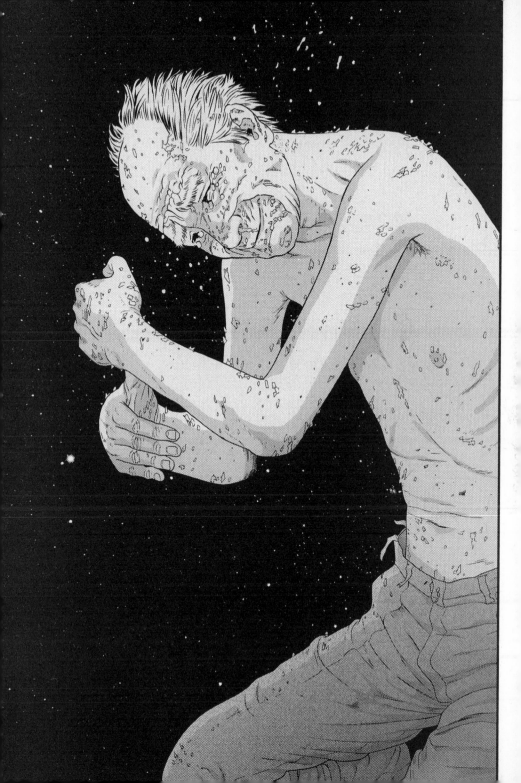

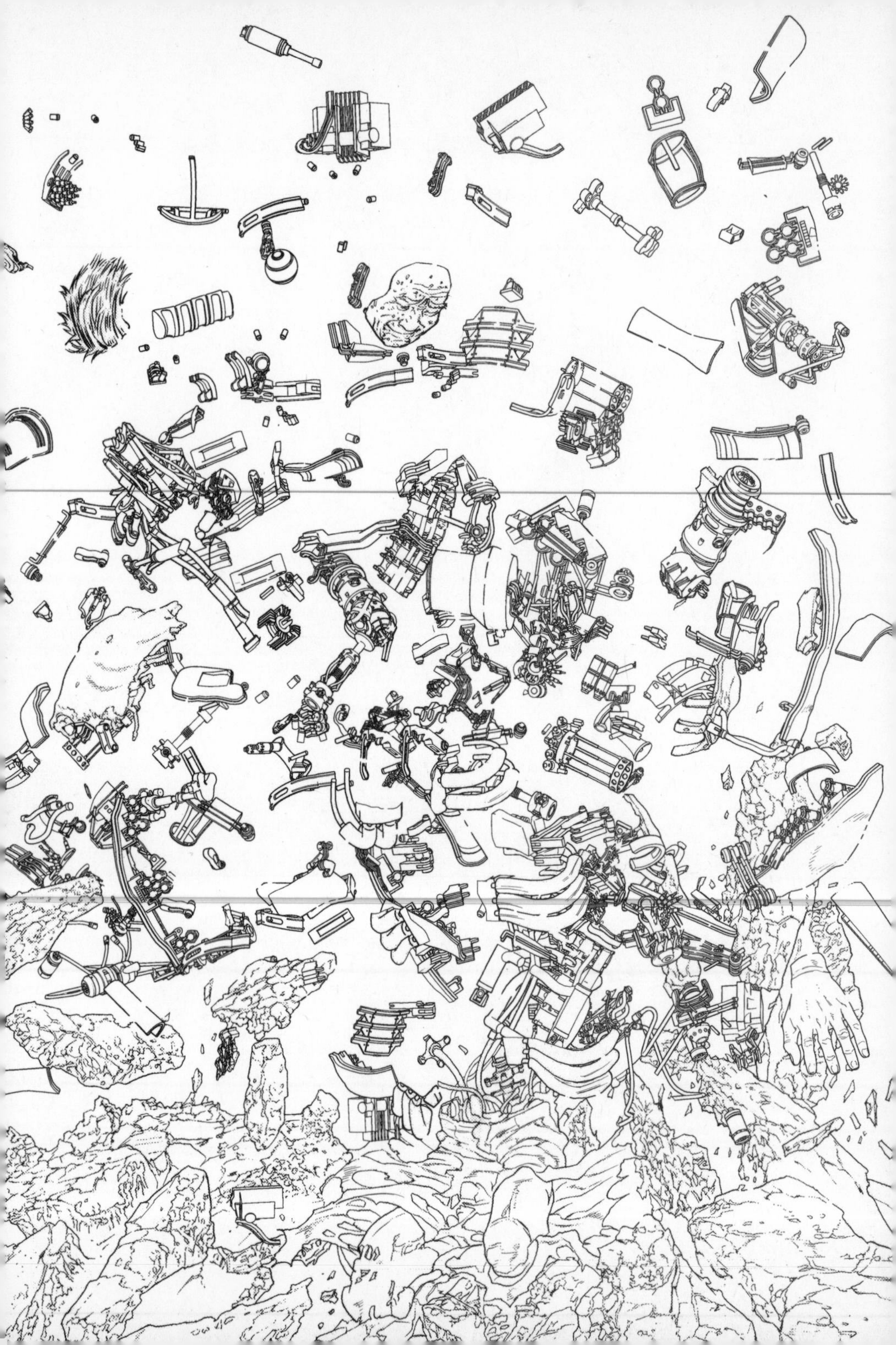

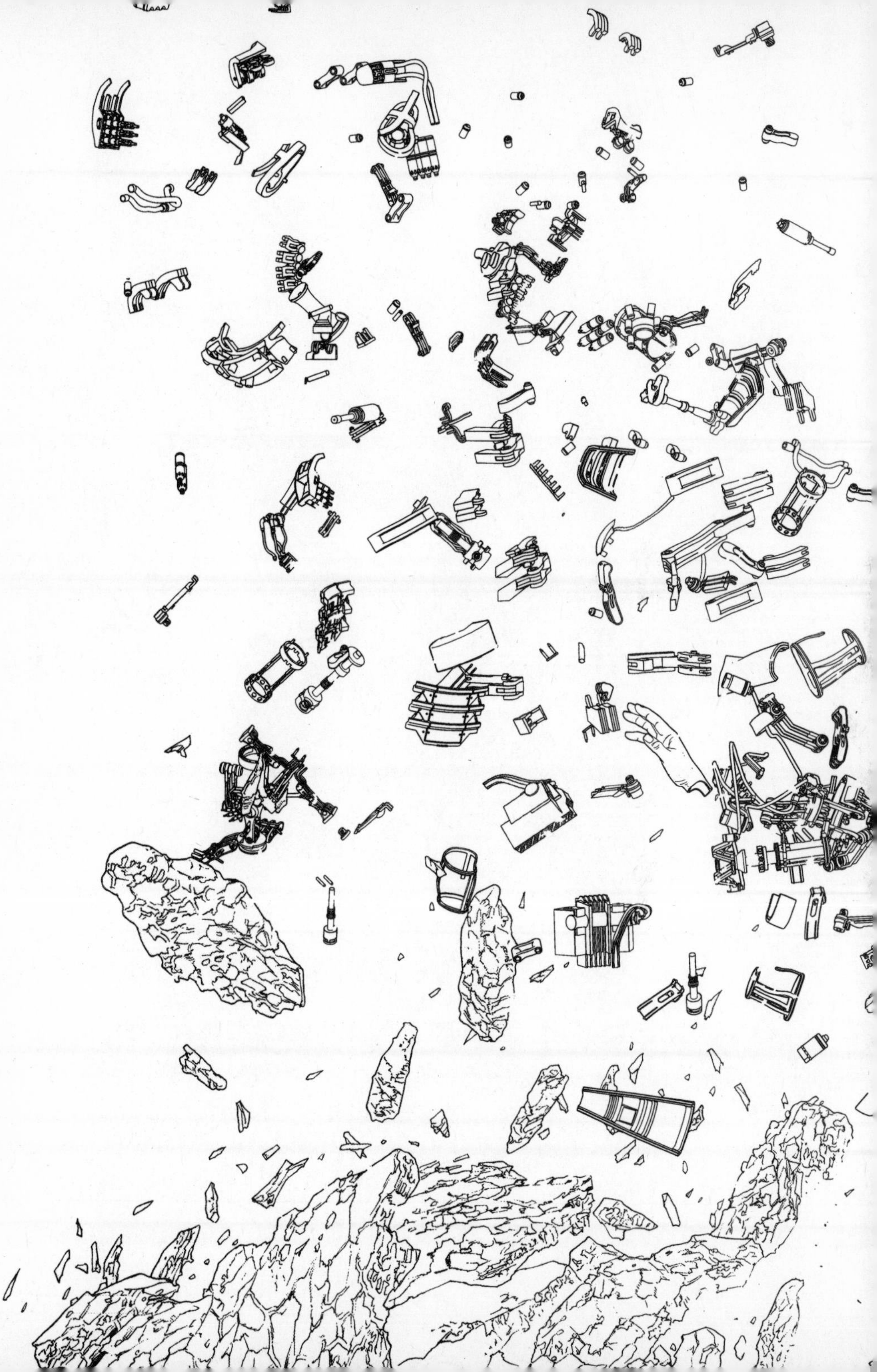

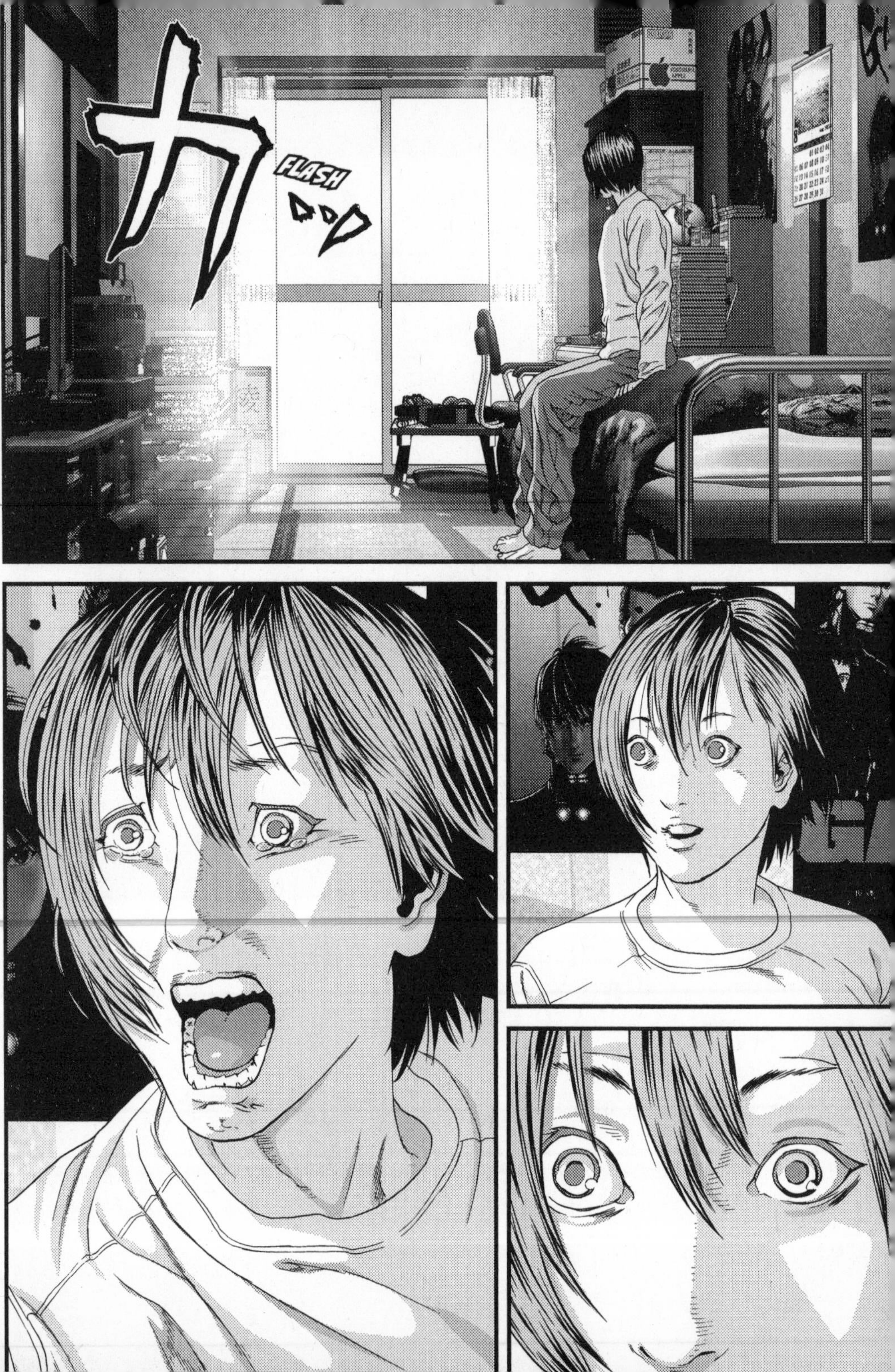
カ
FLASH

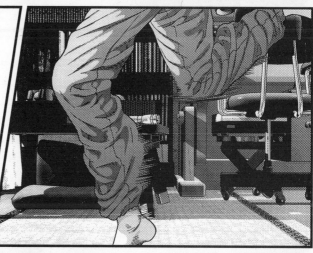

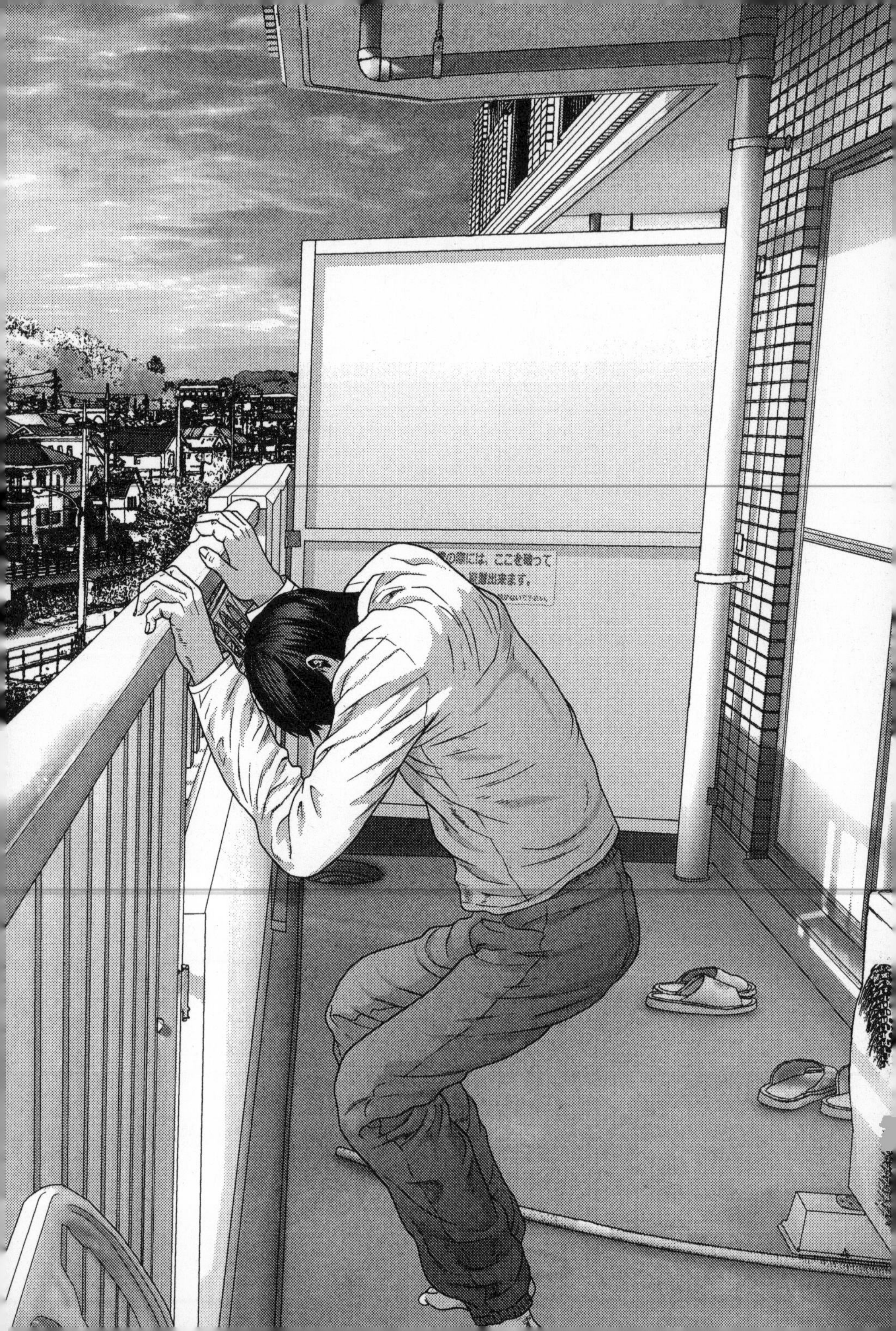
の際には、ここを破って
避難出来ます。

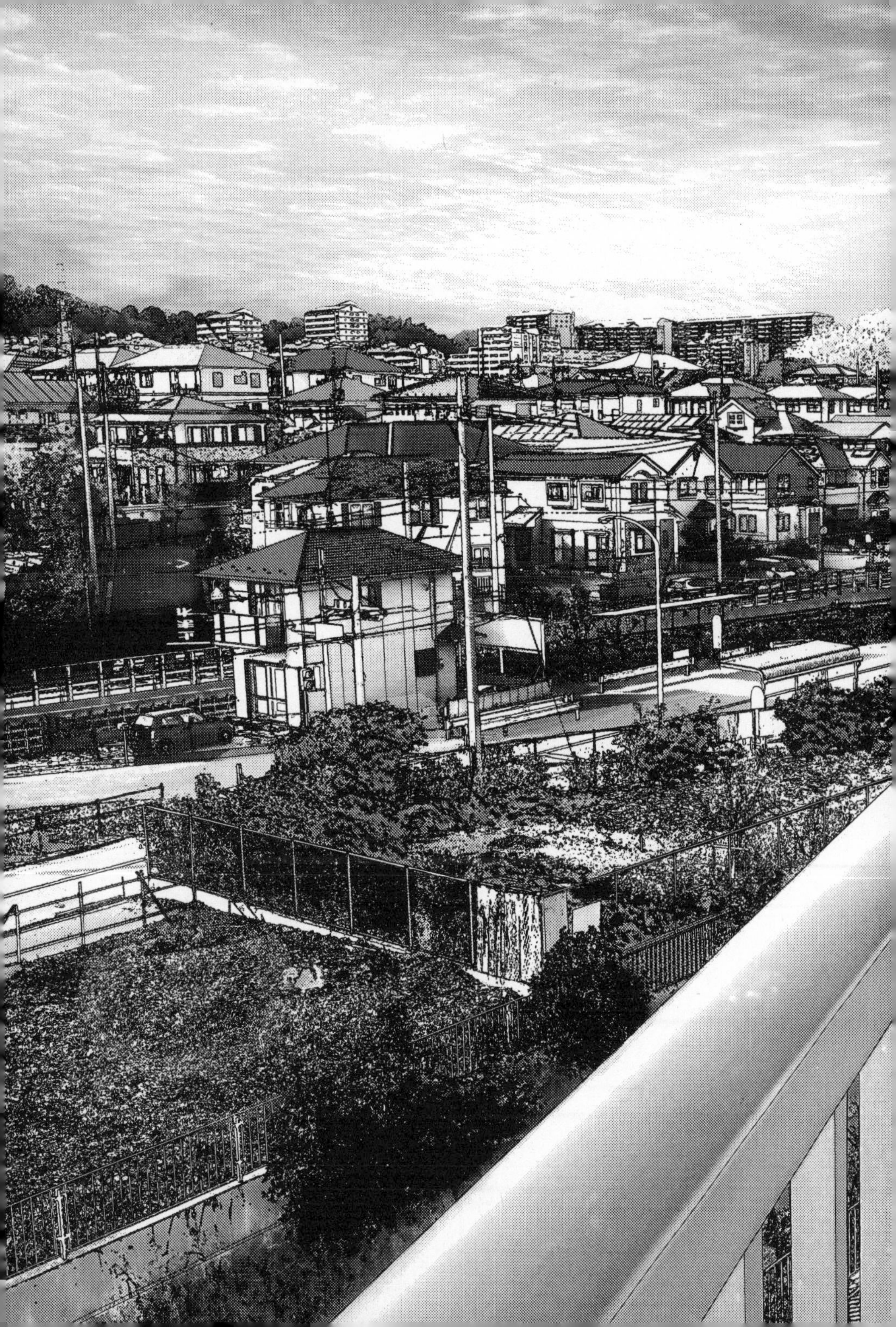

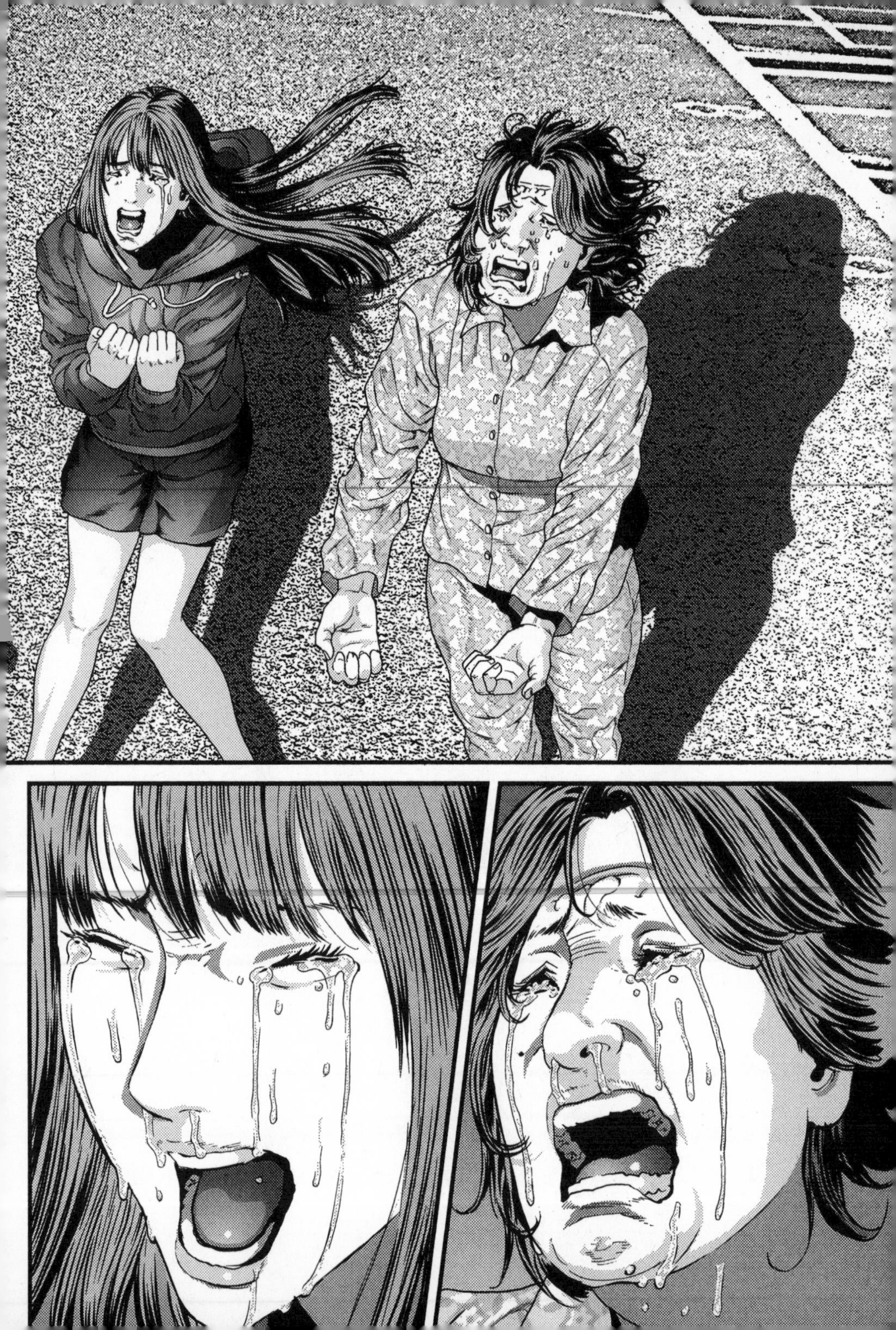

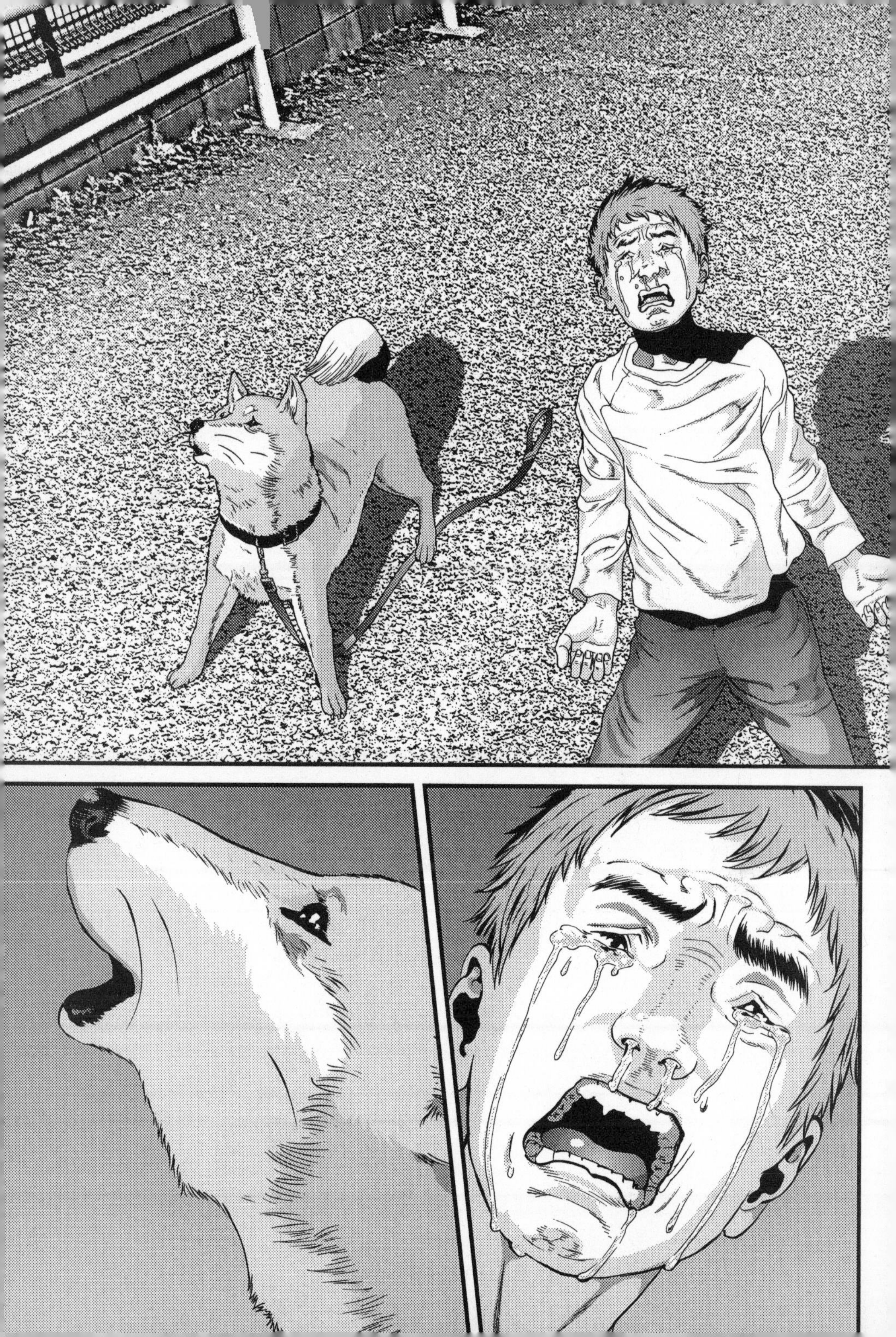

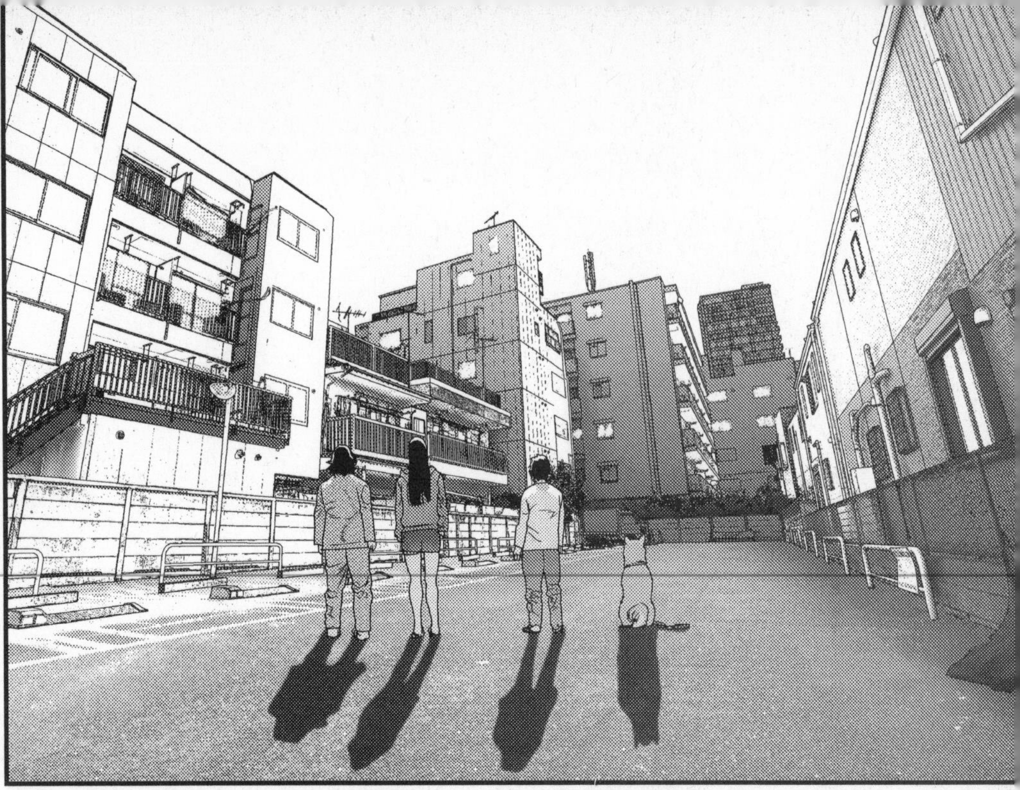

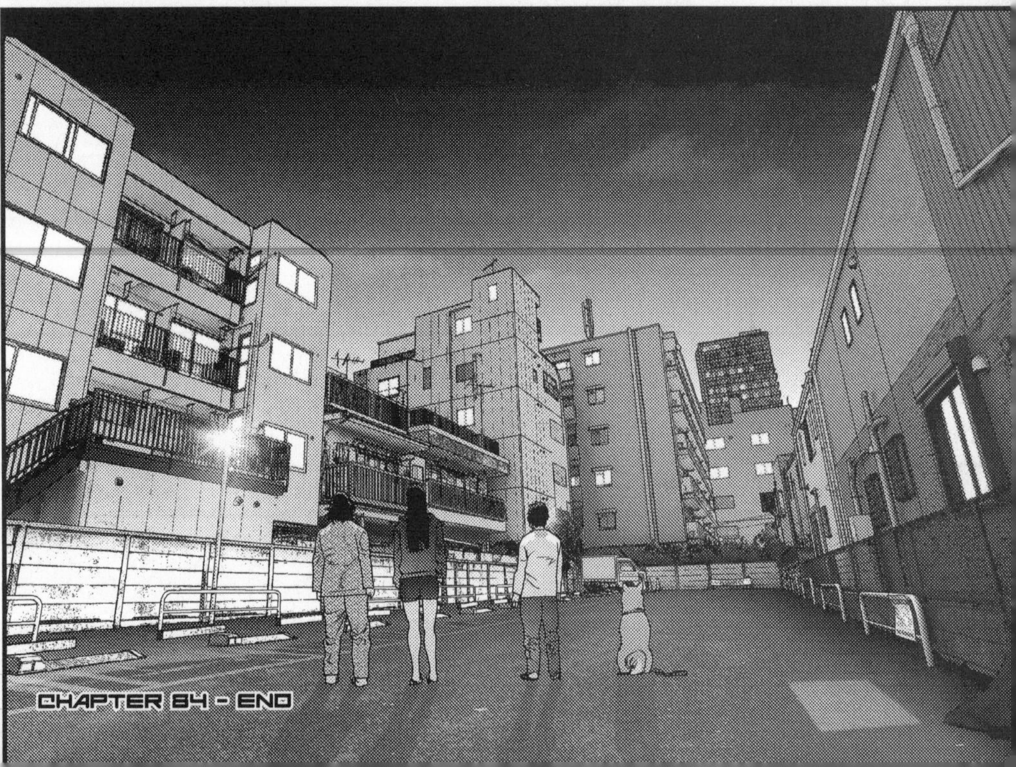
CHAPTER 84 - END

INUYASHIKI

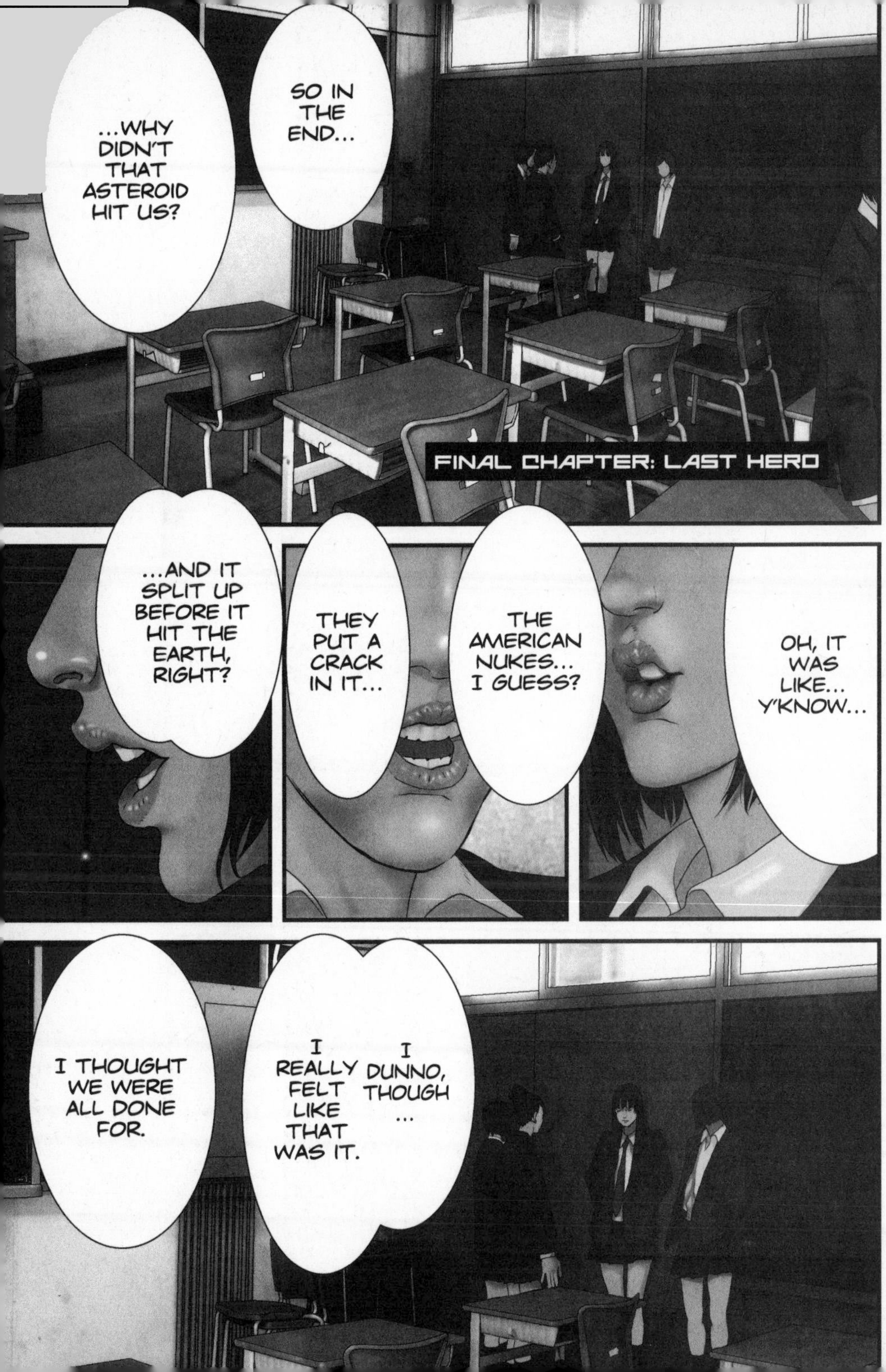
SO IN THE END...
...WHY DIDN'T THAT ASTEROID HIT US?
FINAL CHAPTER: LAST HERO
OH, IT WAS LIKE... Y'KNOW...
THE AMERICAN NUKES... I GUESS?
THEY PUT A CRACK IN IT...
...AND IT SPLIT UP BEFORE IT HIT THE EARTH, RIGHT?
I DUNNO, THOUGH ...
I REALLY FELT LIKE THAT WAS IT.
I THOUGHT WE WERE ALL DONE FOR.

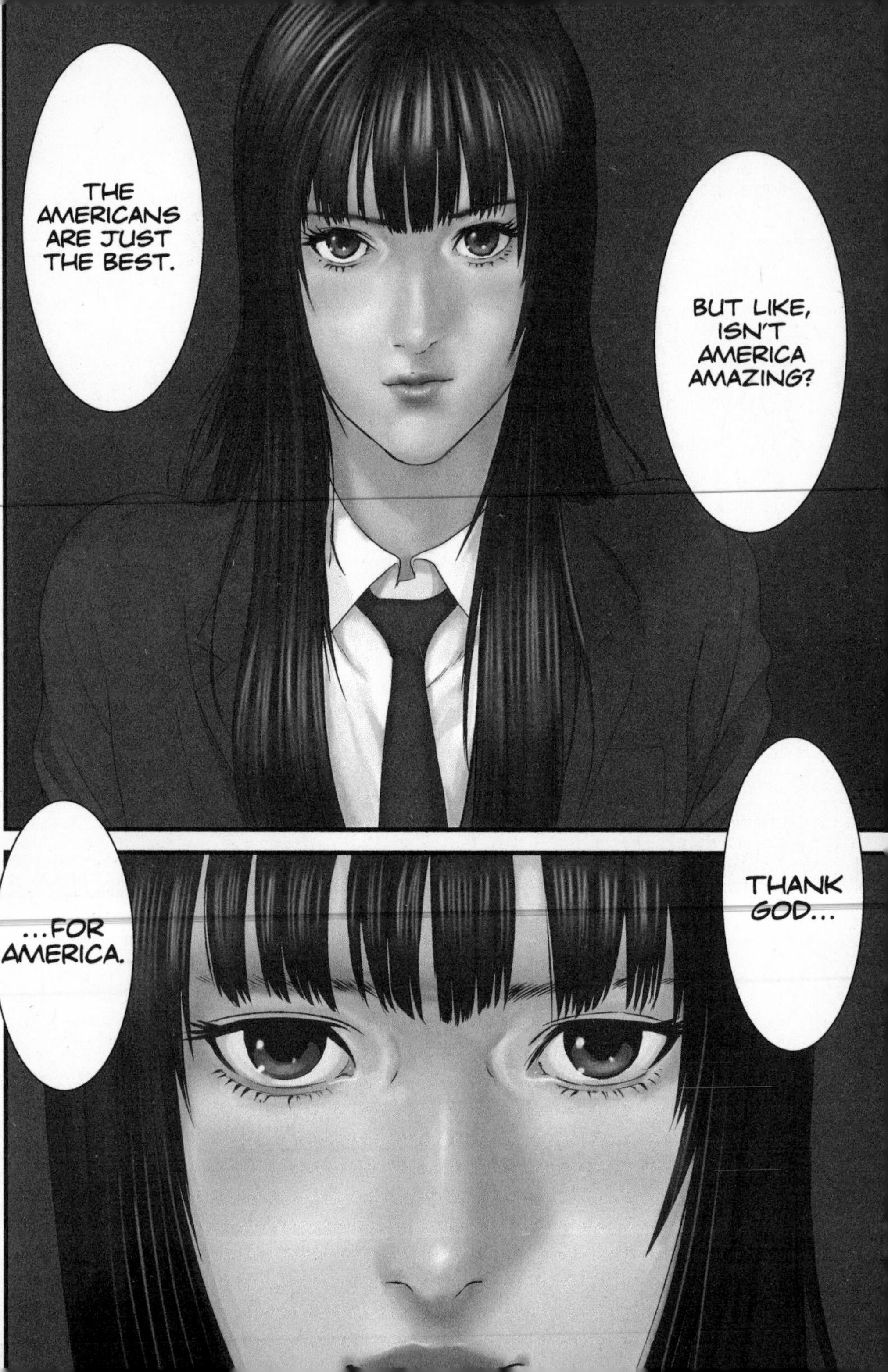
BUT LIKE, ISN'T AMERICA AMAZING?
THE AMERICANS ARE JUST THE BEST.
THANK GOD...
...FOR AMERICA.

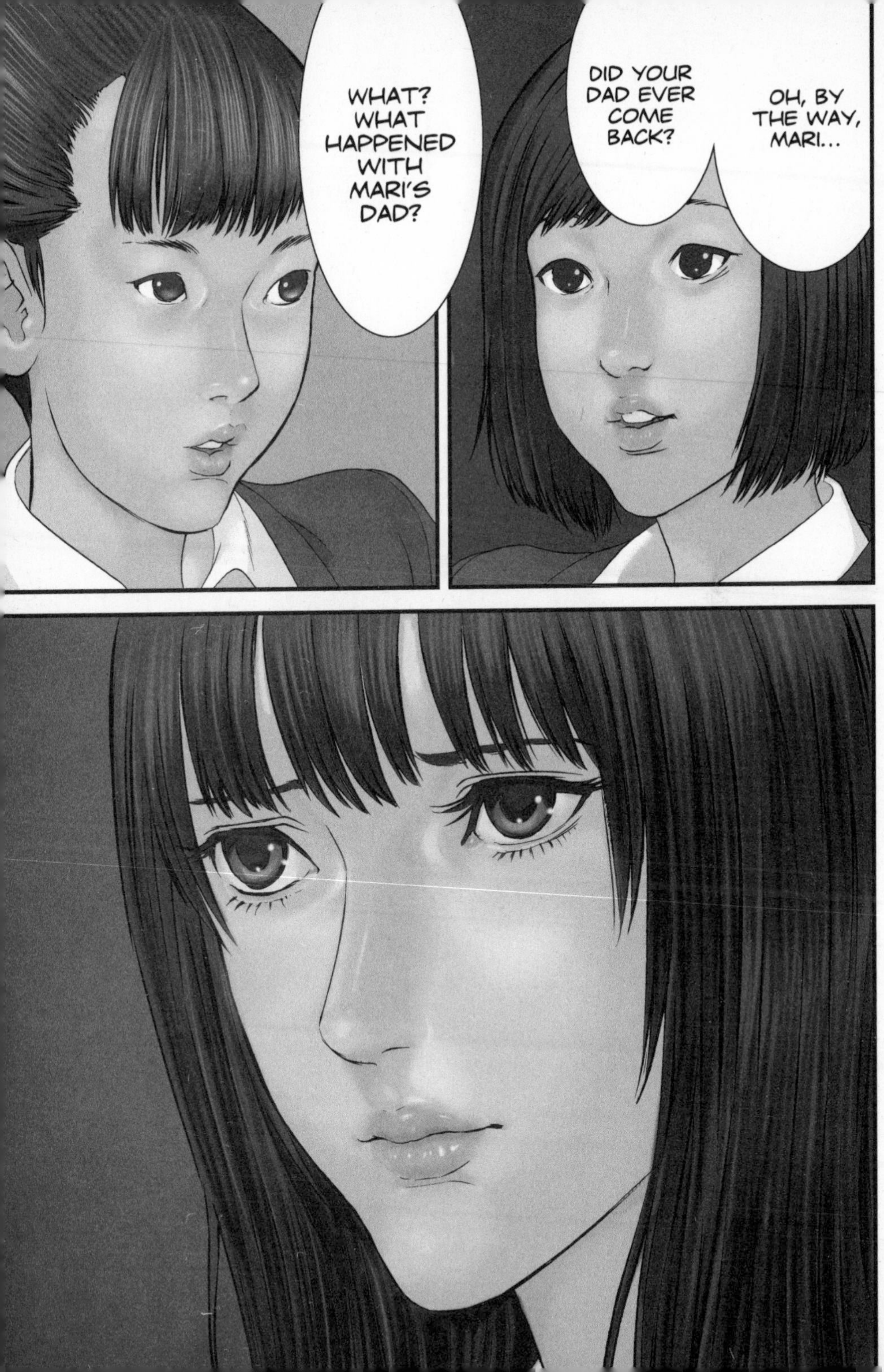
OH, BY THE WAY, MARI...
DID YOUR DAD EVER COME BACK?
WHAT? WHAT HAPPENED WITH MARI'S DAD?

MARI!

ARE YOU OKAY?

OH! I'M SORRY!

HUH? MARI...?

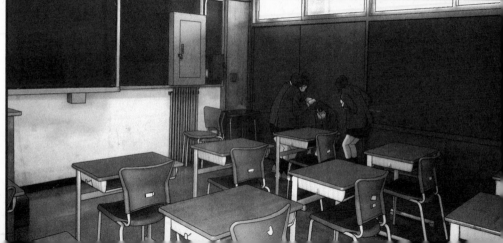

INUYA-
SHIKI-
SAN!!

INUYA-
SHIKI-
SAN.

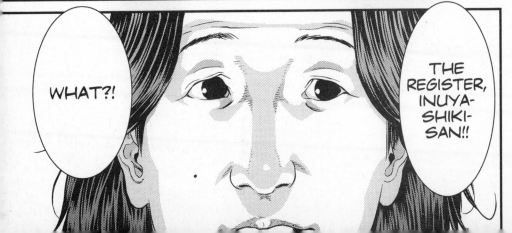

WHAT?!

THE
REGISTER,
INUYA-
SHIKI-
SAN!!

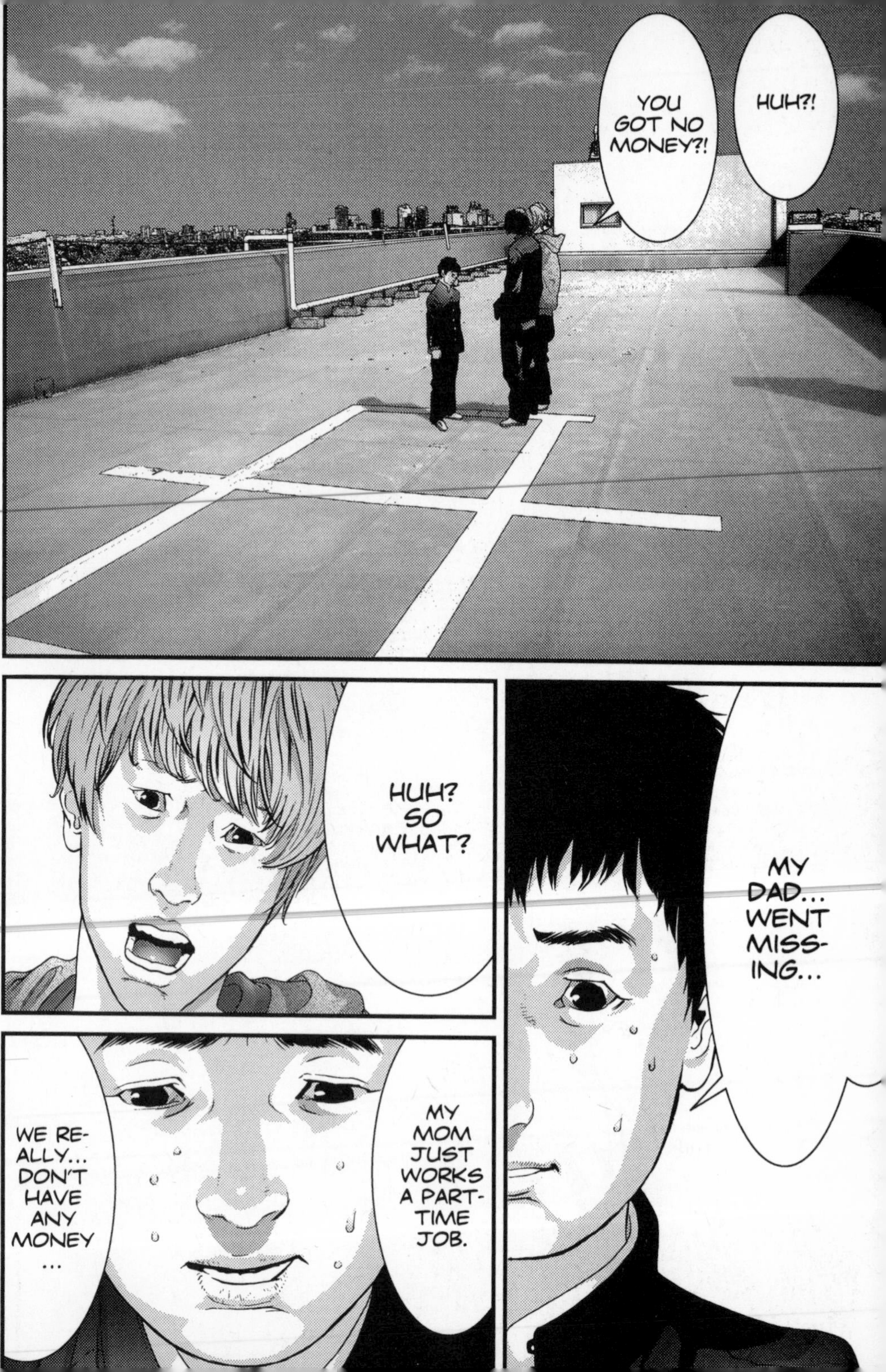
HUH?!
YOU GOT NO MONEY?!
MY DAD... WENT MISS-ING...
HUH? SO WHAT?
MY MOM JUST WORKS A PART-TIME JOB.
WE RE-ALLY... DON'T HAVE ANY MONEY ...

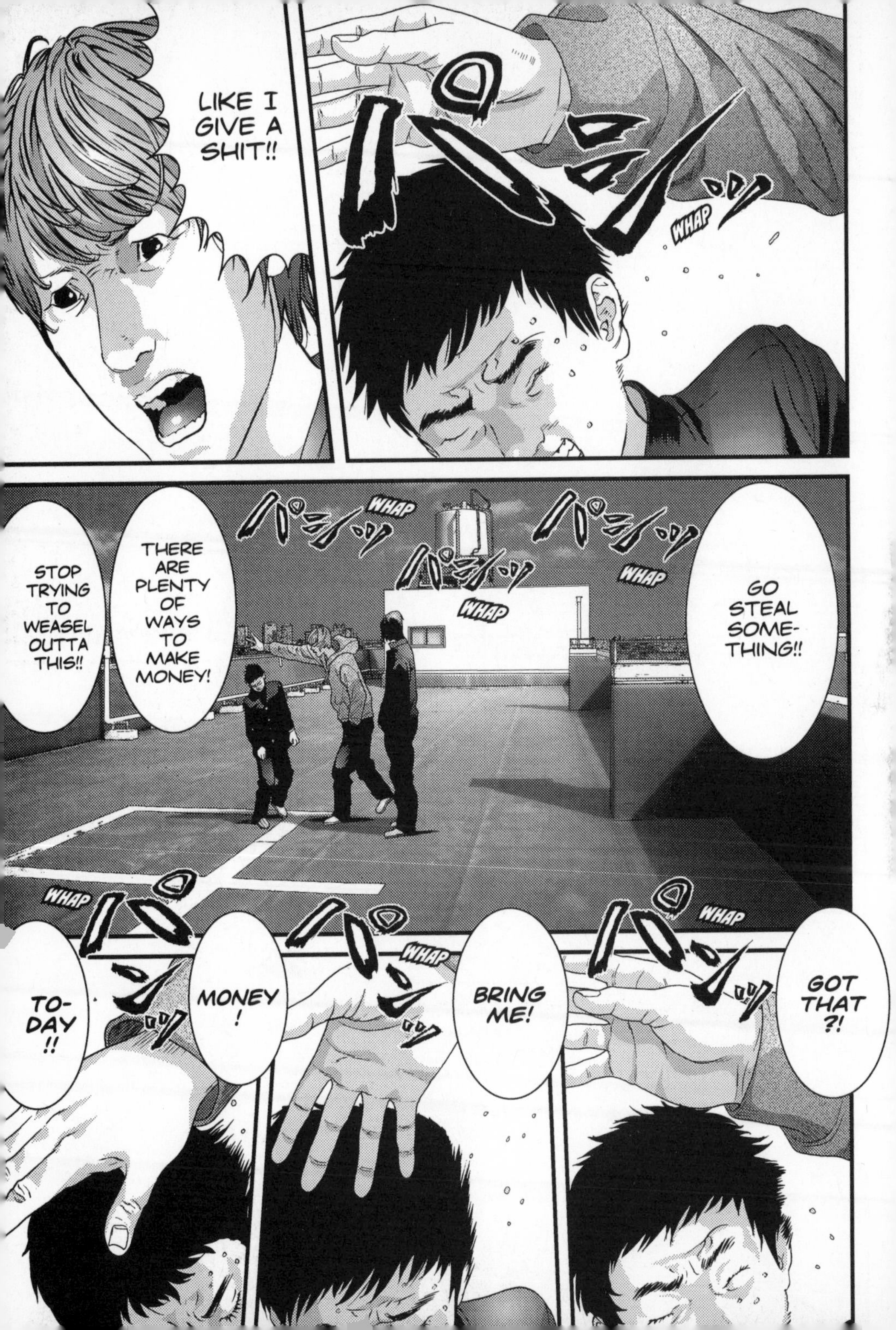
WHAP
LIKE I GIVE A SHIT!!
WHAP
WHAP
WHAP
GO STEAL SOME-THING!!
WHAP
THERE ARE PLENTY OF WAYS TO MAKE MONEY!
STOP TRYING TO WEASEL OUTTA THIS!!
WHAP
GOT THAT?!
BRING ME!
WHAP
MONEY!
WHAP
TO-DAY!!

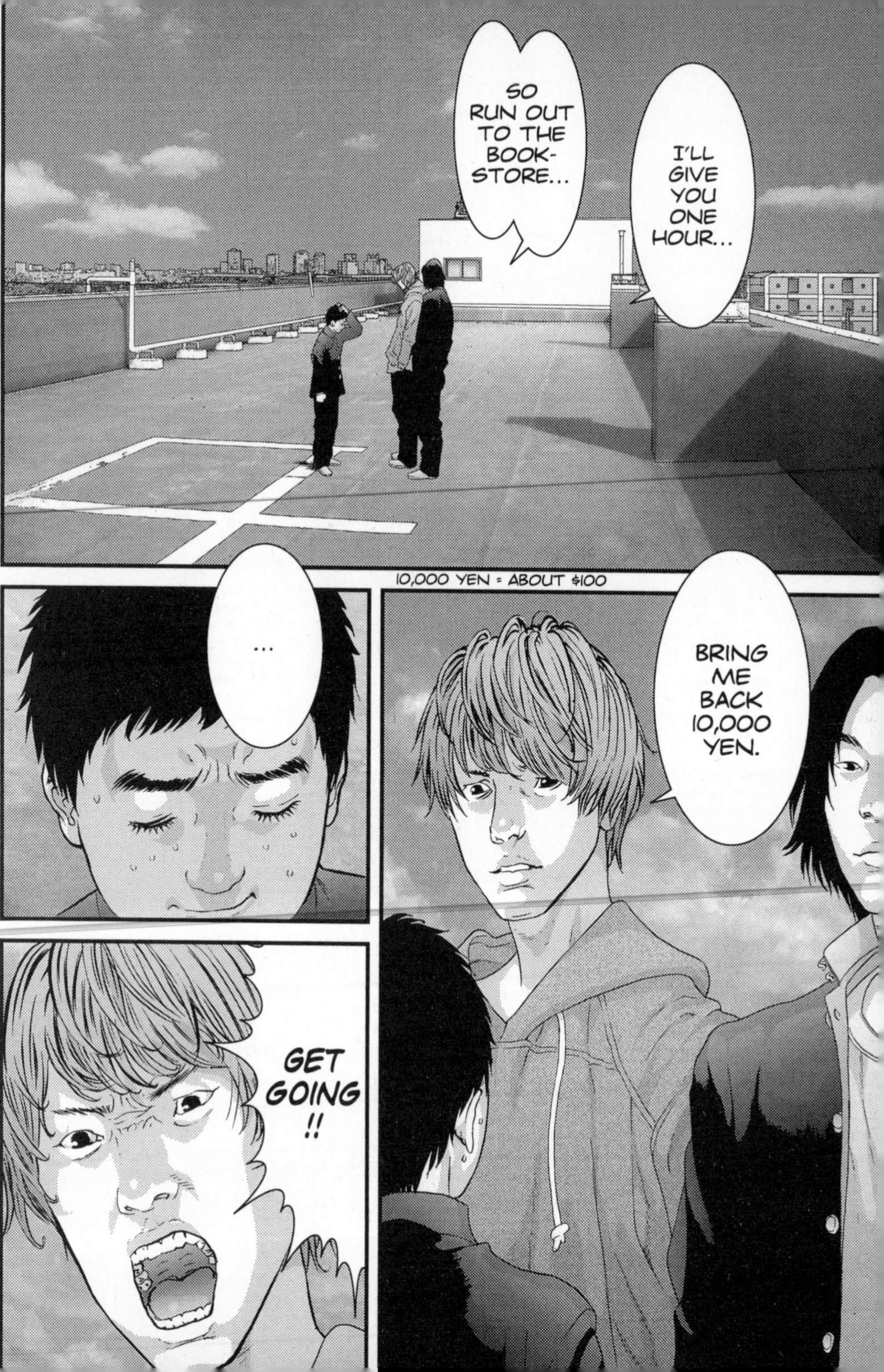
I'LL GIVE YOU ONE HOUR...
SO RUN OUT TO THE BOOK-STORE...
10,000 YEN = ABOUT $100
BRING ME BACK 10,000 YEN.
...
GET GOING!!

RUN!

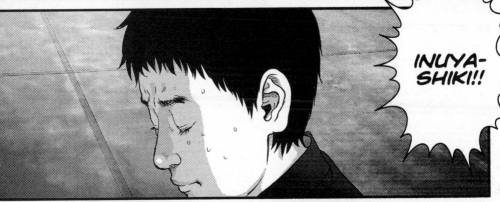

INUYA-SHIKI!!

GET OFF YOUR ASS AND RUN!!!

YOU THINK I'M FUCKIN' JOKING?!

KEEEEE

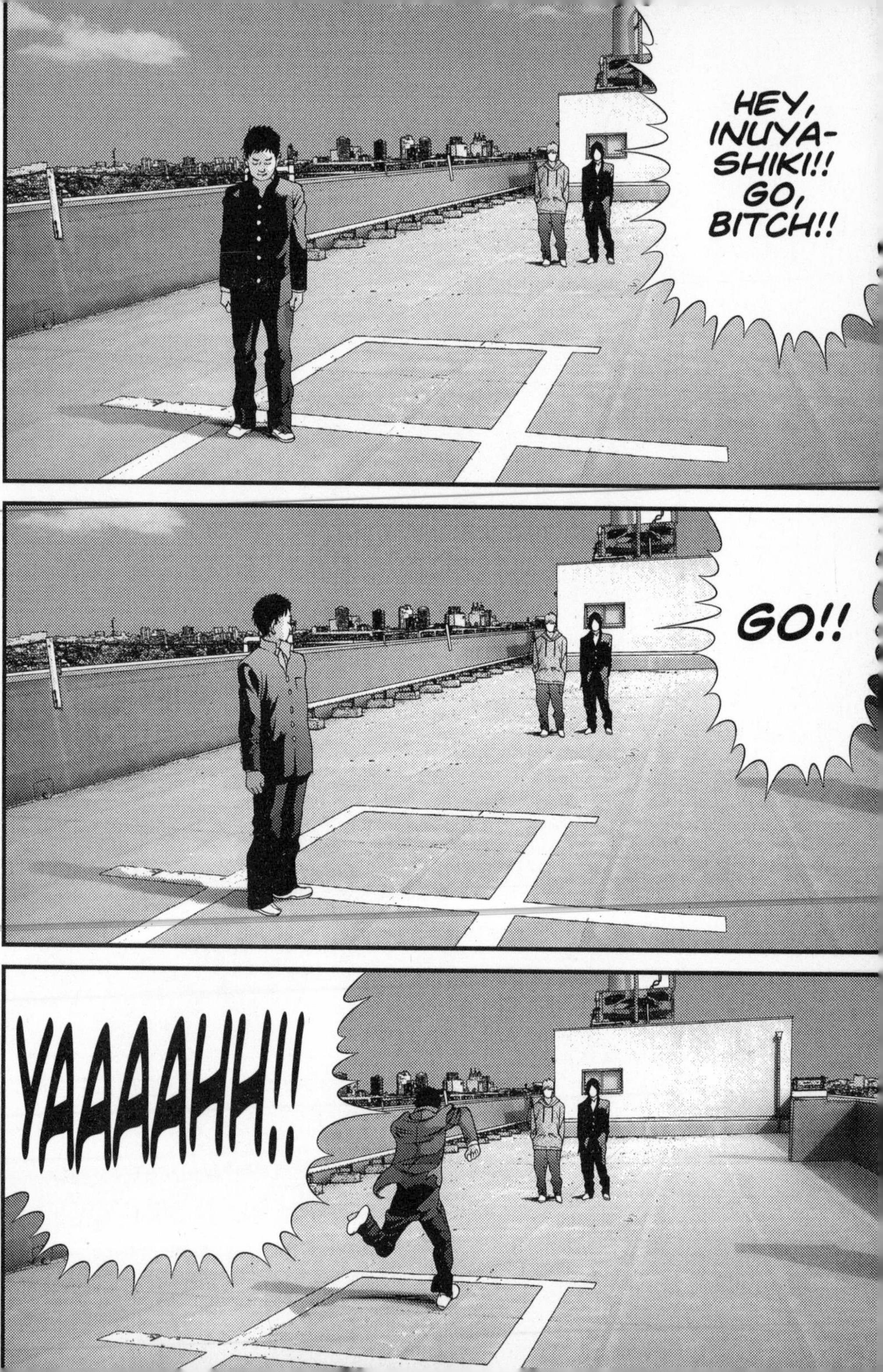
HEY, INUYA-SHIKI!! GO, BITCH!!
GO!!
YAAAAHH!!

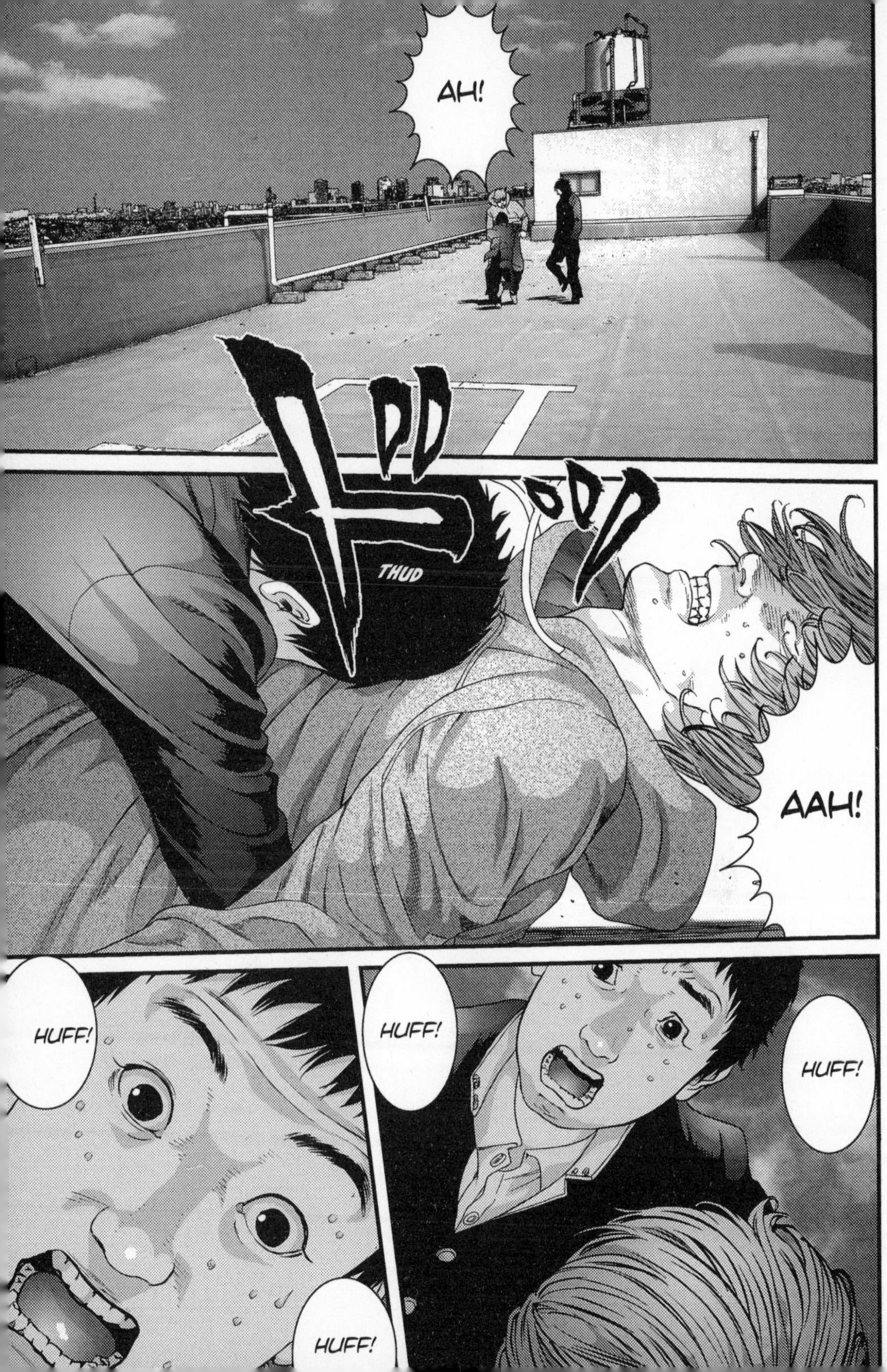
AH!
THUD
AAH!
HUFF!
HUFF!
HUFF!
HUFF!

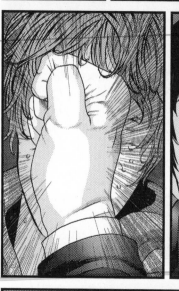

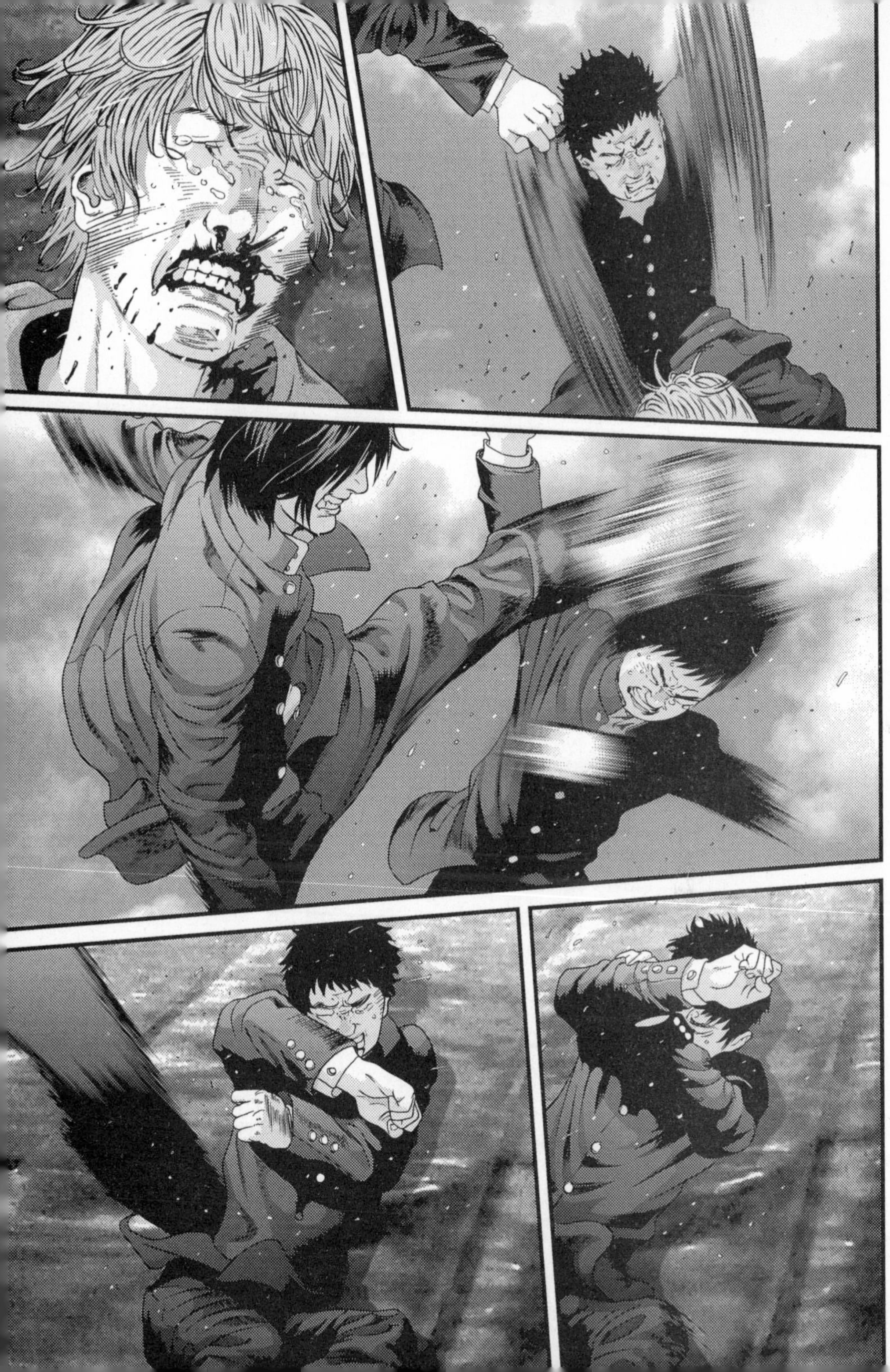

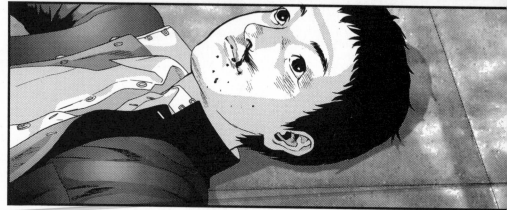

DID YOU SEE THAT?

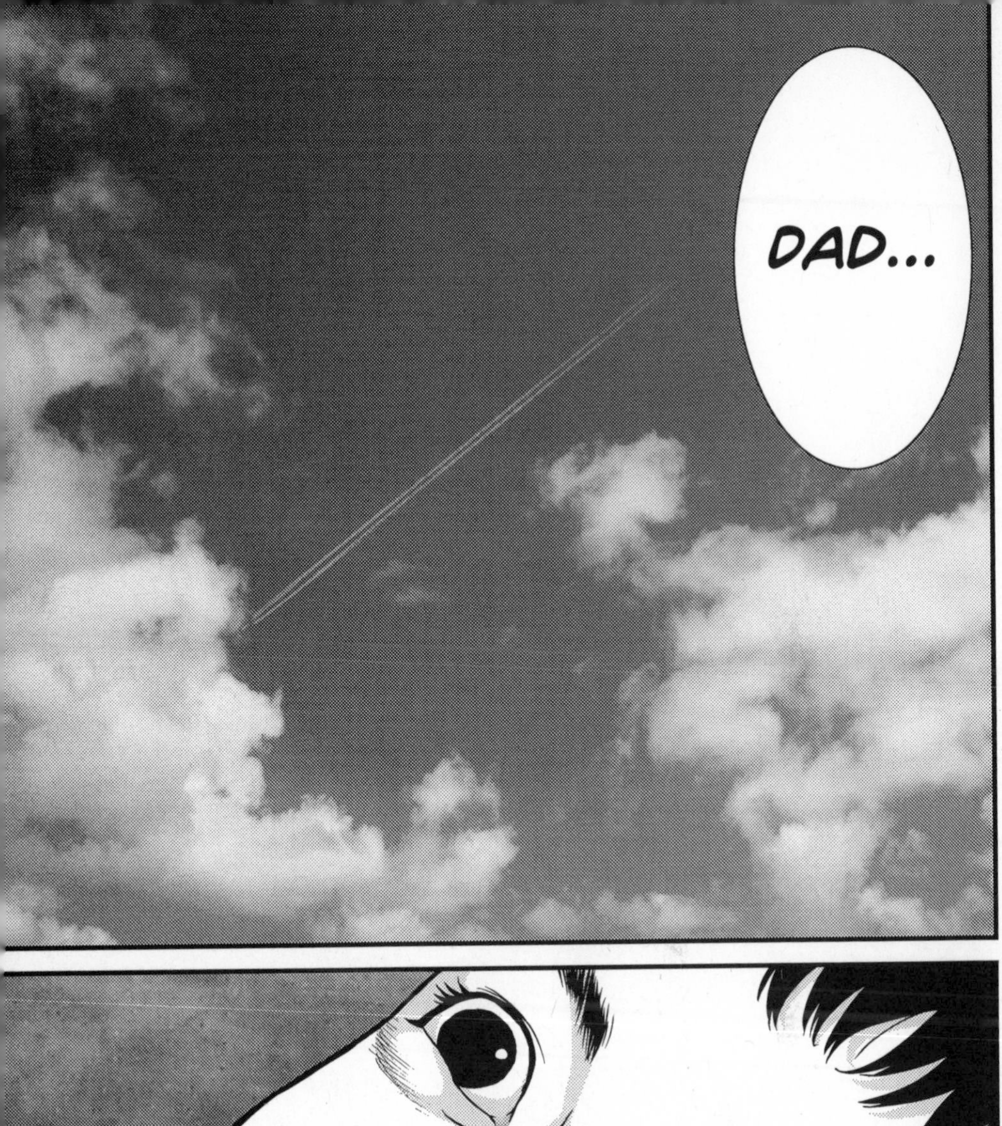
DAD...

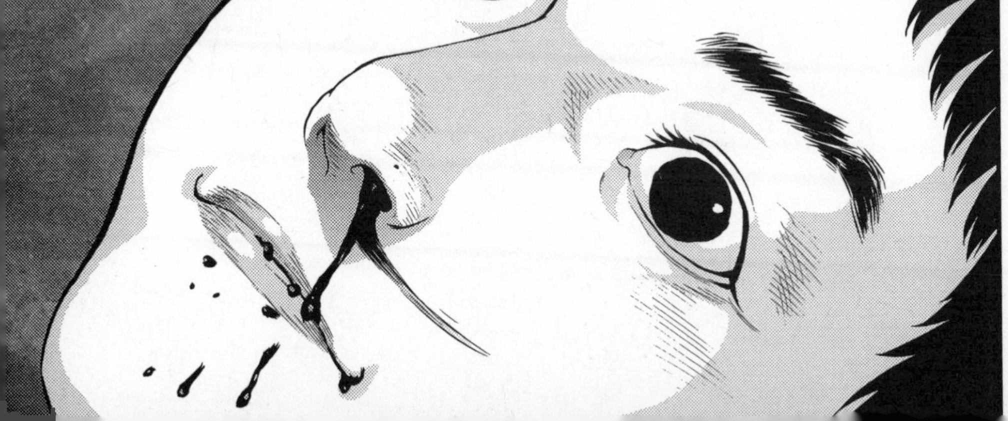

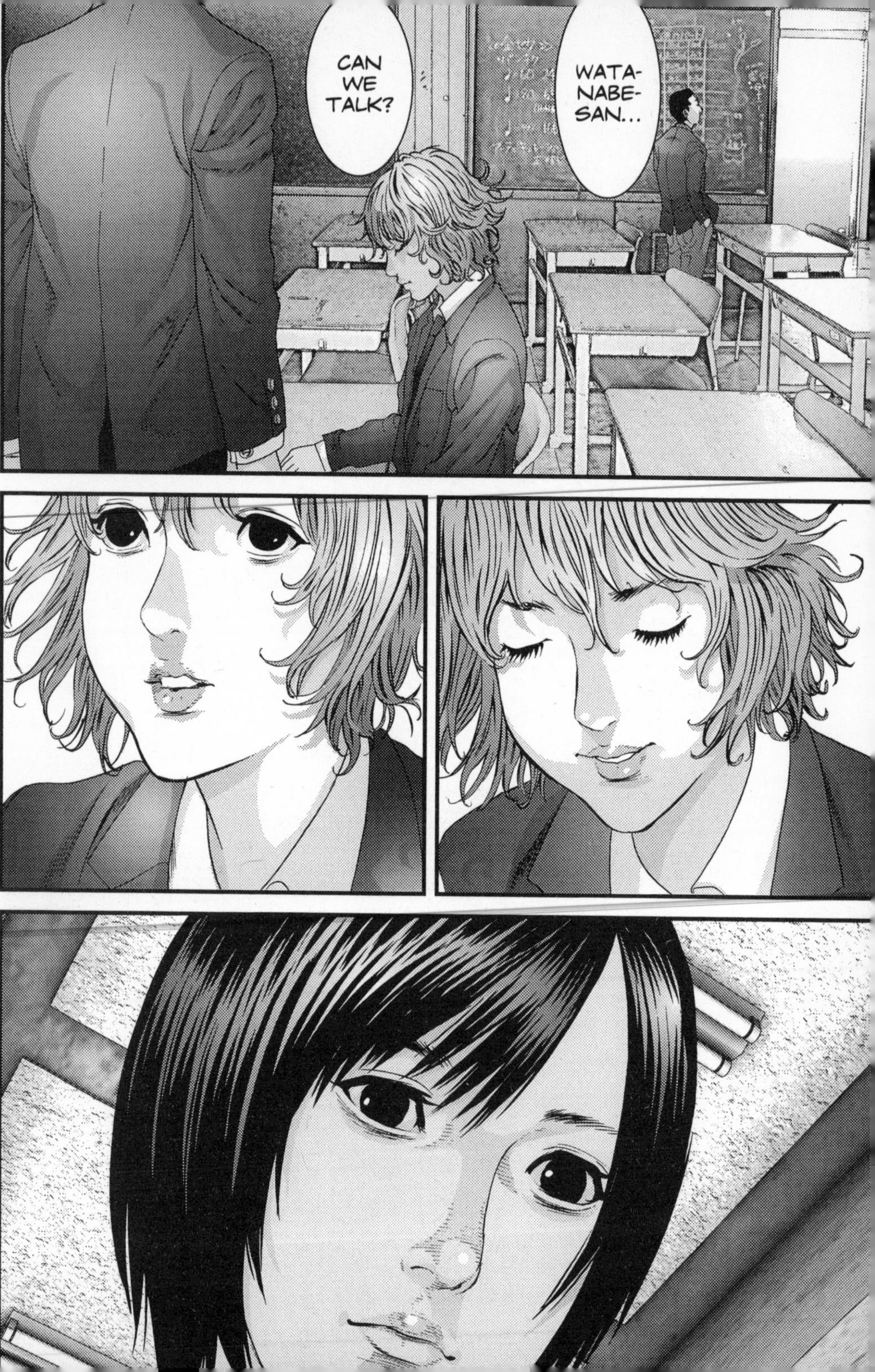
WATA-NABE-SAN...
CAN WE TALK?

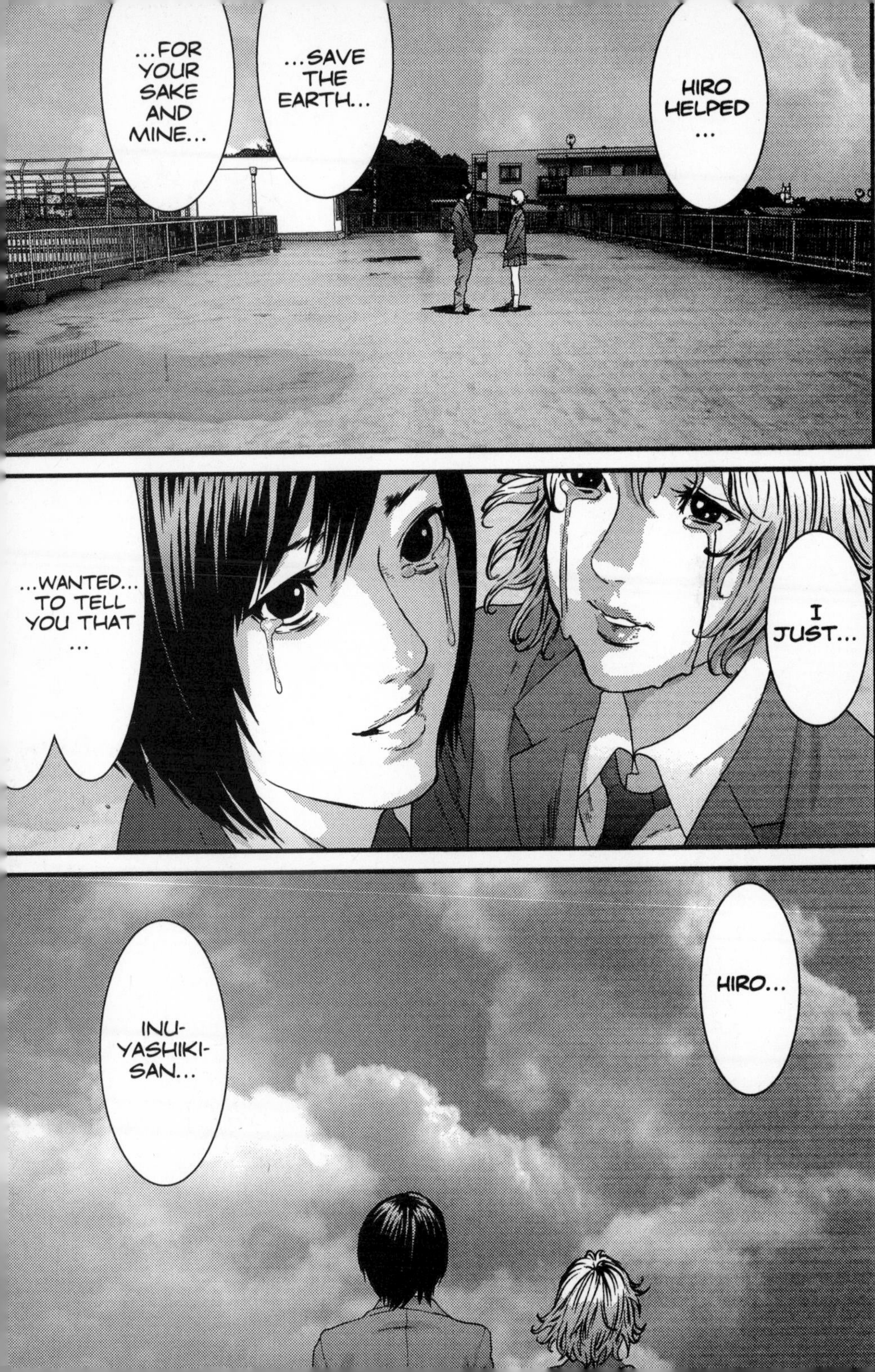
HIRO HELPED ...
...SAVE THE EARTH...
...FOR YOUR SAKE AND MINE...
I JUST...
...WANTED... TO TELL YOU THAT ...
HIRO...
INU-YASHIKI-SAN...

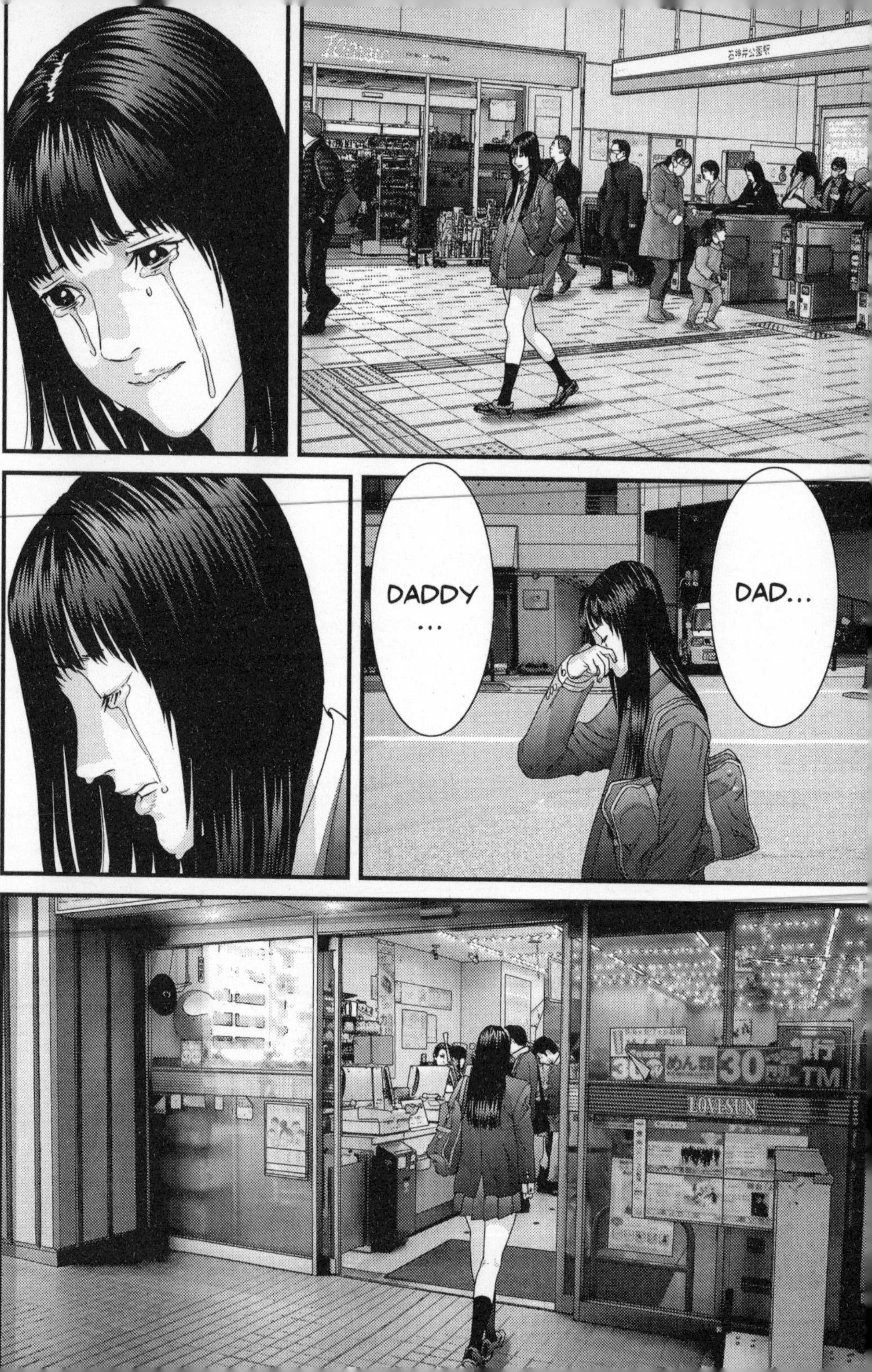
DAD...
DADDY ...
LOVESUN

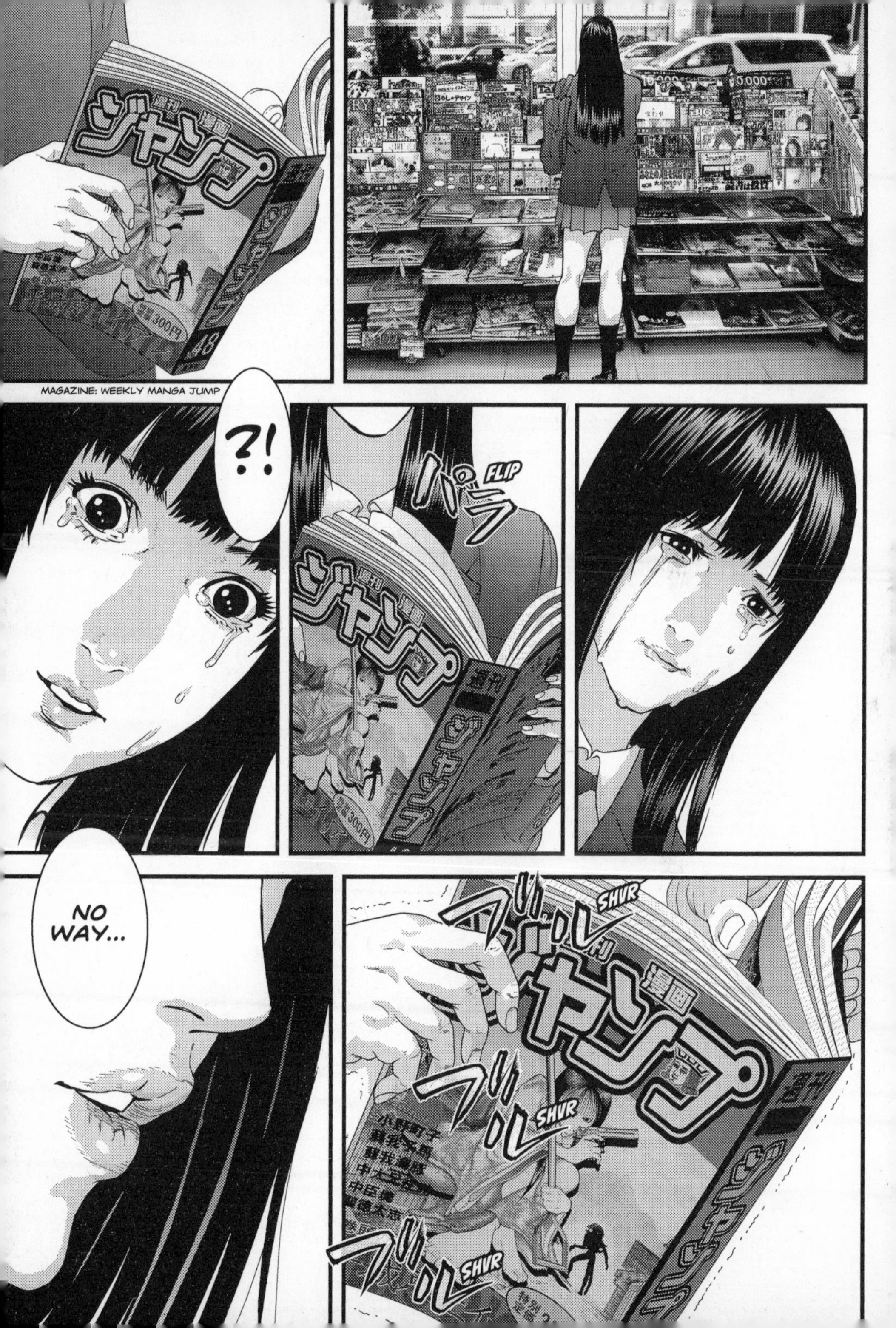
MAGAZINE: WEEKLY MANGA JUMP
パラ FLIP
?!
SHVR
SHVR
SHVR
NO WAY...

A Winner Is Chosen

遂に入選作出る!!

The 81st

腕塚賞 発表!!!

Udezuka Award Winner Announced!!!

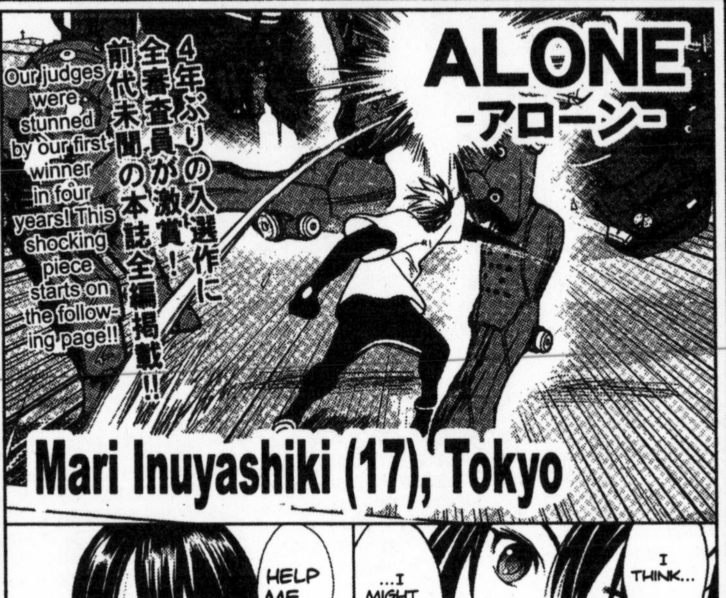
ALONE
-アローン-
4年ぶりの入選作に全審査員が激賞! 前代未聞の本誌全編掲載!!
Our judges were stunned by our first winner in four years! This shocking piece starts on the following page!!
Mari Inuyashiki (17), Tokyo
I THINK...
...I MIGHT BE PRETTY TOUGH!
HELP ME...
HELP?
Winner! Prize Money: 5 million yen
Just turn the page to read the entire piece!
...GO OUT-SIDE!

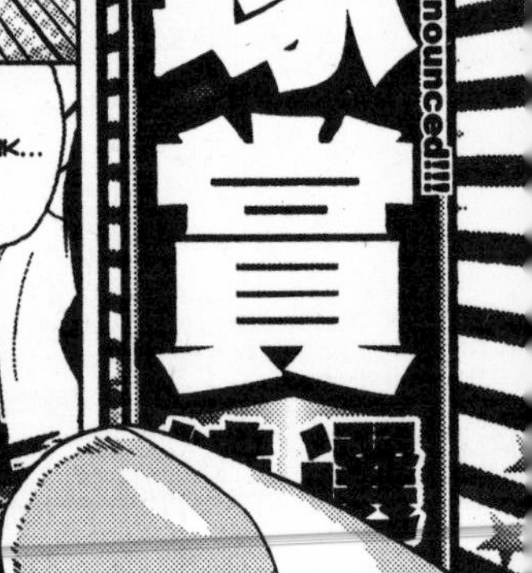

Story: The protagonist, Kakeru, is afflicted with an incurable disease. He goes into cryo-sleep, betting that future medical progress will help him. In the year 3075, Earth is nothing like the human civilization of the past. With his nav-drone companion, he winds up in an alternate world and saves a girl who will change his fate forever…

Critique: The characters, both human and robot, are already so charismatic, they're at pro level. The story is unique and has a strong hook, and I'd love to see this artist try other genres. If I had to be critical, I'd say it could be improved with more variation in pacing, anticipating the reader's emotions and taking advantage of that for dramatic effect. <Otomo>

Critique: Despite the absurd setting, the characters and art were so breathtaking that I could easily buy all of it. The clever combination of interesting hand-drawn art and digital touches is already brimming with originality. I just want to see where she takes this style from here. I can't believe this is coming from a teenage girl! <Abimoto>

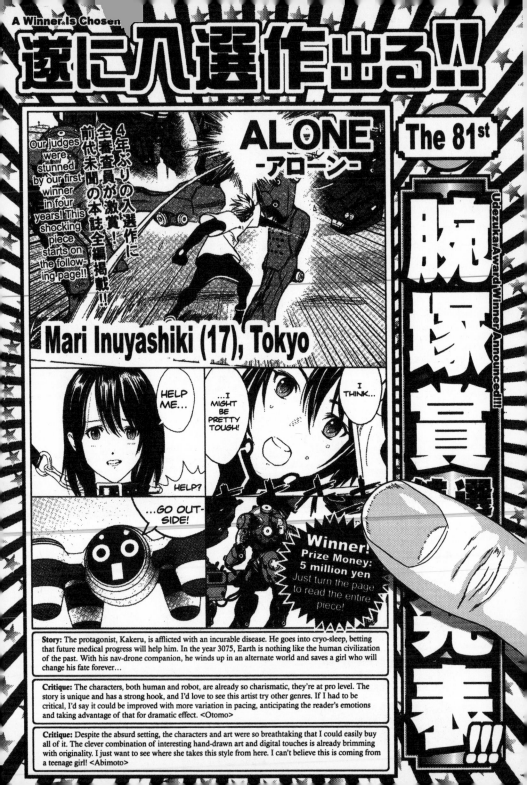

The entire one-shot manga from this stunning new rookie, winner of the 81st Udezuka Award!

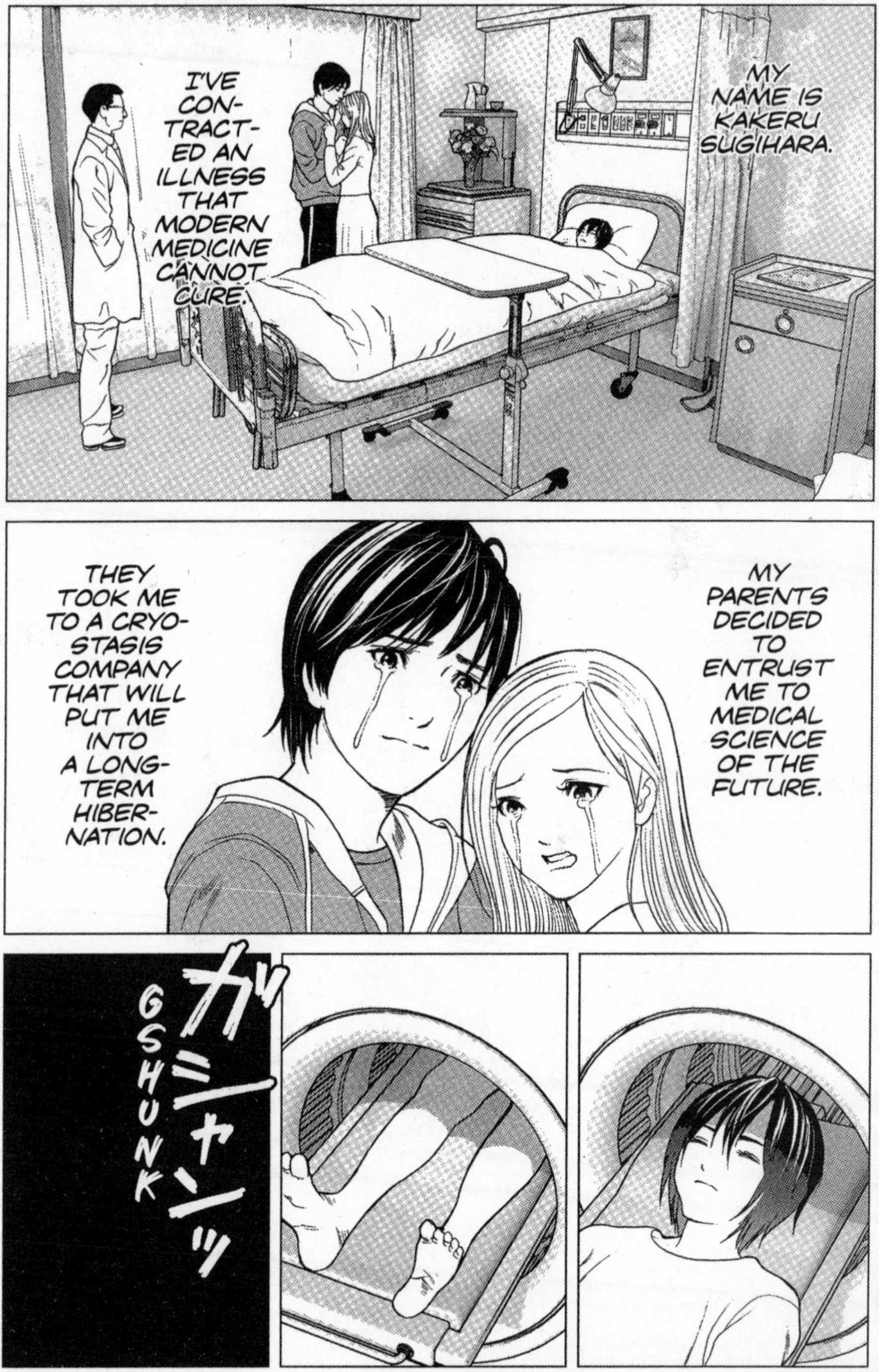
MY NAME IS KAKERU SUGIHARA.
I'VE CONTRACTED AN ILLNESS THAT MODERN MEDICINE CANNOT CURE.
MY PARENTS DECIDED TO ENTRUST ME TO MEDICAL SCIENCE OF THE FUTURE.
THEY TOOK ME TO A CRYOSTASIS COMPANY THAT WILL PUT ME INTO A LONG-TERM HIBERNATION.
ガシャンッ
GSHUNK

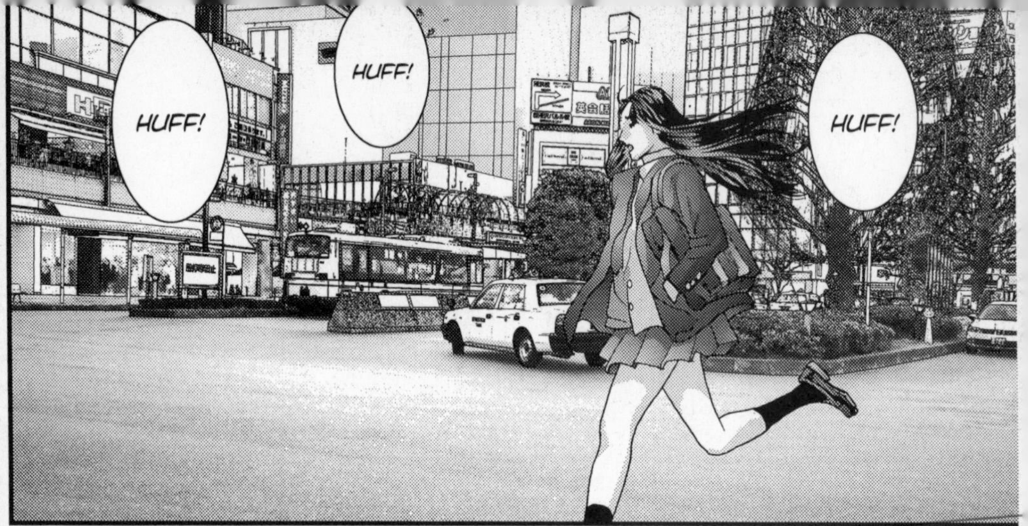
HUFF!
HUFF!
HUFF!

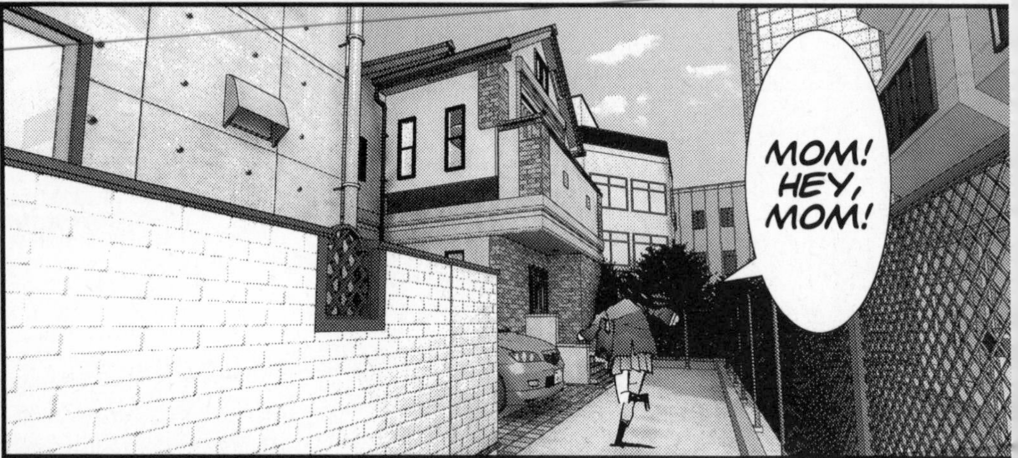
MOM! HEY, MOM!

INUYASHIKI

HIROYA OKU

INUYASHIKI - END

Translation Notes

Thou Shalt Not Die, page 27

A permutation of a famous poem by Akiko Yosano, a feminist writer who published it in the collection *Midaregami*, or *"Tangled Hair."* The tanka poem *"Thou Shalt Not Die"* was written to her younger brother during the time of the Russo-Japanese War, and railed against the war movement of that time.

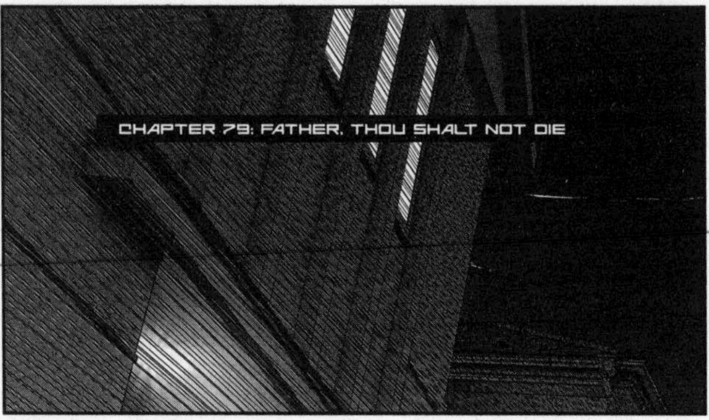
CHAPTER 79: FATHER, THOU SHALT NOT DIE

Udezuka Award, page 180

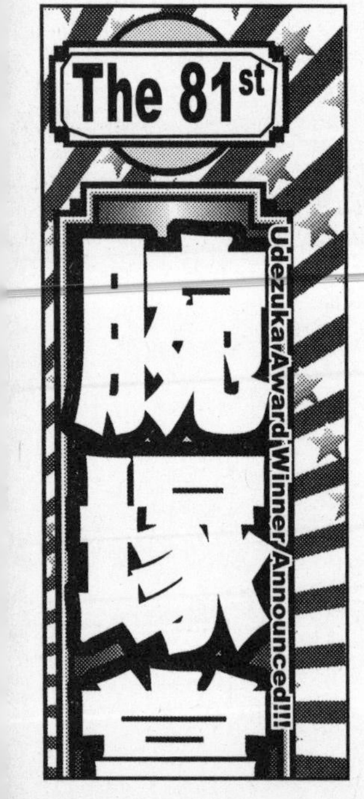
The 81st
Udezuka Award Winner Announced!!!

A parody of the real-life Tezuka Award, which is awarded to new artists by a panel of Shueisha judges, primarily senior artists related to *Weekly Shonen Jump*. The name Udezuka is a pun; the first kanji in Osamu Tezuka's family name has been changed from hand (*te*) to arm (*ude*). The panel is not obligated to choose a winner for the cash prize, so it is quite ordinary for no entry to win in a particular year if none are found worthy enough.

"A fun adventure that fantasy readers will relate to and enjoy." –
Adventures in Poor Taste

Mikami's middle age hasn't gone as he planned: He never found a girlfriend, he got stuck in a dead-end job, and he was abruptly stabbed to death in the street at 37. So when he wakes up in a new world straight out of a fantasy RPG, he's disappointed, but not exactly surprised to find that he's facing down a dragon, not as a knight or a wizard, but as a blind slime monster. But there are chances for even a slime to become a hero...

THAT TIME I GOT REINCARNATED AS A
SLIME

"An emotional and artistic tour de force! We see incredible triumph, and crushing defeat... each panel [is] a thrill!"
—Anitay

"A journey that's instantly compelling."
—Anime News Network

WELCOME TO THE BALLROOM

By Tomo Takeuchi

Feckless high school student Tatara Fujita wants to be good at something—anything. Unfortunately, he's about as average as a slouchy teen can be. The local bullies know this, and make it a habit to hit him up for cash, but all that changes when the debonair Kaname Sengoku sends them packing. Sengoku's not the neighborhood watch, though. He's a professional ballroom dancer. And once Tatara Fujita gets pulled into the world of ballroom, his life will never be the same.

KC KODANSHA COMICS

The Black Museum The Ghost and the Lady

By Kazuhiro Fujita

Deep in Scotland Yard in London sits an evidence room dedicated to the greatest mysteries of British history. In this "Black Museum" sits a misshapen hunk of lead—two bullets fused together—the key to a wartime encounter between Florence Nightingale, the mother of modern nursing, and a supernatural Man in Grey. This story is unknown to most scholars of history, but a special guest of the museum will tell the tale of The Ghost and the Lady...

Praise for Kazuhiro Fujita's *Ushio and Tora*

"A charming revival that combines a classic look with modern depth and pacing... **Essential viewing both for curmudgeons and new fans alike.**" — Anime News Network

"**GREAT!** The first episode of Ushio and Tora captures the essence of '90s anime." — IGN

The prince in his dark days

By Hico Yamanaka

A drunkard for a father, a household of poverty... For 17-year-old Atsuko, misfortune is all she knows and believes in. Until one day, a chance encounter with Itaru–the wealthy heir of a huge corporation–changes everything. The two look identical, uncannily so. When Itaru curiously goes missing, Atsuko is roped into being his stand-in. There, in his shoes, Atsuko must parade like a prince in a palace. She encounters many new experiences, but at what cost...?

Based on the critically acclaimed classic horror manga

The first new *Parasyte* manga in over 20 years!

NEO
ParaSyte f

BY **ASUMIKO NAKAMURA, EMA TOYAMA, MIKI RINNO, LALAKO KOJIMA, KAORI YUKI, BANKO KUZE, YUUKI OBATA, KASHIO, YUI KUROE, ASIA WATANABE, MIKIMAKI, HIKARU SURUGA, HAJIME SHINJO, RENJURO KINDAICHI, AND YURI NARUSHIMA**

A collection of chilling new *Parasyte* stories from Japan's top shojo artists!

Parasites: shape-shifting aliens whose only purpose is to assimilate with and consume the human race... but do these monsters have a different side? A parasite becomes a prince to save his romance-obsessed female host from a dangerous stalker. Another hosts a cooking show, in which the real monsters are revealed. These and 13 more stories, from some of the greatest shojo manga artists alive today, together make up a chilling, funny, and entertaining tribute to one of manga's horror classics!

KC
KODANSHA
COMICS

KC
KODANSHA COMICS

New action series from Hiroyuki Takei, creator of the classic shonen franchise Shaman King!

In medieval Japan, a bell hanging on the collar is a sign that a cat has a master. Norachiyo's bell hangs from his katana sheath, but he is nonetheless a stray — a ronin. This one-eyed cat samurai travels across a dishonest world, cutting through pretense and deception with his blade.

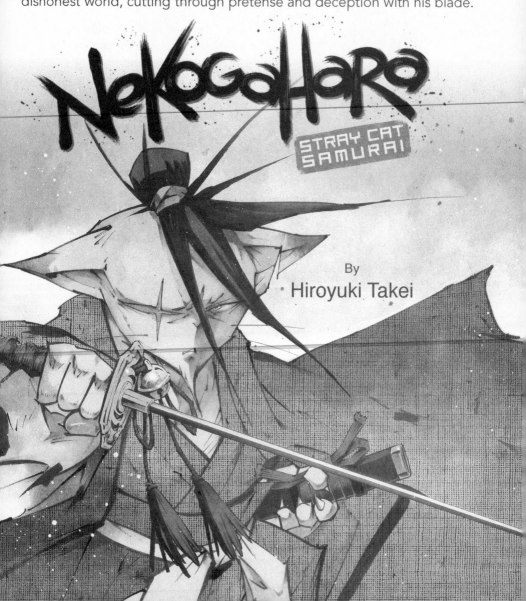

NEKOGAHARA

STRAY CAT SAMURAI

By

Hiroyuki Takei

KC
KODANSHA
COMICS

Japan's most powerful spirit medium delves into the ghost world's greatest mysteries!

Story by Kyo Shirodaira, famed author of mystery fiction and creator of *Spiral, Blast of Tempest,* and *The Record of a Fallen Vampire.*

Both touched by spirits called yôkai, Kotoko and Kurô have gained unique superhuman powers. But to gain her powers Kotoko has given up an eye and a leg, and Kurô's personal life is in shambles. So when Kotoko suggests they team up to deal with renegades from the spirit world, Kurô doesn't have many other choices, but Kotoko might just have a few ulterior motives...

IN/SPECTRE

STORY BY KYO SHIRODAIRA
ART BY CHASHIBA KATASE

HAPPINESS

——ハピネス——

By Shuzo Oshimi

From the creator of *The Flowers of Evil*

Nothing interesting is happening in Makoto Ozaki's first year of high school. His life is a series of quiet humiliations: low-grade bullies, unreliable friends, and the constant frustration of his adolescent lust. But one night, a pale, thin girl knocks him to the ground in an alley and offers him a choice. Now everything is different. Daylight is searingly bright. Food tastes awful. And worse than anything is the terrible, consuming thirst...

Praise for Shuzo Oshimi's *The Flowers of Evil*

"A shockingly readable story that vividly—one might even say queasily—evokes the fear and confusion of discovering one's own sexuality. Recommended." —The Manga Critic

"A page-turning tale of sordid middle school blackmail." —Otaku USA Magazine

"A stunning new horror manga." —Third Eye Comics

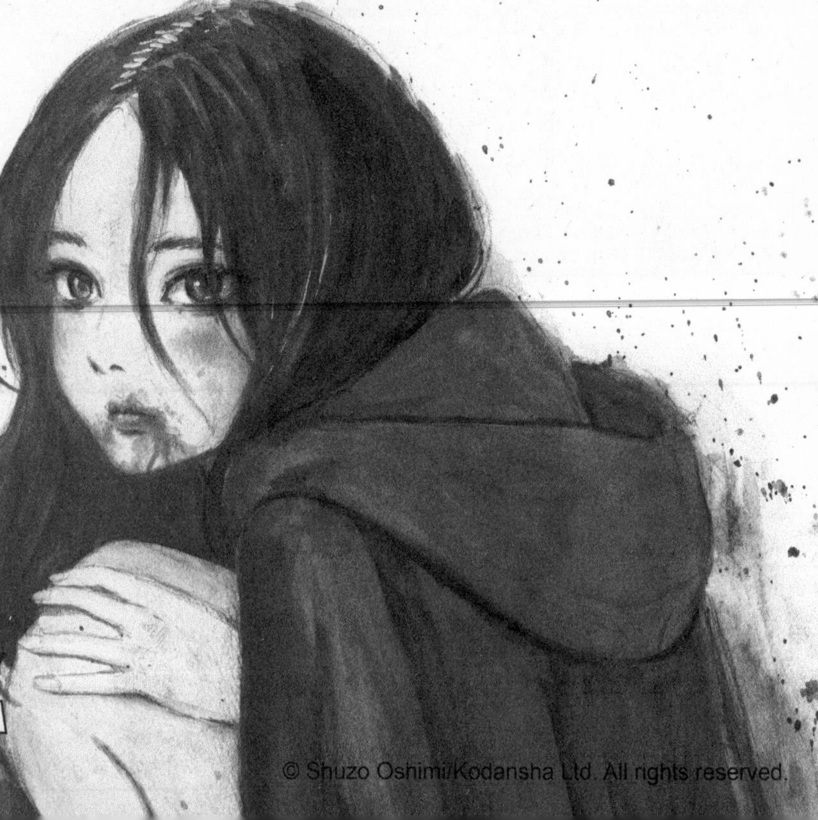

KODANSHA COMICS

The award-winning manga about what happens inside you!

"Far more entertaining than it ought to be... what kid doesn't want to think that every time they sneeze a torpedo shoots out their nose?"
–Anime News Network

Strep throat! Hay fever! Influenza! The world is a dangerous place for a red blood cell just trying to get her deliveries finished. Fortunately, she's not alone…she's got a whole human body's worth of cells ready to help out! The mysterious white blood cells, the buff and brash killer T cells, even the cute little platelets— everyone's got to come together if they want to keep you healthy!

Cells at Work!

はたらく細胞

By Akane Shimizu

Inuyashiki volume 10 is a work of fiction. Names, characters, places, and incidents are the products of the author's imagination or are used fictitiously. Any resemblance to actual events, locales, or persons, living or dead, is entirely coincidental.

A Kodansha Comics Trade Paperback Original.

Published in the United States by Kodansha Comics, an imprint of Kodansha USA Publishing, LLC, New York.

Publication rights for this English edition arranged through Kodansha Ltd., Tokyo.

First published in Japan in 2017 by Kodansha Ltd., Tokyo, as *Inuyashiki* volume 10.

ISBN 978-1-63236-607-8

Printed in the United States of America.

www.kodanshacomics.com

9 8 7 6 5 4 3 2 1

Translation: Stephen Paul
Lettering: Scott O. Brown
Editing: Ajani Oloye
Kodansha Comics edition cover design: Phil Balsman